THE ROCKHOUND'S HANDBOOK

BY V. A. FIRSOFF

Working with Gemstones

THE ROCKHOUND'S HANDBOOK

V. A. Firsoff MA, FRAS
and
G. I. Firsoff MA (Cantab)

Illustrated by the authors

DAVID & CHARLES
NEWTON ABBOT   LONDON   VANCOUVER

0 7153 6810 9

Set in 11 on 13pt Baskerville and printed in Great Britain
by Devonshire Press Ltd Torquay for David & Charles
(Holdings) Limited South Devon House Newton Abbot
Devon

Published in Canada by Douglas David & Charles Limited
132 Philip Avenue North Vancouver BC

CONTENTS

CONTENTS

INTRODUCTION

BETWEEN PRACTICE AND THEORY

A handbook is an easy reference work, intended to provide practical guidance and useful information in compact, readily accessible form.

This book is primarily addressed to the amateur rockhound who seeks practical advice in the pursuit of his hobby rather than abstract academic knowledge. Nevertheless, a certain amount of theory is necessary to provide economy of description and to impose order on what would otherwise be chaos of disjointed facts. At a high scientific level, mineralogy (the science of minerals), petrology (the science of rocks), and geology, which is concerned among other things with the processes by which rocks and minerals are formed, involve a terminology of formidable complexity, most of which is redundant for the present purpose. Long Latin and Greek words are avoided wherever possible, but inevitably some scientific terms are included as no adequate alternatives exist. The reader is advised to try and master the basic concepts, as these are a great help in looking for minerals and in consulting this and other similar works.

No theory can be a foolproof substitute for practice. Classifications deal with pigeon-hole concepts, and reality does not always fit such pigeon-holes with equal ease. Rocks and minerals may assume such variety of form as to defy accurate description,

9

and although a visual image may be more telling than words, it can never be exhaustive for the same reason. All aspiring rockhounds are recommended to study actual specimens in museum collections.

Rockhound's Handbook is not an encyclopedia, and, while every care has been taken to make it as comprehensive as possible, only the most important minerals can have been dealt with, giving special preference to gemstones. Two chapters at the end are devoted to the cutting and polishing of stones, but this is a vast subject, and the reader is advised to refer to specialised works, such as eg *Working with Gemstones*, by the same publisher and one of the present authors.

DEFINITIONS

A rockhound

A rockhound is a person interested in rocks, stones and minerals not for professional, industrial, or commercial reasons, but purely as a hobby. He (or she) will usually be a collector of specimens and may be a lapidary who cuts and dresses some of the finds.

It is also nice to think that the rockhound is a nature-lover and will avoid wholesale removal of the minerals he collects, keeping a brake on what a Roman poet has described as ' the criminal love of possession '.

A rock

To a geologist anything that makes up the body of Mother Earth is *rock*. In other words, rock need not be hard and solid: gravels, sands, silts, and volcanic ash all qualify.

For one thing, such *clastic* (fragmented) materials in due course become compacted, baked and hardened into rocks of common parlance with which cottages, bridges and cathedrals are built, and the transition is gradual.

A mineral

A rock may be of any composition, which may, but need not, be homogeneous, ie uniform throughout. A mineral, however, is a chemical compound in which the constituent chemical elements are combined according to the laws of constant and multiple proportions, so that its composition can be summed up in a formula. For example, quartz is silica, or silicon dioxide, and has the formula SiO_2 (one part of silicon to two parts of oxygen). There are, however, other minerals which have the same formula but are not quartz. To qualify as quartz the substance must have a definite crystalline structure and certain other characteristics, such as refractive index, hardness and specific gravity, to be considered in detail in later chapters.

In some minerals the chemical composition varies more or less continuously within certain limits, and all minerals may contain impurities, to which their colouring is often due. But this does not affect the principle.

Marble is an almost pure carbonate of lime, $CaCO_3$, as is calcite and aragonite. Thus it is a mineral, but it is also a rock, inasmuch as it occurs in large masses – there are whole mountains of marble. On the other hand, obsidian is a glassy lava whose ingredients are so intimately intermingled that it would require chemical analysis to winkle them out. Nevertheless, it is only a mixture and not a chemical compound: its constituents are not bound in molecules of fixed composition. Indeed, these constituents are the same as in granite, where they occur separately in a way discernible to the naked eye.

A gemstone

Any stone of attractive appearance and sufficient hardness to take a good polish and ensure permanence in use as a personal ornament may be considered a gemstone. In other words, a gemstone need not be, although it usually is, a mineral. Diamond, ruby and opal are all distinct mineral species, but pebble jewellery may make use of good-looking pieces of coloured rock. As a rule rocks make at best a lower grade of 'ornamental stone', suitable for small articles, where, incidentally, the exposure to wear is less than in dress trinkets and the requirements for hardness are correspondingly relaxed; or they may be used only for special building purposes such as mantelpieces or columns. But the line of division is fluid. The Derbyshire Blue John is purple fluorite and as such a mineral, but it is used for standing ornaments in its crude impure form, which may be more accurately described as a rock.

Some soft stones, such as sphalerite, look beautiful as faceted gems, and in *Faceting for Amateurs* Glenn and Martha Vargas give instructions for the cutting of such materials as calcite and sulphur, which are even softer. Mineralogical museums often contain as exhibits faceted specimens of minerals that are normally opaque but occasionally attain gem quality, are more or less unknown to the trade, and are not listed as gemstones in mineralogical compendia. On the other hand, not all diamonds or rubies achieve gem status, and some may be only good enough for industrial abrasives.

V.A.F., G.I.F.

I
ROCKS

All rocks are divided into three classes: igneous, sedimentary and metamorphic.

Igneous rocks begin their existence in molten state. Such molten rock is called *magma*, but when it flows out on to the Earth's surface from a volcanic vent or fissure it becomes *lava*. As we shall see later, this distinction is not mere pedantry.

Loose fragmentary deposits are all sediments, although for example volcanic ash and bombs are of igneous origin, so that here these two classes of rock meet. Hard sedimentary rocks are formed by the consolidation of such loose materials, due to pressure, chemical binding or cementation, for example shingle or gravel may become embedded in a limestone matrix.

Metamorphic rocks arise from sedimentary and igneous rocks by the action of heat, pressure and/or the chemical effect of penetration by *magmatic emanations*, ie fluids, which means both gases and liquids, exuded by magma. The chemical changes induced by the latter are known as *pneumatolysis*. There are also various processes of chemical weathering affecting the structure and composition of all rocks to some extent and resulting in *secondary minerals* which were not present in the rock when it was formed – eg olivine decays to serpentine, and they are a primary and a secondary mineral accordingly. Other minerals are minutely soluble in hot or even cold water (especially if this is alkalised or acidulated), are washed out of their parent rocks in the course of ages, and redeposited elsewhere, along cracks and in cavities. These processes are going on all the time. They are akin to *metamorphism*, although not usually described as such.

As stated, igneous rocks are not exempt from the effects of heat, pressure and pneumatolysis in particular, both during and after consolidation, and this may appreciably alter their structure and composition. Since they have been crystalline from birth, however, such a rehash does not affect them to quite the same extent as it does sedimentary rocks, which become partly or wholly crystallised, various minerals arising from the chemicals contained in them.

IGNEOUS ROCKS

Igneous rocks are fundamental: they form the main body of the Earth, and other rocks are derived from their decay at its surface. The igneous rocks embody the essence of ' rockiness', being hard, tough, crystalline or glassy, unless weakened by geological decay. As a rule they are harder and tougher than those of the sedimentary, although not necessarily of the metamorphic, division.

The crystals of the individual minerals that make up the rock may or may not be readily recognisable with the naked eye and could, in fact, be partly or wholly lost in a glassy matrix. This depends chiefly on the speed of cooling of the originally molten mass (magma). Large masses of very hot magma which have set deep underground, cooling slowly under the cover of the overlying strata, yield coarse-grained rocks, described as *abyssal* (formed deep down, in the abyss). Smaller, less deep-seated, less hot intrusions of magma will cool faster, allowing less time for the crystals to grow before the melt begins to harden, which results in *hypabyssal* rocks of progressively finer grain. At a certain stage large crystals (usually felspar or quartz) are scattered in a fine-grained matrix. Such structure is called *porphyritic*, and the corresponding rocks are *porphyries*. A still more rapid cooling, in lavas, yields a glassy matrix in which smaller crystals, rounded by *magmatic corrosion* (melting round the edges), are sparsely embedded. *Rhyolite* is this type of rock. It looks like a kind of ' fossil soup with noodles '. Finally, very rapid chilling produces volcanic glass free from crystals, as in *obsidian*, which resembles bottle glass, is brittle and splinters into razor-sharp sherds. Aztec priests used obsidian knives to cut out the throbbing hearts of their human sacrifices and, no doubt, for other purposes.

The rate of cooling, and so grain-size, will vary within the same igneous intrusion (or *pluton*), being rapid on the margins and slow near the middle, the rock grading from glass to medium or coarse grain. And there are other complications.

Most of the Earth's surface is clothed in soil and various sediments, consolidated or not. The sediments may be hundreds and thousands of feet or metres thick, and are arranged in layers, or *strata* (plural of *stratum*). But deep down below are molten igneous masses of various composition, laden with compressed gases and ready to seep or roar through any weaknesses of the overlying crust. Land movements, and more particularly the folding responsible for alpine mountains, open the upward way to magma. It rises at the root of the mountains into ' molten peaks ', called *batholiths*, which set hard and may in due course become exposed on the surface by erosion. Or else the magma may well up through a channel, as though a stem, reach daylight and produce a volcano, or fail to reach it and spread out between the strata into a kind of mushroom, known as *laccolith*. A thinner sheet of igneous rocks intercalated between sedimentary layers is a *sill*, and a more or less vertical one, cutting across them, is called a *dyke*.

' Dyke ' may mean either a ditch or a wall. This is admirably suited to geological reality, for a geological dyke exposed on the surface may either erode faster than the country rock and produce a ditch, or be more resistant than the rock and stand up

15

like a wall. Such small intrusions cool quickly and yield fine-grained rocks with certain special features, described by the term *lamprophyre*.

An igneous intrusion is often itself intruded while cooling by further hot and 'virulent' magmas, laden with fluids. This may result in a rock of giant grain with well-formed crystals from an inch (2½cm) to a foot (30cm) long, or even larger. Such rocks are called *pegmatites*. They often contain rare minerals and precious metals, and have a maggoty look owing to an abundance of gas bubbles in the hot melt. The resulting cavities are known as *druses* (*vuggs* or *vughs* in Cornwall, and *loughs* in the north of England). Call them what you will, they are the rockhound's delight, for here the rock constituents can grow unopposed into large clear crystals.

Pegmatites are frequently accompanied by *aplites*, characterised by small grain and lighter colouring, as a product of differentiation or fractionation of the original magma: the aplites are a kind of left-overs after the less fusible and less vaporisable compounds have solidified. They, too, may contain chain-cavities.

All this is true of any igneous rock, regardless of its chemistry, so that any family or *clan* of these rocks can be divided vertically according to the size of grain.

DIVISIONS OF IGNEOUS ROCKS

The horizontal classification of igneous rocks is based on the proportion of silica in their make-up. Silica may be bound in silicates, eg felspars, micas, pyroxenes and so on, or be present in pure form, commonly as quartz.

There are four main groups of igneous rocks: (1) *acid*; (2) *intermediate*; (3) *basic*; and (4) *ultrabasic* or *ultramafic*. Chemically, silicates are metallic salts of silicic acid and silica is the silicic acid anhydride, or what is left of the acid H_2SiO_3 after the removal of water, H_2O. But there are other silicon acids, and all of them are theoretical as they do not occur as natural substances. This, however, serves to explain the names ' acid ' and ' basic '. The rocks from (1) to (4) are progressively heavier, darker and rarer on the Earth's surface. Indeed, acid rocks are typical of the crust of our planet – they are continental rocks. The basic and ultrabasic rocks come from deep down below, as heavier magmas tend to sink, and are to be found mainly on oceanic floors and on islands in association with past or present volcanic activity, like Skye in Scotland or Iceland, although basic lavas carpet thousands of square miles in India, the USA and elsewhere.

A rock is acid if it contains over 66 per cent of silica, more than 10 per cent of which is quartz. In the intermediate division the corresponding proportions are between 55 and 66, and less than 10 per cent respectively. In basic rocks the silica content drops below 55 per cent and quartz crystals are rare or absent. The ultrabasic division marks a further decline in silica to less than 45 per cent, and felspars fade out.

Each horizontal division is subdivided vertically according to grain: coarse, medium, fine, and (absent) glassy. The last two named are *vulcanites*, which have no special names outside the acid division. There are also corresponding pegmatites and aplites.

Granite is the most common igneous rock. It is a pudding from Pluto's kitchen, made of three *essential* minerals: quartz, felspar (mainly of the orthoclase variety, see p 106), and mica. The rock is not a granite unless it consists predominantly of these, but it may include various *accessory* minerals: tourmaline, fluorite, topaz, beryl, garnet, corundum, zircon etc., even diamond in small proportions. All granites contain a little gold and other metals and ores. The quartz is mostly milky-white or transparent, but it may be brown, smoky, black, seldom greenish, pink or blue (in some Indian granites). The felspar is white, yellowish, flesh-pink or red, rarely transparent or green. The mica is characteristically the pale muscovite, but the dark biotite likewise occurs; coloured micas are rare.

17

The overall colour of the rock is due mainly to felspar. The contribution from quartz and mica is less important, and accessory minerals, except for black tourmaline (schorl) and occasionally fluorite, are seldom noticeable in bulk. Typically, granite has a greyish, pepper-and-salt look, but it may be from nearly white to almost black; and red granites are not uncommon, eg in Scotland and Scandinavia. Coloured granites and porphyries make attractive polished sections, baroque stones and minor articles, such as ashtrays or vases.

Silica is only a marker, and the decline in its content is paralleled by other chemical changes, foremost of which is the steady increase in the proportion of iron and magnesium, present in the dark-coloured pyroxenes and amphiboles. These may steal over into the acid division, just as quartz crystals may infiltrate the basic gabbros. The reason why this does not happen more often is that the acid magmas are not only lighter, but also have higher melting points than the basic and so tend to congeal first and float on these rather like wax on water. Acid rocks are characteristically greyish or reddish; the greenish and bluish hues are typical of the more basic types. An intimidating nomenclature has been devised to describe the minor rock varieties, but here we must confine ourselves to the essentials, which is best done in the form of a table (see Table 1).

SEDIMENTARY ROCKS

A rockhound is on the look-out for handsome minerals and gemstones, which are mainly to be found in, or are derived from, the igneous and metamorphic formations. Sedimentary rocks are less promising. This, however, is only approximately true. In any case, most of the Earth's land surface is coated more or less thickly with sediments, consolidated or not. The latter clastic ones can again be classified by ' grain ' size, ranging from boulders and blocks (over 250mm in diameter) to fine silt (less than 0·005mm).

These sediments are divided into: *rudaceous*, ie blocks, pebbles and gravels; *arenaceous*, or sandy, including angular grits, sands of rounded grain, and silts; *argillaceous* or clays; *calcareous*, ie chalks and limestones, containing over 50 per cent of carbonate of lime; *siliceous* of organic or inorganic derivation; *carbonaceous* of organic origin, recent or petrified; *ferriferous*, ie ironstones deposited from water; *chemical* deposits of salts, including the homely sodium chloride in the impure form of rock salt; *phosphates*, which comprise *coprolites*, or excrement-stones, guano, bone-beds, but also contain a gemstone – apatite. *Pyroclastic* rocks or *tephra*, consisting of fragmental volcanic ejecta, are not usually included in this list but could be assimilated in the rudaceous category.

This group embodies products of rock decay which inherit the contents of the parent formations. The latter may be igneous of any type, metamorphic or sedimentary, jointly or separately. Generally speaking, the toughest and hardest fragments will survive longest the geological hurly-burly. Thus flint pebbles, silicified fossils and marcasite weather out of chalk and find their way to a beach or stream bed. Crystalline gemstones are the hardest of all, and by the same token the river gravels of Burma, Sri Lanka and the Transvaal are a rich source of these. Gold and platinum grains become concentrated in the sand and grit by a similar process, combined with segregation by weight, for, being heavier than other minerals, they stay behind when these are washed away. Such secondary deposits of precious materials are called *placers*.

In the course of time rudaceous sediments become compacted into solid rock, unlearnedly referred to as *puddingstone*. If the fragments in the ' pudding ' are angular, the rock is called *breccia* (which is the Italian for ' broken stuff ' and is pronounced ' brecha '), and if of pyroclastic origin, *agglomerate*. Rounded fragments yield a *conglomerate*, which may be fine or coarse, and in *tillite*, a rock derived from the boulder-clays of ancient glaciations, becomes a boulder *conglomerate*.

Conglomerates incorporate the content of the original pebble and gravel beds with such waterworn gems as these may have contained, *potato stones* and *agates* weathered out of lavas, gold etc. But it all depends on what parent rocks they are derived from. The hard components of a conglomerate will again weather out of it, and the process may be repeated several times until everything has been reduced to fine sand and silt.

The matrix that holds the puddingstone together may be sandy, clayey, calcareous (limey) or ferruginous. Lime can be washed out with acetic acid (eg vinegar), and a ferruginous ground-mass will yield to oxalic acid. Successive steepings in these should usually suffice to break up the stone and make it disgorge its riches, if any, unless it has been indurated by heat.

Volcanic ashes coalesce into *tuff*, which is usually more or less featureless, although heat and chemical action may cause crystals to develop in it, and secondary vein minerals may be found in its cracks and cavities.

OTHER SEDIMENTARY ROCKS

The consolidation of arenaceous deposits yields *sandstones* (not all sand is quartz), *gritstones* and *siltstones*. Clay becomes compacted into massive *mudstones*, hard *argillites*, flaky *shales* and, when its content of sand is high, into *flags*.

These rocks may contain fossils, but are innocent of primary gemstones or crystals, although these may arise in them by deposition from solutions, pneumatolysis or other chemical action.

The material of calcareous sediments is shells and skeletons of marine animals. They may take the form of *chalk*, soft *coral limestone*, *Blue Lias* and other limestones used for buildings, *magnesian* and *dolomitic limestones*, which form the magnificent cliffs and towers of the Dolomitic Alps. Limestone is impure carbonate of lime, which is slowly soluble in water, so that limestone country abounds in caves and cavities, often encrusted with calcite crystals or adorned with stalactites and stalagmites formed by deposition from dripping water. In hot springs the dissolved carbonate of lime is precipitated in the form of *aragonite* and *calcareous tufa* – a kind of kettle-stone, in fact. *Dolomite* is carbonate of calcium and magnesium and may be crystalline or massive. All unaltered limestones are fossiliferous, but are not mineralised unless subject to pneumatolysis or metamorphic action which may introduce galena, fluorite and other minerals.

Siliceous deposits may be *organic* or *inorganic*, the latter including *geyserite* and *chert*. Fossils, both vegetable and animal, are often silicised or opalised.

The carbonaceous deposits yield *mineral coals* and *bitumens*. The latter include *crude oil, asphalt* and *ozokerite* which, however valuable industrially, are of little interest to a rockhound. The coals are obviously fossiliferous and may contain various minerals. A rockhound may like to make a collection of various kinds of coal. In any event, *lignite* has been used for ornaments, for instance in Ireland, and its hard black variety called *jet* is reckoned a gemstone.

The main interest of ironstones is likewise industrial as a source of iron.

Salt forms extensive rock masses in Iran, Utah in the USA, Thuringia in Germany, and elsewhere. The salt mines of Wieliczka, near Cracow, Poland, have been worked for 600 years and are still going strong. In addition to halides, there are deposits of borates, nitrates and alkali carbonates. *Rock salt* (mainly $NaCl$) may assume various colourings, and one of the authors (VAF) remembers vividly a beautiful display of coloured salts he saw as a child somewhere in Germany (probably Helmstedt). Salts absorb atmospheric moisture and deliquesce (dissolve in it), so that they have to be kept in airtight containers (eg sealed jars).

Phosphatic deposits include the following minerals: *collophane, apatite, dahlite, variscite* and *vivianite*.

21

This looks deceptively neat and tidy. In reality, however, the lines of distinction are blurred: there are calcareous sandstones and ironstones, bituminous shales, and so on. Still, the idealised theoretical types of rock do actually occur and are recognisable as such.

2

METAMORPHIC ROCKS

METAMORPHISM

Metamorphism is the process and/or the result of the process whereby the structure and mineralogy of rocks are changed. The rocks thus altered are called metamorphic. The forces responsible for such changes are threefold: pressure, and more particularly directed pressure or *stress* generated by crustal movements; magmatic heat; and chemical action either at contact with magma or through pneumatolysis (p 13). To this may be added the processes of chemical weathering, including oxidation, action by water and such substances as may be dissolved in it, and especially carbonic acid, which is formed when carbon dioxide from the air dissolves in water, resulting in the gradual conversion of silicates to carbonates.

As already mentioned, no kind of rock is exempt from metamorphism, but its effect on sediments is the most telling. Clastic rock may become welded into a hard solid mass. But even the consolidated sedimentary rocks, such as sandstone or limestone, are relatively soft and friable, and become hardened or *indurated* by pressure and heat in the same way as potter's clay is turned into hard earthenware by firing. Sediments contain the chemical ingredients of various minerals, but it requires heat and stress to conjure them into crystalline compounds. Stress and heat applied separately have different effects on both structure and mineral content. Some minerals have high-stress

23

and high-temperature forms (or *allomorphs*), of the same chemical composition, but having different physical properties and crystal shape.

Heat alone will suffice for induration and crystallisation. Crustal stresses, involving the creep of enormous rock masses, produce a foliated or leafy rock structure, exemplified by the laminar splitting of slate. From the rockhound's point of view the effect of strong stress is unfortunate inasmuch as crystals, unless housed in cavities, tend to be stretched and fractured in the process. Foliated rocks are referred to as *schists*.

Pressure itself generates heat. But it operates most effectively when the sediments are buried under thousands of feet of overlying strata and are already heated to begin with, since the temperature of the rocks rises with depth. Thus such metamorphism, which affects large land areas, and thus is known as *regional metamorphism*, must inevitably involve some heat, even though it is mainly due to stress. Increasing regional metamorphism, typified by the Scottish Highlands, converts shales into slates, phyllites, mica-schists and eventually gneiss (nice), which has the same composition as granite with the essential minerals arranged in layers, Swiss-roll fashion. This progressive alteration of the rocks is paralleled by the successive appearance of almandine garnet, kyanite, staurolite, sillimanite and cordierite, the garnet enduring throughout the series right into gneiss. Beryl, epidote, hornblende, corundum and other gem and non-gem minerals may also form, and are often sorted out into quartz veins.

Granite, too, is transformed into gneiss, and basic rocks into ' greenstone ' or, to be more precise, into hornblende and epidiorite schists and serpentinite (a crude serpentine rock), which are softer than the original formations. Sandstone turns into quartzite, and limestone crystallises into marble.

A list of metamorphic rocks and their properties is given in Table 2.

CONTACT METAMORPHISM

Contact metamorphism is due mainly to the heat of magmatic intrusions. Such an intrusion is surrounded by a *metamorphic aureole*, within which country rock has been metamorphosed. This may be from a few centimetres up to 5km wide, depending on the size and temperature of the intrusion. There is also chemical action along the contact line. Some of the country rock is engulfed and digested by the magma, which alters its composition, or else larger ' islands ' of country rock, known as *rafts*, are surrounded by magma and strongly baked. The magma branches off into the enclosing strata, insinuates itself between them in sills, ascends along the faults and fractures in dykes (p 15), and forms minor veins and veinlets. These penetrate not only the original rocks but the cooling igneous mass itself as new batches of hot melt surge up from the depths.

Limestone is still baked to marble; and garnets, corundum, spinel, beryl and quite a few other minerals may crystallise out in it. Sandstone, in which amethysts may develop, often changes colour from red to green, eventually to be fused into quartzite as the flow of heat continues. However, in the absence of shearing stress, schists cannot arise, and shales and like rocks are baked into tough *hornfels* instead, spangled with quartz, felspar, mica and alusite, cordierite, diopside, wollastonite, grossularite, and occasionally sapphire. Olivine and calcite may form in siliceous dolomitic limestone, and as olivine subsequently decays to serpentine by chemical weathering, the rock becomes *ophicalcite*, a green-and-white ornamental stone.

Crystals arising from contact metamorphism are usually free from stress fractures.

PNEUMATOLYSIS AND THERMAL VEINS

Pneumatolysis is metamorphism due to the penetration by magmatic fluids, associated with the late stages of consolidation of igneous intrusions. As the heat of the emanation declines, the hot corrosive gases are succeeded by hot water carrying various substances in solution and giving rise to *hydrothermal veins*.

Most metals have lower melting points than most silicates, and so remain in the fluid state when the latter begin to solidify. Thus metals form a ' mobile ' component or *fraction* of magmas (especially acid magmas), which also hold large amounts of steam and other gases. The amount of these a magma can retain decreases with temperature and pressure, both of which are reduced in its ascent towards the surface. Therefore, these gases and metallic vapours are given off by igneous intrusions and insinuate themselves into the cracks and crannies of the pre-existent rocks, additionally shattered by the pressure exerted by the rising magma.

In this way such metals as lead, tin, zinc, copper, silver and gold are entrained by the magmatic gases and become deposited in metalliferous *lodes* in the company of characteristic *gangue* minerals, arising partly from the emanations themselves and partly through their thermal and chemical interaction with the country rock. Quartz, tourmaline, fluorite, chlorite, barite, calcite and topaz are typical gangue minerals.

The general effect of pneumatolysis in sedimentary formations will vary according to their composition as well as that of the magmatic emanations themselves, but the crystallisation of various garnets, axinite, epidote, apatite, fluorite, topaz, tourmaline, zinnwaldite, lepidolite etc may be looked for. Quartz and calcite are ubiquitous rock constituents and commonly occur in veins. Basic rocks rich in magnesia may be altered to serpentinite, a crude serpentine rock of speckled appearance resembling the skin of a serpent. Precious serpentine is a yellow–green mineral, and as already mentioned is formed by the chemical decay of olivine.

Wherever igneous rocks outcrop, pneumatolysis may be expected within, and sometimes beyond, the metamorphic aureole; and it must be borne in mind that the outcrops are only the summits of the concealed underground intrusions.

There is, of course, no difference between the magmatic and volcanic fluids, so that similar changes take place in the vicinity of lavas – except that a lava can vent its vapours more or less freely into the air, yielding surface incrustations (eg of sulphur), and its temperature will generally be lower than that of a confined body of magma.

PNEUMATOLYSIS IN IGNEOUS, ESPECIALLY ACID, ROCKS

The effects of pneumatolysis on the rocks of the granite clan are of especial interest, partly because they are the typical igneous formations of the Earth's crust, and partly because they contain some of the most attractive minerals.

Superheated steam accounts for up to 90 per cent of all volcanic and magmatic exhalation, and it can be highly corrosive. Its action on igneous rocks consists mainly in attacking the felspars and converting these to kaolin, a soft white clay much sought after for the making of china ware. This causes such felspar-rich rocks as granite or syenite to disintegrate, releasing the other crystalline minerals they contain, eg amethyst, cairngorm and tourmaline. Turquoise, chrysocolla and other hydrated species will tend to form. Since carbon dioxide is another copious magmatic emanation, hot carbonic acid will attack silicates, as well as metals and their salts, transforming them into carbonates, some of which are brightly coloured, eg azurite, malachite and rhodochrosite. These also form by the slow process of chemical weathering.

Boron vapours convert felspars and micas into tourmaline. Chlorine and fluorine often occur together, yielding topaz, apatite and fluorite, and giving granite a loose crumbly structure, described by the term *greisen* (grysen). Once again this is a boon to miner and rockhound alike as this makes the interior of the rocks easier to reach – and most well-formed crystals are unaffected by the transformation. Enrichment in metals and their salts may also be expected.

Sulphurous and phosphorous fumes will interact with the

rock chemicals, yielding corresponding mineral compounds. Apatite is a common pneumatolytic product requiring the presence of phosphorus.

At a later stage thermal solutions circulating along the fractures and chain-cavities will deposit in these various soluble minerals, and chalcedonic silica and opal in particular. This applies especially to the porous (vesicular) lavas, both acid and basic; the cavities of the latter often contain zeolites.

3
CLASSIFICATION OF MINERALS

COMPOSITION
As will be recalled from the Introduction, most rocks are of
mixed composition, containing different minerals. Minerals
are more or less pure chemical substances, and their composition can be expressed by a chemical formula showing that the
substance is built up from atoms occurring in constant and
multiple proportions.

Minerals are quite often classified according to chemical
composition: as elements, oxides, sulphides, silicates etc. This
is more of theoretical value than practical use as it does not
enable us to identify minerals in the field without chemical
tests, and the composition of a mineral is not immediately
recognisable from its appearance. We will not often want to
carry out chemical analysis of minerals, particularly as this
involves the destruction of some of the material, and we may
want to preserve the finds intact in a display or for cutting as
gems.

Composition is not all we need to know about a mineral either.
It is possible for chemical compounds with the same formula to
have different internal structures, and this means different
external shapes, and usually these are distinct minerals with
contrasting physical properties, known as *allomorphs* (see p 24).
A good example is the hard precious gem diamond, which is
the same chemical, pure carbon, as graphite, the latter being

29

found as opaque, very soft, shiny, grey or black plates or masses and used for lubrication and the making of pencil ' lead '. The two forms arise from different conditions, very high pressures being needed to crystallise diamonds, and hence these are harder, more compact (chemically and hence also in physical density) and rarer than graphite deposits, at least in surface rocks – diamond being an accessory mineral in ultrabasic rocks, which originate at great depths. Titanium oxide, TiO_2, occurs as rutile, anatase and brookite, minerals having different crystal forms and properties. Conditions of origin also distinguish crystals of quartz from shapeless chalcedony, which is deposited from water solutions. Both are silica, SiO_2.

Most minerals can form crystals in which the internal structure is repeated symmetrically. These crystals vary in size, a quartz crystal from Madagascar being 12ft long. Frequently, crystals are too small or intergrown to be immediately recognised as such. Thus the crystalline appearance of minerals is distinguished from the *amorphous* (meaning shapeless) or *massive*. However, most massive minerals have a concealed crystalline structure and are known as *crypto-crystalline*. Thus chalcedony actually consists of tiny crystals which can only be seen under magnification. A typical massive mineral is haematite, an iron oxide which forms rounded lumps massed together in structures that may be *reniform* (kidney-shaped) or *botryoidal* (like a bunch of grapes). If these lumps are broken open it can be seen that each is a mass of radiating crystals growing from a centre and looking like a fan in cross-section; and like some other massive minerals, haematite can also occur in recognisable crystals.

Amorphous materials containing water bound into the structure form from colloidal suspensions and are known as *gels*. This is the same in principle as the formation of gelatine or soap jelly and is represented by the mineral opal, which is formed from silica. Other minerals of this type include chrysocolla, glauconite and limonite.

The only other minerals which are truly non-crystalline are

glasses, such as obsidian (p 15), formed from a melt which has cooled too rapidly to crystallise.

In a complex chemical lattice structure, particularly with the silicates, there can be variations in the composition without much difference in properties. This is the case with tourmalines and garnets. In garnets there are two metals which fit into the silicate structure, and these may be calcium, magnesium, iron or manganese in the one case, and either iron, aluminium, chromium or titanium in the other, totally or partly replacing each other. These substitutions do not affect the lattice, so that although the physical properties of the garnets vary slightly, the crystal shapes remain the same. The colour depends on composition, however, including shades of red, brown and green. Olivine is a silicate of iron and magnesium, or a mixture of both, and similar remarks apply. Other silicates of variable composition include pyroxenes, amphiboles, micas, felspars, epidotes and zeolites.

Where gemstones are concerned, the colour is of great interest and importance in the trade and to the collector as well, and this can be the cause of great confusion. Both the red ruby and the blue sapphire are forms of corundum, which is aluminium oxide, Al_2O_3. With the aid of a spectroscope it is possible to show that the colour is due to chromium in the first case, and to the presence of iron and titanium in the second, both occurring as impurities in minute traces. Moreover, there are violet, green, yellow, grey, black and colourless sapphires as well. In the gem trade fanciful and misleading names are given to these stones. Violet sapphire is called ' oriental amethyst ', although an amethyst in fact is violet or purple quartz. Yellow sapphire and quartz are similarly confused with topaz which, although commonly yellow, can be brown, pink, red, green, blue or colourless. Quartz may range from the colourless rock crystal through white, rose-pink, yellow, brown and smoky to black, and from green and blue to the purple of amethyst. Zircon and spinel also vary widely in colouring.

It is clear that although due to variations in composition, such colours are of no assistance in identifying and classifying minerals. In some other cases colour is more helpful. If we can establish that we are dealing with a garnet, its colour will then indicate the type of garnet. In opaque minerals, such as rhodochrosite, turquoise, malachite and lapis lazuli, the colours are reasonably constant, and together with surface appearance, with which we shall deal next, are a fair guide to identity.

APPEARANCE

The minerals we find may be in their natural form as crystals or massive shapes, or in an earthy or powdery condition. They may also be broken or deformed, or occur as waterworn pebbles, which makes identification more difficult. They may be coated with rust or other foreign substance which could disguise their colour and even distort their shape. When all this is considered there are still some quite superficial properties that are helpful in classification.

Minerals are either *transparent* and show a sharp image of the objects viewed through them, or if they give a slightly blurred image, they are *semi-transparent*. If light passes through in a diffuse way so that no image is seen, the stone is *translucent*. If no light passes through it is *opaque*. It is worth bearing in mind that the thinner the material the more easily light passes through, so that even opaque materials may be transparent or at least translucent in thin slices. For example, flints, which are impure silica, are translucent in thin chips, but opaque in mass. Sometimes the colour of the light transmitted in thin sections may be characteristically different from that of the surface; eg gold is green in transmitted light. This classification will, however, be found helpful.

As we have seen, the colour of transparent minerals can be very variable, particularly if the pure substance is colourless. The colouring of opaque minerals is more reliable, but may be altered by tarnishing. The tarnished surface often shows a display of rainbow colours similar to those of oil spread on water and called *iridescence*. This is also found in transparent or translucent crystals with internal fractures or fissures.

Some materials, notably felspars, may change colour with the angle of viewing. This is due to the interference of light on thin plates of mineral impurities, and rocks containing such felspars from southern Norway are used in ornamentation. Owing to structural properties some crystals vary in colour with orientation. This is called *pleochroism* and is considered with the optical properties of minerals. Different again is the play of colour when fine gems, especially the diamond, are moved about. This arises from the prismatic structure of the crystal or faceted gem and its high refractive index.

The quality of reflection or *lustre* of the surface is another distinguishing feature. This may be *metallic*, that is opaque and shiny, as on the metals and many of their ores. It may be *vitreous*, or *glassy*, as in quartz; *adamantine* (fine) like that of diamond; *resinous*, which is typical of amber and garnets; *pearly*, where the material is in thin layers, examples of which are talc and topaz on fracture planes; *silky*, where the structure is fibrous, as in some forms of calcite and gypsum, both known as ' satin spar '; and *waxy*, like that of chalcedony, turquoise and jasper. The lustre of materials reflecting an image brilliantly like a mirror is *splendent*; or if a little indistinctly, merely *shining*. If no image is seen it is termed *glistening*, fading to *glimmering*. If there is no lustre the mineral is *dull*.

Among the many terms used to describe the shapes of crystalline and massive minerals, it may be useful to explain the following:

Acicular   fine thin crystals like needles, eg natrolite
Amygdaloidal   almond-shaped, as materials found enclosed in cavities
Bladed   tapering plates, eg kyanite
Botryoidal   like a bunch of grapes (p 30)

Dendritic or *Arborescent*   in thin branches, as deposited in crevices

Fibrous   in thin threads

Filiform   like wire or string, especially native silver and copper

Foliated   in thin sheets, also described as *lamellar*

Granular   consisting of grains, eg marble

Mammilated   a mass of interpenetrating balls, eg malachite

Oölithic   in small, roughly spherical bodies

Reniform   kidney-shaped (p 30)

Reticulated   in cross-mesh or net array

Tabular   broad flat crystals

It is doubtful if we need go much further than this, although it is possible to classify the feel of minerals, and a few even have a taste or smell to distinguish them by, such as the garlic smell of the arsenic compounds when heated. It is not recommended to test these particular minerals for taste. The feel of minerals may be *smooth*, *greasy* or *unctuous*, *soapy*, *harsh*, *meagre* or *rough*, and some adhere to the tongue as an additional test.

When we come to describe the various minerals in the later chapters, we will refer to the colour and lustre as well as shape, but we will group them mainly according to the rocks and circumstances in which they are found.

CRYSTAL FORM

The atoms in a substance bear certain constant structural relations to each other, and in a mixed melt or solution not only do particles of the same substance tend to cling together, but they do so in an orderly way, just as we might build up models of similarly shaped blocks. The crystals of a mineral may not always have the same shape, but the angles and symmetry of form are preserved in a certain way as a consequence of the molecular structure. The flexibility of form may be illustrated by calcite, or crystalline calcium carbonate, $CaCO_3$, which occurs in over 700 different shapes, all related to the basic hexagonal structure. Of these about six distinctive common forms are described and named.

The first step to clarifying this rather daunting complexity is to recognise that there are six different crystal families or *systems.* These are the *cubic* or *isometric, tetragonal, hexagonal, orthorhombic, monoclinic* and *triclinic,* working roughly in the order from the most to the least symmetrical, and all crystal forms are developed within these systems.

Crystals, being three-dimensional, must be defined by at least three directional axes. For this purpose use is made of *structural* or *crystallographic axes.* These are not the same as geometrical axes, nor do they denote all the axes of symmetry in the crystal, of which there may be various numbers, from none to thirteen. These crystallographic axes each have a measurable length through the centre of symmetry from one crystal face to its opposite number. If there is no centre of symmetry, as can occur for example in quartz crystals, the axes still meet in a point. Only in the simplest case are all the axes at right angles to each other and equal in length. The six crystal systems are based on the relative lengths and inclinations of these axes.

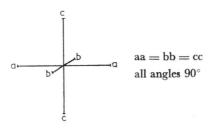

aa = bb = cc
all angles 90°

Where all the axes are equal and at right angles we have examples of the *cubic* or *isometric* (of equal measure) system (Fig 1), in which the cube and the octahedron are the simplest shapes. Another basic form is the tetrahedron, bounded by four equilateral triangles. The simple shapes are usually modi-

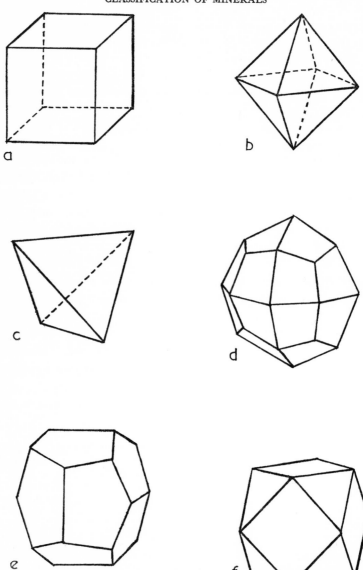

FIG 1 Cubic system: A=cube (pyrites, fluorspar); B=octahedron (spinel, magnetite); C=tetrahedron (tetrahedrite); D=trapezohedron (leucite, garnet); E=pyritohedron (pyrites); F=cube and octahedron (galena).

fied in nature with bevelled or depressed edges, pyramidal projections or depressions on the faces, or the points may be cut off into additional facets. This kind of development is common to all the crystal systems, each mineral having its favoured forms of occurrence. It will be seen, however, that this cannot affect the basic symmetry of the system, and in the cubic family the result is always a symmetrical bead which can be inscribed within a sphere. The family is a large one in nature, comprising minerals such as diamond, the garnets, spinel, fluorite, iron pyrites, galena and other metal sulphides, as well as native gold, silver and copper.

aa = bb ≠ cc
All angles 90°

The *tetragonal* system (Fig 2) is an extension of the cubic with one axis different from the other two, but all still at right angles to each other. The simplest shape is thus a square column with rectangular cross-sections through the odd axis. Often there will be pyramidal endings to the column, or bevels, or the two

aa = bb ≠ cc
∢ aOc = ∢ bOc = 90°
α = β = 120°

pyramids may meet each other with or without an intervening girdle. Chalcopyrite can form into disphenoids, which are

37

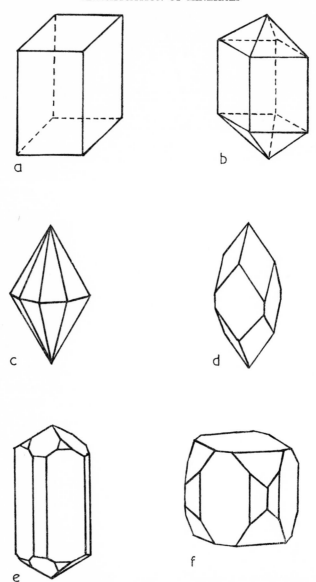

Fig 2   Tetragonal system: *A*=basic form; *B*=zircon; *C*=double pyramid;
D=apophyllite; *E*=rutile; *F*=apophyllite.

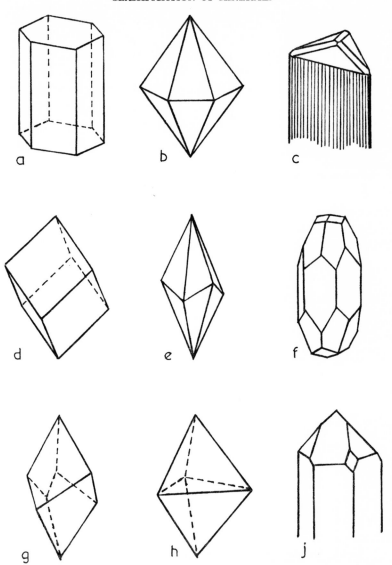

FIG 3 Hexagonal system: A=hexagonal prism (beryl); B=hexagonal pyramid; C=tourmaline; D=rhombohedron; E=scalenohedron; F= calcite (trigonal forms typical of calcite); G=trapezohedron; H=pyramid; J=quartz (trigonal forms typical of quartz).

irregular tetrahedra. Zircon, rutile, scheelite and cassiterite are other tetragonal minerals.

The *hexagonal* system (Fig 3), like the tetragonal, has an odd axis at right angles to the equal ones, but in this case there are three of the latter at 120° to each other. The forms are thus derived from prisms with a hexagonal or triangular cross-section. Six- or even twelve-sided (dihexagonal) prisms are usual in the case of beryl, while in tourmaline three of the prism faces may be developed at the expense of the others, giving a predominantly triangular form. Quartz usually forms hexagonal prisms ending up in a pyramid at one or both ends, but it also occurs in bipyramidal crystals. Corundum may be spindle- or barrel-shaped. Hexagonal plates are another possibility, and an interesting variation is found in both quartz and calcite in which crystals have six quadrilateral sides. In calcite these are diamond-shaped (rhombohedral), and in quartz trapezium-shaped (like triangles with the tops cut off), (see Fig 3, d and g). These crystals, having irregular sides, are not cubic, but have trigonal symmetry. Apatite, haematite and nepheline are other examples of the hexagonal system.

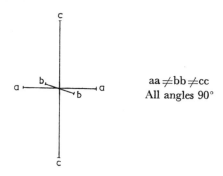

$$aa \neq bb \neq cc$$
All angles 90°

The *orthorhombic system* (Fig 4) is once more right-angled, but unlike the tetragonal it has three axes of different lengths, so that the crystal shapes are derived from a brick-like solid, actually represented by crystals of prehnite. Pyramidal forms

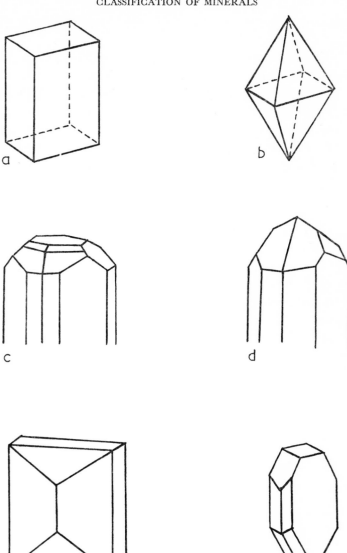

Fig 4   Orthorhombic system: A=basic form (prehnite); B=pyramid (sulphur); C=topaz; D=topaz; E=staurolite; F=hemimorphite.

41

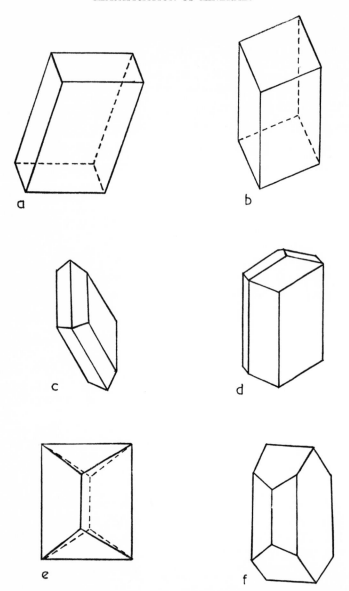

FIG 5   Monoclinic system: A=inclines to right; B=inclines on diagonal (basic forms); C=gypsum; D=hornblende; E=sphene; F=orthoclase.

are more common. In topaz the number of side faces in the prism is usually doubled. If a crystal ' stands straight ' and is neither tetragonal nor hexagonal, it must be orthorhombic. Barite, olivine, staurolite, aragonite, sulphur and natrolite are other members of this system.

In the *monoclinic* system (Fig 5) one of the three unequal axes slopes away from 90° to the plane of the other axes, which stand

$$aa \neq bb \neq cc$$
$$\sphericalangle aOb = \sphericalangle bOa = 90°, \ \sphericalangle cOa \neq 90°$$

at right angles to each other. Kunzite, a variety of spodumene, has crystals of this type – like a distorted matchbox leaning to one side. Orthoclase, augite, hornblende and gypsum are monoclinic.

$$aa \neq bb \neq cc$$
no angle $= 90°$

We reach the limits of variation in the *triclinic* system (Fig 6) where no two axes are equal or at right angles to each other. Any face of the crystal matches only its opposite mate and is different from all the others. Kyanite shows crystals of the simplest type, like a distorted brick which will lean sideways whichever way it is stood up – a geometrical solid enjoying the name of parallelepipedon. Plagioclase felspar, axinite and rhodonite belong to this family.

We have mentioned some of the complexities by which faces

43

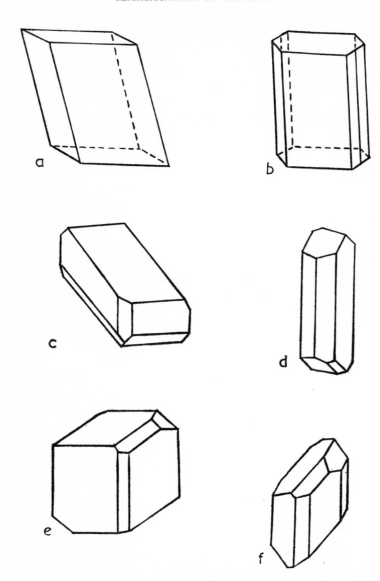

Fɪɢ 6   Triclinic system: *A*=basic form; *B*=kyanite; *C*=rhodonite; *D*=albite; *E*=axinite; *F*=axinite.

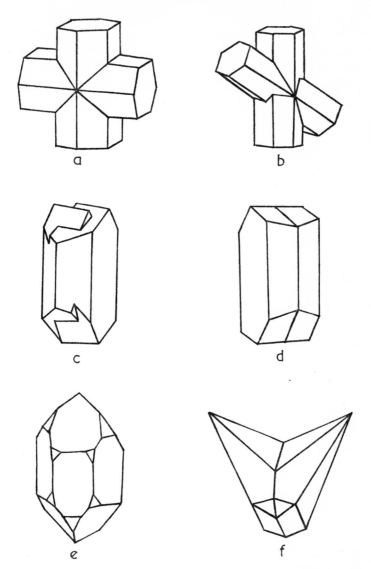

FIG 7   Twinned crystals: *A* and *B* staurolite twins; Carlsbad twins of orthoclase; *C*=penetration twins; *D*=contact twins; *E*=Brazil twins of quartz; *F*=calcite twins.

are built up and it should be noted that unequal development of faces is frequent in nature, owing to obstruction or lack of material in some direction or other. On the whole, small crystals are the most likely to be perfect in shape. However, the angle between the adjacent faces of the particular solid always remains constant, relating it to its crystal system which can normally be identified. Small angular differences are not easy to estimate, which may give rise to confusion. Thus a crystal whose one axis is inclined at 87° is monoclinic and must be distinguished from an orthorhombic crystal where the angle is 90°.

It is possible for crystals to interpenetrate or meet each other by sharing a common plane. This is known as *twinning* and gives rise to some beautiful shapes, such as the cruciform crystals of staurolite (Fig 7). Crystals may grow in an aggregate with edges or faces parallel, or be jumbled up quite irregularly. The crosswise pattern of staurolite is an example of *stellate* twinning: there may be six crystals forming a star, as in chrysoberyl, or many crystals may be bunched up radially in three dimensions. The radial arrangement of crystals in a solid botryoid has already been mentioned (p 30).

Finally, it is worth noting that some crystals are *striated*, ie lined or grooved, in a characteristic way, or there may be typical etch marks on the faces, aiding recognition. The prisms of beryl and topaz are usually lined lengthwise; those of quartz are lined across, with faint ridges; pyrite is lined on the faces, the lines on the faces of a cube being at right angles to one edge and to the lines on the adjacent faces. Zinc blende octahedra have different etch marks on alternate faces; the alternate oblique faces of quartz crystals are likewise differently marked with ' scoops ' and ' birdies '.

To look at the named and described crystals in collections of minerals will help to illustrate the various laws and points outlined here. Textbooks of mineralogy and crystallography go into greater depth for those who are interested, but the above should suffice as a general practical introduction to the subject.

4

THE PHYSICAL PROPERTIES
OF MINERALS

HARDNESS AND STREAK

Minerals differ greatly in hardness, which provides an important and simple way of testing and distinguishing them. A softer mineral will be scratched when the point of a harder one is gently drawn over it. In making a scratch one must choose a clean undecayed surface that is not coated with foreign matter, eg haematite (rust); otherwise the result of the test may be misleading. Furthermore, crumbs of the softer material, known as the *streak*, may be confused with the scratch, so that it is best to wipe or blow away the dust and examine the scratch with a magnifying glass. In this way also a small scratch can be observed with minimum damage to the specimen.

If a slightly softer mineral is applied with sufficient pressure a kind of scratch may be produced on the harder one by crushing, but this spoils the test as well as the specimen. It also demonstrates that hard materials can be brittle; and diamond, the hardest substance found in nature, disintegrates readily when given a sharp blow. Therefore, scratching should be reasonably delicate.

As a harder stone will always scratch a softer one, it is possible to arrange minerals according to hardness, and the system now in common use was devised by Friedrich Mohs (1773–1839) by assigning numbers from one to ten to important

47

minerals in the order of increasing hardness. It must be understood, however, that these numbers are not quantities: as scientifically tested, diamond is some 140 times harder than corundum – and this is the biggest difference in the table – while the hardnesses of felspar and quartz compare as $2\frac{1}{2}$ to 3.

This is *Mohs' scale of hardness*

1 Talc
2 Gypsum (or rock salt)
3 Calcite
4 Fluorite
5 Apatite
6 Orthoclase felspar
7 Quartz
8 Topaz
9 Corundum
10 Diamond

Borazon (crystalline boron nitride) is harder than diamond, but has not to date been found in nature. Two other hard synthetic materials, silicon carbide (carborundum) and boron carbide, both used as abrasives, fall between diamond and corundum. Minerals of intermediate hardness are given fractional placings: thus euclase and andalusite are $7\frac{1}{2}$, while beryl is $7\frac{3}{4}$, and tourmaline $7\frac{1}{4}$. It must be repeated that this scaling is arbitrary and not related to quantitative measures of hardness.

For testing materials on this scale small pointed fragments of the test minerals can be mounted, eg with an epoxy-resin adhesive or lapidary's dopping wax, on a wooden stick, small tube or the like, to make *hardness pencils*. A pencil may be double-ended, with different minerals at the two ends. Common objects which can be used for rough hardness estimates include steel files ($6\frac{3}{4}$), penknives ($5\frac{1}{2}$ to $6\frac{1}{2}$), window glass (5), copper coin (3) and fingernail (variable, $2-2\frac{1}{2}$).

Some anomalous results may be obtained. Kyanite, also

known as disthene which is the Greek for two-strengths, has a hardness of only 5 along the prism, but 7 across it. Thus it can be readily identified with a pocket knife.

The colour of the powder produced by scratching minerals can be useful in distinguishing them. As previously mentioned, this is known as the *streak*. Most transparent stones have a white streak, and the streak of others (eg anatase and fluorite) is colourless. But the streak of pyrope garnet is red, and most softer minerals have coloured streaks. Those of opaque minerals may differ in colour from the stone itself. Haematite, which is usually iron-grey or black, has a characteristic cherry-red streak. Pyrite, or ' fool's gold ', can be easily distinguished from true gold by its greenish-black streak – the genuine article has a golden streak, knowing which we need not be fooled. For streak tests use is often made of a hard ceramic plate (*streak plate*) over which the mineral is drawn like a pencil over paper, leaving a mark that is the streak; or else one may employ a piece of fine carborundum or emery paper. The latter will take the streak from any natural mineral short of corundum, and the former will work for all minerals except diamond.

FRACTURE AND CLEAVAGE

In many crystals the chemical bonds between the atoms are weaker in one plane than another, and such minerals tend to break evenly parallel to this plane or planes. This is called *cleavage* and is characteristic of the mineral species, although it may be subject to slight variation within it. The ' books ' of foliated minerals, such as micas and molybdenite or scaly graphite, can be easily split into thin leaves. Cubes of galena cleave parallel to the cubic faces, and the cleavage is thus cubical. In diamond and fluorite the cleavage is across the corners of the cube, leaving an octahedral remnant. Calcite is reduced to rhombohedral fragments when broken or crushed, regardless of the original crystal shape. In the case of topaz

49

there is a strong tendency for breaks to occur at right angles to the long axis of the prism, and this should be guarded against.

Cleavage may be useful to a skilled lapidary in *bruting* or roughly shaping a stone, and this technique is commonly used in working with diamonds. Otherwise in faceted gems the cuts are made at a small angle to the cleavage planes to prevent subsequent chipping. The use of cleavage as a means of identification is limited, inasmuch as we are unlikely to want to break up a fine crystal simply to observe its mode of cleavage. The results of natural cleavage may, however, be present in the specimens as found.

A break in an uncleavable mineral or in a cleavable mineral across a cleavage plane will display a characteristic *fracture*. One of the common forms of fracture is *conchoidal*: it is concave and in concentric steps, like rings, recalling the inside of a conch shell. This occurs in quartz, beryl and in glasses, including most window glass. Although a form of quartz, amethyst has a *rippled* fracture which may be found in some uncoloured crystals as well. The fracture may be *even*, but in many cases it is *uneven* and in a series of jerks or steps as in the examples described above. *Hackly*, exemplified by the fracture of cast iron and native copper, and *splintery*, are self-explanatory terms. Minerals with a fibrous structure, such as asbestos, have a *fibrous* fracture. In loosely coherent minerals the fracture is *earthy*, as in chalk.

Once again this is a property we are more likely to observe than to produce deliberately.

SPECIFIC GRAVITY

The density or relative weight of minerals is an important and characteristic property and can be measured with simple apparatus, normally consisting of some form of balance. The density is more precisely standardised as *specific gravity* (SG) which is expressed as a multiple of the density of water. In metric units this is the same as the weight in grammes per cubic centimetre, because a cubic centimetre of water weighs one gramme.

It is not necessary to measure the volume of an odd-shaped stone directly. As Archimedes discovered (while sitting in his bath, so the story goes), a body immersed in water is lighter by the weight of water it displaces, and this gives the volume of a body in terms of the weight of water. It is, therefore, only necessary to weigh our specimen first in air and then in water, and the specific gravity is given by

$$\frac{\text{Normal weight in air}}{\text{Difference in weights}}$$

There are several ways of doing this. With an ordinary chemical balance, the specimen can be weighed normally and then suspended from a thread and immersed in a beaker of water which rests on a wooden bridge standing over the scale pan. It is important to remove any bubbles of air with a brush, and some allowance needs to be made for holes or inclusions in the specimen.

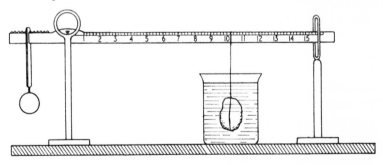

Fig 8 Walker's steelyard.

A simple way of weighing the specimen in and out of water is with Walker's *steelyard* (Fig 8). Here the test object is moved along the arm of a graduated rule until it balances against a counter-weight. The weight in each case is inversely proportional to the distance on the rule measured from the pivot, and

51

it is not even necessary to know the value of the counter-weight. If the reading in air is a and in water is b, then:

$$SG = \frac{\dfrac{1}{a}}{\dfrac{1}{a} - \dfrac{1}{b}} = \frac{b}{b - a}.$$

Another method is to use a long helical spring which hangs vertically next to a rule, as in *Jolly's spring balance*. If the spring is stretched down over a distance a unloaded, over b with the specimen freely suspended in air, and over c with the specimen immersed, then:

$$SG = \frac{b - a}{b - c}.$$

A quick measure of the volume can be found with reasonable accuracy by immersing the specimen or specimens in a graduated measuring cylinder and noting the increase in volume in cubic centimetres. All that is now required to obtain the specific gravity is a weighing in air, preferably in grammes, as otherwise a conversion will have to be made.

A method that is sometimes used involves heavy liquids. A solid will sink in a liquid that is less dense than it, float in one of greater density, and if the densities are exactly equal it can come to rest in any position below the surface. Among the liquids used are bromoform (SG $2 \cdot 9$), methylene iodide ($3 \cdot 35$) and Clerici's solution ($4 \cdot 0$), which is a mixture of thallium formate and thallium malonate. The former two can be diluted with benzene or methylated spirit, but both require careful storing as they are affected by exposure to light. Clerici's solution is stable, but is both expensive and poisonous. It can be diluted with water.

An elegant way of determining the density of small pieces with heavy liquids is to use a *diffusion column*. Two miscible liquids, one of high and the other of low density, are used. The latter is poured gently on top of the former in a long tubular container, avoiding mechanical mixing. In a day or two the liquids will have diffused into each other, forming an intermediate band of graded density. Marker chips of, say, quartz (SG 2·65), topaz (SG 3·5) and other minerals, each of which will sink to the depth corresponding to its density, can be used for calibration. It is then a simple matter to drop in small samples or cut gems and find their specific gravity against these standards. As diffusion continues, the markers will change position, but this does not affect the calibration, and the column will remain useful for some weeks until the diffusion is more or less complete and the mixture has settled to a substantially uniform density. The same method is employed to separate the components of crushed or mixed materials for identification.

MISCELLANEOUS PROPERTIES

There are a few other properties of minerals which may be of interest, even if less of a practical help in identification. One such depends on surface tension effects and serves to separate diamonds and some metal ores from mixed rock fragments and pebbles by making use of the fact that these valuable components adhere readily to grease and oil. A similar method relies on the dust of crushed ores being attracted by air bubbles and thus rising to the surface in a turbulent stream of water.

The conduction of heat varies in minerals and other materials. Gemstones conduct heat reasonably well and better than glass. Hence genuine diamonds and other gems are colder to the touch than paste imitations when first handled, although, of course, they warm up if left in the hand.

Most minerals acquire an electric charge when rubbed with a flannel, and will then attract dust or chaff. Amber, which is called *elektron* in Greek, was well known for this in classical antiquity, and electricity has been named after it. Tourmaline and topaz share the interesting *pyroelectric* property of becoming charged by heating alone and attracting small particles in the same way as rubbed amber.

Magnetite and pyrrhotite are magnetic enough to be attracted by an ordinary bar magnet. The more powerful magnetism of an electromagnet can be used to influence siderite, iron garnets, chromite, ilmenite, haematite and wolfram among others, this trick again being applied to the industrial extraction of ores.

5

OPTICAL PROPERTIES

REFLECTION, REFRACTION AND DISPERSION

The optical properties of opaque minerals have been discussed in Chapter 3. In dealing with transparent minerals we have to consider the behaviour of transmitted as well as of reflected light. Indeed, it is to the properties of transmitted light that most of the fire and special appeal of precious stones is due.

Light striking a crystal face or gem facet at right angles passes through in a straight line. If the angle is less than a right angle, however, the ray of light is bent or *refracted*. This is the same effect as when a stick dipped in water appears bent at the surface, and is due to the slower speed of light in water, which is optically denser than air.

Fig. 9 illustrates the behaviour of a ray of light entering a stone from the air. The *angle of incidence* α is measured between the ray and the line drawn at right angles to the surface of the stone. The *angle of refraction* β is, similarly, the angle between this line and the refracted ray in the stone. The denser the material is, optically speaking, the smaller will be the angle β in relation to α: or, optical density measures the reduction in the speed of light as compared to its speed in air. In fact, the speeds of light in air and stone compare as in sin α to sin β, or as $a'\,a''$ to $b'\,b''$ in our drawing. This ratio is the same for all values of α, and is called the *refractive index* or RI for short.

Since this ratio depends solely on the speed of light in the

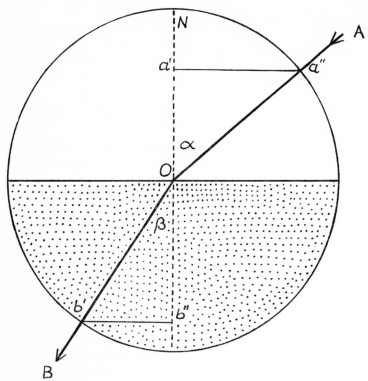

Fɪɢ 9 Refraction of light at air–stone interface (stone is stippled): $AO=$ incident ray, $OB=$refracted ray; $\alpha=$angle of incidence; $\beta=$angle of refraction; $O=$point of incidence; $NO=$normal to interface at point of incidence; $RI=\dfrac{\sin\alpha}{\sin\beta}=\dfrac{a'\ a''}{b'\ b''}$

two media, the diagram can be viewed upside-down to show the reverse path of the ray from the stone into air. As α is always larger than β, it is clear that as β increases a point will be reached where $\alpha=90°$, so that light from inside the stone skims along the boundary between the stone and air. This is called the *critical angle*. If it is exceeded, there will be *total internal reflection*, and the ray will rebound back into the stone at the same angle at which it hit the face, but on the other side of the vertical line (Fig 10).

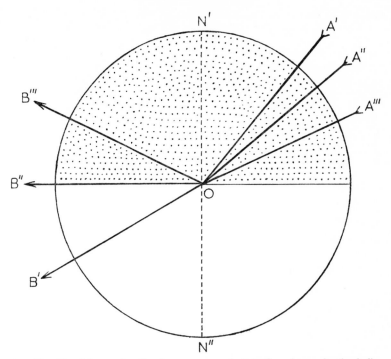

Fig 10 Total internal reflection at stone–air interface (stone is stippled): $N'ON''$=normal at point of incidence O. A' refracted as B'. A'' at critical angle of incidence refracted as B''; A''' totally reflected as B'''.

Clearly, the more easily internal reflection occurs the more light will concentrate in certain directions, giving a sparkling effect. To enhance this a gem is cut to ' trap ' as much light as possible: in other words the cut is contrived to reflect back into the eyes most of the light shining into the gem and to allow only an unavoidable minimum to pass through the gem to the underside. This is achieved by giving the facets of the top half of the gem, or *crown*, and the bottom half, or *pavilion*, such inclinations that light entering the stone vertically from above strikes the pavilion facets at angles greater than the critical and is reflected back to the crown facets at angles below the critical.

57

To return to our original train of thought, $RI=\dfrac{\sin \alpha}{\sin \beta}$ and for the critical value of β, $\alpha=90°$, and so $\sin \alpha=1$, whence the sine of the critical angle is $\dfrac{1}{RI}$, the reciprocal of the refractive index. In this way we can find the critical angle from RI, without any calculation, simply by looking up in the mathematical tables the angle whose cosecant is equal to RI. This can be very useful to a lapidary.

It can be seen that the higher the RI, the smaller is the critical angle and the more easily internal reflection occurs. This makes a stone particularly valuable for cutting, and in this respect diamond $(RI=2\cdot42)$ excels over all natural stones except the titania minerals: brookite, anatase and rutile.

The RI is measured by means of an optical instrument known as a *refractometer*, the principle of which is illustrated in Fig. 11. It is based on the critical angle.

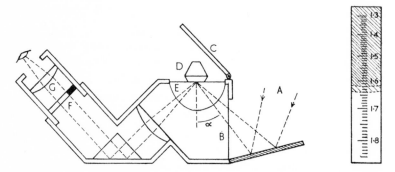

Fig 11 The refractometer: α is the critical angle; $A=$convergent light beams; $B=$glass window; $C=$adjustable screen and cover; $D=$ gemstone; $E=$glass hemisphere; $F=$calibrated scale; $G=$eyepiece. View of the scale in the eyepiece. Note: the stone is birefringent, giving two shadow edges. The faint shadow at $1\cdot81$ shows the RI of the oil.

In a construction commonly used for testing gems, the specimen is placed on the base of an inverted glass hemisphere.

This is convenient because a beam of light directed at or coming from the centre always strikes the surface at a right angle and passes through without deflection. A drop of oil with a high refractive index is placed under the specimen and is pressed into a thin film excluding air and forming a boundary at which total internal reflection can occur. The face of the specimen must be perfectly smooth and polished, as in the table of a cut gem, otherwise the method will not work. A convergent beam of light is shone on the stone through the hemisphere, and that part which is reflected passes into an optical system where it is viewed through an eyepiece with a scale. The beam of light, having converged on the stone, diverges after reflection and at the point where reflection ceases, which corresponds to the critical angle of incidence onto the face of the stone, there is a sharp boundary between light and dark areas on the scale. This has normally been converted into RI, the value of which can be read directly off the scale. It should be remembered that reflection can only occur at the surface of the stone if its RI is less than that of the oil. In the case of birefringent minerals (see p 61), there will be two cut-off points and two values of RI.

The refractive index can be measured for white light, but white light is the mixture of all the colours of the rainbow and the refractive index differs with colour, being higher for the shorter wavelengths of violet than for red. The consequence of this is that light passing through a prism is split into a rainbow band or *spectrum*, and refraction through raindrops gives rise to natural rainbows in the same way.

The RI of diamond for violet light is 2·451 and for red 2·407. It thus has a high *dispersion* of 0·044, which is the difference between the two refractive indices, and so measures the spread of the spectrum. This is exceeded by that of cassiterite, 0·071; demantoid garnet, 0·057; and sphene, 0·051; and also by the dispersion of some synthetic stones, with which we need not be concerned. The longer the path

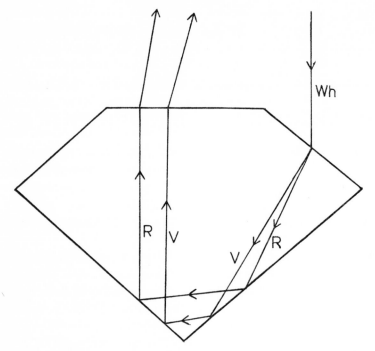

Fig 12 Dispersion and total reflection of light in a brilliant. *Wh*=white
light; *R*=red; *V*=violet.

of refraction the greater is the actual dispersion of the colours, which is demonstrated in the faceted stone, or brilliant, in Fig 12. The fire or brilliance of diamond and other gemstones is thus enhanced by flashes of spectral colour seen in the top facets as the stone is moved around.

Since the refractive index varies with the colour of light, it is necessary to fix a standard and this is taken as the yellow light of glowing sodium vapour as seen in sodium street lights, which corresponds to the maximum energy of sunlight as well as to the greatest sensitivity of the human eye. The sodium-yellow refractive index thus coincides for practical purposes with that for ordinary white light which is, of course, sunlight.

DOUBLE REFRACTION AND PLEOCHROISM

In crystals of the cubic system the structural properties in all directions are equal, and the refractive index is the same whatever the direction of the light ray within the crystal. Crystals of all other systems are somewhat *anisotropic*, that is, they vary in optical density in different directions. Just as the hardness of kyanite alters with direction (p 49), so do its refractive index and colour.

Light consists of electromagnetic vibrations at right angles to its path. In ordinary *unpolarised* light these vibrations are in any and every direction, like the bristles on a sweep's brush. However, on being reflected by a shining surface, the light becomes polarised so that its vibrations are aligned with the reflecting surface.

When an unpolarised ray of light enters an anisotropic crystal at an angle to its *optic axis*, every vibration is split into two components at right angles to each other and these components travel at different speeds, depending on the optical density in the two directions of vibration, and so are differently refracted. The ray is divided into two divergent rays.

No polarisation occurs along the longitudinal axis of tetragonal and hexagonal crystals, as all directions at right angles to it are equivalent, and no effect is seen in observing along this axis. Such crystals are *uniaxial*. In orthorhombic, monoclinic and triclinic crystals the position is more complex: suffice to say that there are two directions or optic axes along which the ray travels without splitting, and such crystals are called *biaxial*.

Except along these axes, all anisotropic crystals are *birefringent*, ie show double refraction and have different refractive indices in different directions. This effect is very pronounced in calcite, through which, in many orientations, objects appear distinctly doubled. The *birefringence*, or the difference between the maximum and minimum RI, is $0 \cdot 17$ in calcite, and is also high in sphene – up to $0 \cdot 15$. In quartz it is very low $(0 \cdot 009)$, and in this and most other cases birefringence can only be detected with a *polarimeter*.

The operative part of the instrument consists of two rotatable *Nicol prisms* or *Nicols*. These are each made up of two crystals of calcite (Iceland spar) which are so cut and cemented as to let through only the light polarised in one plane, while the light vibrating at right angles to this plane is reflected out to the side. If the Nicols are crossed at right angles to each other, none of the unpolarised ray of light will be allowed to pass and the appearance in the eyepiece will be dark. The light passed through a birefringent crystal is split in two differently polarised rays. If such a crystal is now placed between the crossed Nicols, and either these or it are rotated, there will be two positions in which the plane of polarisation of the first Nicol coincides with that of the one polarised ray of the crystal. The light will pass through, but will be suppressed by the second Nicol – the result is darkness. The same will happen if the Nicol-polarised ray fits in with the second plane of polarisation in the crystal. Thus there will be four positions of darkness. In between the light from the first Nicol will be split in the crystal into two components and their corresponding planes of polarisation, neither of which is at right angles to the polarisation plane of the second Nicol, which will thus allow some of the light through. Polarising filters may be used instead of Nicols.

In this way the position of the optic axes of the crystal and its planes of polarisation can be determined.

Birefringence adds to the fire of a gem by multiplying the images. On the other hand, weak birefringence makes the image fuzzy and this is not so helpful to the lapidary, who can conceal it by cutting across the optic axis.

Associated with birefringence, but not necessarily proportional to it, is the variation in the colour, or its intensity, in a coloured mineral according to its orientation. This is strongly marked in tourmaline crystals, which look very dark along the prism and pale across it. Cordierite is *pleochroic* (of more than

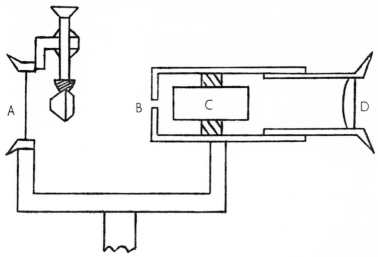

FIG 13 The dichroscope: A=instrument pointed at sky; B=narrow slit; C=calcite rhomb divides image; D=eyepiece focused on slit.

one colour). In the blue variety the crystal looks deep blue along the prism, but yellow and colourless in the two directions at right angles to each other across it. This is not unusual in biaxial crystals, but as a rule the third colour is intermediate between the other two so that the effect is generally described as *dichroism* (double-colouredness).

A simple instrument known as the *dichroscope* (Fig 13) enables the two divergent light rays of different colours to be seen separately and simultaneously. In the dichroscope the green sphene gives a deep green and a reddish-brown image, aquamarine a pale yellow and a sky-blue one which distinguishes it from the yellowish green and bluish green of emerald. The colours in biotite are dark brown and yellow. Corundum, quartz, topaz and zircon are also dichroic.

All dichroic minerals are birefringent, but the converse is not true, as some birefringent ones are colourless, and in others the effect is too slight to be noticeable.

OTHER SPECIAL EFFECTS

In some minerals there are sets of minute channels running parallel to one or several axes inside the crystal. The reflection from these produces *chatoyant* (playful) or moving bands of light on the surface, particularly if the stone is artfully fashioned into a rounded *cabochon* (p 182). The *asterism* of star-rubies and star-sapphires is due to this. Here there are three sets of canals at 120° to each other, and a six-armed star pattern appears on the surface.

Fibrous inclusions in quartz and other minerals have a similar effect, stones with a chatoyant band of light now being generally known as *cat's-eyes*, whatever the mineral.

In adularia (moonstone) and labradorite, which are both felspars, numerous tiny plates, arranged parallel to the cleavage planes in the crystal, give rise to a play of light and colour, sometimes referred to as *adularescence*. This is mentioned on p 33 together with iridescence, which it resembles. *Opalescence* is the rainbow play of colours caused by thin films in precious opal, which is a translucent stone.

Some minerals emit light after being heated, rubbed or exposed to radiation, and this is known as *phosphorescence*. Some varieties of fluorite glow after being powdered and heated. Pieces of quartz emit light when rubbed together in a dark room. X-rays cause phosphorescence in diamond, ruby and willemite, among other minerals.

More accessible to the amateur is the *fluorescence* which substances show while illuminated by invisible ultra-violet rays. This is apparent in most specimens of fluorite, which glow with an unearthly violet, or sometimes blue, green or red light. Scheelite fluoresces lilac, and this property is not confined to minerals.

6

TESTS FOR CHEMICAL ELEMENTS

The bright yellow glow of sodium vapour in street lights also appears when sodium compounds are strongly heated, and several other elements produce colours of this kind by which they can be identified.

A short piece of unreactive platinum wire is normally used for such *flame tests*. The end of a glass tube, or rod, is heated until it becomes soft, and the heated wire is inserted into the glass. When cooled, this forms a firm holder to protect the hand from heat.

The wire is dipped in hydrochloric acid, and then heated in the flame of a bunsen burner or a spirit lamp. This is to clean the wire between tests, and the procedure should be repeated until no colour flash is seen in the flame. The yellow colour of sodium is the strongest and most persistent, and can conceal other colours if they are present. Otherwise, when a small quantity of material, such as powdered mineral, is picked up on the wire moistened with the acid, the characteristic colour will appear brightly glowing in the flame. However, some colour flashes are very brief and difficult to see, so the test may have to be repeated to make sure of them.

Lithium gives a deep crimson or magenta flame, deeper in colour than the crimson of strontium, while the calcium flame is brick red.

Yellow–green is characteristic of barium. If we treat the specimen with sulphuric acid, the presence of boron is shown by a very brief greenish flash which is caused by a compound that immediately evaporates in the flame. A bright green flame is produced by a rare element, thallium. Other indefinite greenish flames appear with molybdenum, phosphorus and zinc.

Copper gives a strong sky-blue colour, but if nitric acid is used instead of hydrochloric acid the flame is emerald green. Less definite blue flames correspond to antimony, arsenic and lead.

A lilac colour denotes potassium compounds, but so readily is this masked by slight traces of sodium that it is best seen through a blue glass or a minus-yellow photographic filter which eliminates the yellow light.

If the light of these incandescent flames is observed in a *spectroscope*, where light is spread into a long rainbow ribbon by dispersion (p 59) with a series of prisms or a diffraction grating, then bright coloured *emission lines* are seen against a dark background. The major lines correspond to the flame colour, eg for sodium there are two main lines in the yellow part of the spectrum, for potassium one in the violet.

Conversely, at a low temperature the light of the same colours is absorbed so that when transparent minerals are viewed in front of a white light source, dark *absorption lines* or *bands* appear in the place of the emission lines against a bright rainbow background, thus identifying the elements. In this way small traces of elements have been found in the ruby and sapphire to which their colours seem to be due (see p 31). The presence of chromium in a beryl stamps it as an emerald.

Few amateurs may need or want to invest in a spectroscope, but it is worth remembering that the flame test with a platinum wire is a rough form of spectral analysis.

The spectra of some gemstones are shown in Figs 14 and 15.

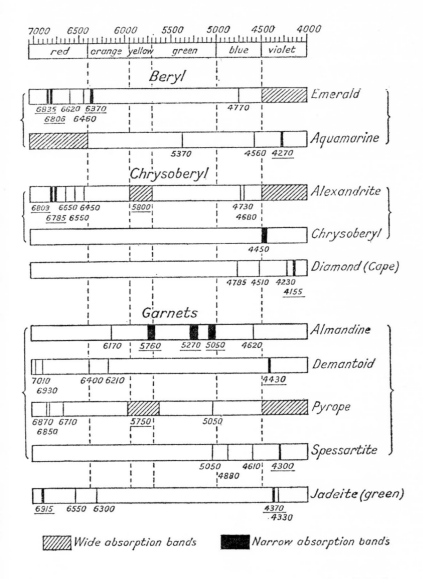

Fɪɢ 14 Absorption: spectra of gemstones (*courtesy of Messrs Oliver & Boyd*).

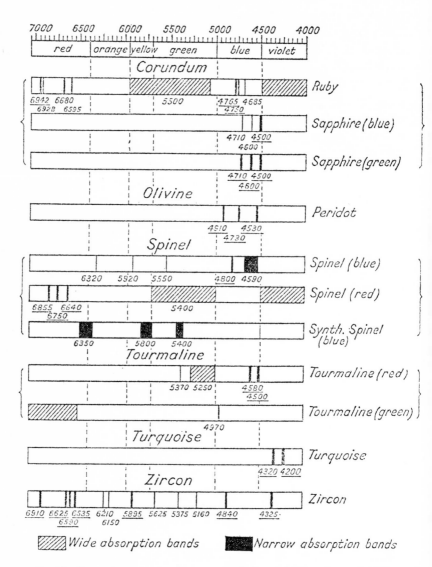

FIG 15 Absorption: spectra of gemstones (*courtesy of Messrs Oliver & Boyd*).

CHEMICAL REACTIONS

The platinum wire can be used for other simple chemical tests such as the *borax bead test*. A small loop is first made at the end of the wire by bending it round a pin, for example. The wire is heated and then dipped in powdered borax, some of which is picked up. On heating it gives up water and melts into a clear droplet – the borax bead. The bead is heated with a pinch of the powdered test substance and takes on varied colours according to the elements present. The presence of sulphur and arsenic can alter the effects of the test, and if this is likely the sample should be first strongly heated on a charcoal block to remove these elements.

A phosphate of sodium and ammonia, known as *microcosmic salt*, is used for bead tests in a similar way. As well as certain metallic elements, shown by the colours, silicates are identified by an insoluble silica skeleton in the bead. *Sodium carbonate* likewise forms beads which are coloured by manganese (opaque blue–green) and chromium (opaque yellow–green).

For these bead tests the effect of the hot pale blue to colourless *oxidising flame*, which appears at the very tip when there is a good supply of air, should be distinguished from that of the luminous *reducing flame* (Fig 16). An oxidation flame is encouraged by blowing into the flame through a bent iron tube known as *blowpipe*, the end of which is actually in the flame. With the tube a small distance outside a reducing

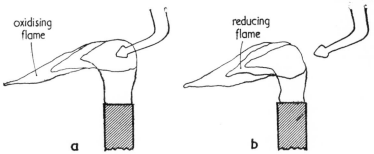

FIG 16 Blowpipe flames: A=oxidising flame; B=reducing flame.

flame is produced. Bunsen burners usually have adjustable air holes for regulating the flame. Borax and microcosmic-salt beads normally differ in colour according to whether the oxidising or reducing flame is used. In the manganese and chromium tests with sodium carbonate use is made of the oxidising flame.

BORAX BEAD TEST

Element	Oxidising flame	Reducing flame
Chromium	Yellowish green	Emerald green
Cobalt	Deep blue	Deep blue
Copper	Blue	Opaque red
Iron	Yellow hot, colourless cold	Bottle green
Manganese	Reddish violet	Colourless
Nickel	Reddish brown	Opaque grey
Uranium	Yellow	Pale green

MICROCOSMIC BEAD TEST

Element	Oxidising flame	Reducing flame
Chromium	Red hot, green cold	Green
Cobalt	Blue	Blue
Copper	Blue	Opaque red
Iron	Colourless to brownish	Reddish
Manganese	Violet	Colourless
Molybdenum	Bright green	Green
Nickel	Yellow	Reddish yellow
Titanium	Colourless	Yellow hot, violet cold
Tungsten	Colourless	Blue–green
Uranium	Yellow hot, yellow–green cold	Yellow–green hot, bright green cold

The test substance may next be heated on a charcoal block in the oxidising flame. This is best done by scraping out a small hollow in the block and placing the sample in it. The distinctive smell of burning sulphur may be detected, or the garlic smell of arsenic. Antimony forms a white crust close to the sample, in the case of arsenic this is farther away, and with bismuth the crust is orange. The other colours which may appear are mostly yellow and not readily distinguished.

If the incrustations are moistened with a solution of cobalt nitrate and heated again strongly the following colours appear:

Element	Colour
Aluminium	Blue but unfused
Antimony	Dirty green
Magnesium	Pink
Tin	Blue–green
Zinc	Grass green
Some silicates, phosphates, borates	Blue and glassy

Heating on charcoal together with potassium iodide and sulphur is a suitable test for mercury, which gives a greenish-yellow incrustation and greenish-yellow fumes. A yellow incrustation is obtained with lead, while with bismuth it is scarlet although yellowish near the sample.

Heating in the oxidising flame with powdered charcoal and sodium carbonate often produces the elemental metals which are readily distinguished, as in the following table:

Element	Bead or residue
Bismuth	Silver-white bead, brittle
Cobalt, nickel	Residue weakly magnetic
Copper	Red, spongy mass
Gold	Soft, yellow metallic bead
Iron	Residue strongly magnetic
Lead	Very soft metallic bead, melts easily, marks paper
Silver	Silver-white bead
Tin	Soft metallic bead, does not mark paper

The flame tests, the bead tests and the four charcoal tests are sufficient to distinguish all the commonly occurring metallic elements. It remains necessary to mention how the salts of various acids can be identified.

The flame test for boron has already been described (p 66), and silicates are detected in the microcosmic bead test. Phosphates do not respond to these tests, but still form a blue glassy mass in the cobalt nitrate test (p 71). For a more specific test the phosphates are heated with some magnesium metal in a small closed tube and water added. The stinking-fish smell of phosphine is observed.

Carbonates give off bubbles of carbon dioxide with hydrochloric and other acids, and this turns lime water milky. Strong sulphuric acid is needed to obtain greasy bubbles of hydrofluoric acid from fluorides, and if a drop of water is held over the tube a white film of silica collects there. Sulphuric acid gives brownish fumes when nitrates are present. (It will be appreciated that these substances are strongly corrosive or poisonous and must be handled with care: the fumes should not be inhaled.)

With sulphuric acid and manganese dioxide, chlorides liberate the greenish-yellow chlorine gas (poisonous) smelling of bleach; bromides give off bromine as a reddish-brown liquid and vapour; iodides yield a violet vapour and crystals of iodine.

Sulphides give a smell of burning sulphur when heated on charcoal, but sulphates do not. Sulphates, however, are reduced to sulphides by heating with sodium carbonate and powdered charcoal, and then a black stain appears on a silver coin or other silver object.

Table 5 (p 204) shows the elements commonly occurring in minerals, their symbols and some salt radicals.

7

THE ART OF 'FOSSICKING'

Small-scale individual search for gemstones and other minerals as a hobby has long been an established feature of life in Australia, where the words ' to fossick ' and ' fossicking ' have been coined to describe it.

Fossicking is both a science and an art. The geological information basic to it has been outlined in the introductory chapters, while lists of minerals with their properties, their classification and identification are presented in Chapters 3 to 6 and the tables at the back of the book. A more detailed description of the most important mineral species, arranged according to their appearance and mode of occurrence, will follow. This is the science, or such of it as the fossicker is likely to need. The art consists in applying this information to good effect in practice.

We may be moving in the certain knowledge that a particular country or district has definite minerals to offer. But this is not good enough. The minerals in question will occur only in certain rocks, perhaps only in a limited part of these rocks, which has to be located. This may be quite difficult, especially in built-up and/or heavily vegetated areas. What is required is a good ordinary map, sufficiently detailed for the purpose in view, supplemented with a corresponding geological map. The latter by itself may be a little confusing, especially to the inexperienced (see next section).

Maps are best held in a map-carrier with a transparent plastic ' window ' and so folded that the relevant part appears in this window. This may be of less consequence when travelling by car, but in the open even a light breeze is quite sufficient to make reading an open map a trial. The map has to be oriented which requires, a compass, preferably with a needle floating in oil or spirit as otherwise it is disconcertingly unsteady. The compass north (or south) will need correcting for the magnetic deviation, which is indicated on all Ordnance Survey or similar maps. It goes without saying that the map and compass will not be much help unless we know how to use them; the necessary skill requires some practice, but is not difficult to acquire.

In a country with a dense network of signposted communications these injunctions may be less vital, and the problem may largely boil down to following numbered roads. Such places, however, seldom afford promising hunting grounds for rare minerals, so that it is generally necessary to stray from the beaten track.

Another essential item in prospecting a *seashore* is *tide tables*, without which we might land ourselves in dire trouble. In some cases an eye must be kept open for quicksands, and sea cliffs may be undermined by erosion and prone to rock fall and landslide. On frequented beaches warning notices to this effect may be posted, but in out-of-the-way places we have to rely on our own judgement. A crash-helmet or some other protective headgear should be worn when tackling such rocks.

In exploring a large area some form of transport will be necessary, but even then we must be prepared to cover a good deal of rough ground on foot.

ROCKHOUND AND GEOLOGICAL MAPS

Rocks are shown on geological maps which a rockhound, or fossicker, should study and learn to understand.

Generally, the more colourful the map the greater the variety of rocks and stones the terrain has to offer. Of especial importance are the exposures or *outcrops* of igneous rocks, usually indicated by various shades of red although basic formations may be marked in purple. On black-and-white maps crosses, xs or ' birdies ' serve the same purpose. Bright red is traditionally reserved for acid rocks.

A large area of uniform red is less promising than small patches of red, which mark only the summits of submerged igneous intrusions or *plutons* and thus are a fair sign of pneumatolysis and mineralisation in the surrounding rocks. Of course, the plutons may not be exposed at all on the surface, and the associated small lodes and veins will not be shown on a small-scale map. This would require more detailed maps, say, 6in to a mile or 10cm to a kilometre.

Other things being equal, the most interesting mineralogically are the lines of contact between different igneous or igneous and other formations. For instance, we may look for corundum, diopside, fluorite and other calcium minerals where the igneous red meets the blue of limestone. Ring complexes mark the site of ancient volcanoes and likewise deserve attention, as do, of course, such volcanic mountains as still stand. The mode of occurrence of minerals must always be borne in mind.

Igneous rocks apart, the formations are often classified on maps according to geological periods, which is not directly informative from the fossicking point of view. The general rule, however, is to avoid recent sediments, unless they be puddingstones derived from pre-existent rocks of the right kind, alluvial placers or gem-rich gravel beds. The ancient Archean of Pre-Cambrian, Paleozoic and Mesozoic rocks will generally have been more or less metamorphosed, and, as we know, metamorphic rocks contain various crystalline and massive minerals of interest and value. The incidental advantage is that schists, quartzites and the like are relatively barren so that such regions are usually sparsely populated, thinly clothed with vegetation, and more often than not mountainous, or at least hilly.

Once we have related the idealised map picture to the actual terrain, we must keep a sharp look-out for natural or artificial exposures of country rock in cliffs, outcrops, road and railway cuttings, river gorges, quarries, gravel pits etc. If none such are available, the stones by the roadside, field and garden walls built with what may be assumed to be locally quarried material, and especially stream and river beds and banks should help to keep us on the right track.

EXCAVATIONS, MINES AND QUARRIES

As a rule no permission is needed to explore the old established road cuttings, but apart from allowing us to ascertain the character of the country rock such cuttings are seldom rewarding to a fossicker. On the other hand, where new roads are being built, particularly in mountainous country, large masses of fresh rock have to be blasted and shifted, some exciting mineral veins, druses and other features being revealed in the process. The construction engineers and their crews are not primarily interested in the rock rubble arising from their activities, and may not object to its inspection by a rockhound. For obvious reasons permission will be granted more readily to an individual or a small group than to a large party.

Construction workers, quarrymen and miners are usually friendly folk who work in lonely places and are not averse to exchanging a few words with a stranger who takes a sympathetic interest in what they are doing. And they may have some good advice to offer – provided our approach is courteous and unassuming.

Disused *mines* and *quarries* may be open to the public, but even if they are closed it should not be too difficult to obtain permission to visit them. But it is not safe to enter old galleries, unless perhaps the rockhound is a mining expert and so in no

76

need of advice. Besides, a gallery is only a passage and thus will rarely contain anything exciting. It may be both safer and more profitable to rummage about in the old mine dumps, which may require some kind of digging tool such as a spade, or at least a gardening trowel.

Opencast workings are self-evidently more accessible, and since only the economically valuable extractions will have been removed they usually have a good deal left to interest a collector. For the same reason the surroundings of a mine may be well worth examining as they may contain thin lodes and outcrops of mineralised rock that, although unprofitable as a mining proposition, are more than adequate for the modest needs of a fossicker. Moreover, if this is, say, a lead mine the operators will have been concerned with the extraction of lead and not of the gangue minerals such as tourmaline, fluorite, apatite or topaz.

For visiting an active mine or quarry, permission must be obtained from the works manager or secretary and referred to the foreman or engineer in charge of the operations on the spot. However, some companies are rather sticky about granting permission. It depends on such factors as how often the mine has been visited by geologists and rockhounds in the immediate past (and so, possibly, on the season of the year) and on the nature of the mine itself – if this is a diamond mine the application might not be viewed with great favour.

The visitor is not usually allowed inside the mine, but if one is content with the dumps, which are of no further use to the company except as a source of road metal, no undue difficulty need be anticipated. The miners are no fools and are well aware of the value of good mineral specimens and gemstones, but their time is limited and they cannot afford to go through a dump with a fine comb. Thus, especially while mine work is in progress, a fresh dump will generally contain something useful.

Quarries are more readily accessible. What has been said

77

about road construction applies here, only more so. The warning about the insecurity of rock walls is even more pertinent than in the case of sea cliffs, especially where the rocks have recently been blasted. On the other hand, each new blast uncovers a new layer of rock and being able to examine it immediately after presents an obvious advantage. The object of a quarry is to obtain building or road material, so that neither the management nor the workers are particularly interested in such minerals as their operations may occasionally bring into the open and will not object to their removal, at least on a small scale, always assuming that this does not interfere with the operations.

A protective helmet is essential, especially if the quarry is visited on a working day and blasting is in progress. This takes place at intervals of a few hours, and ample warning is given by a loud hooter. Moreover, not all ' bays ' are being worked at the same time, so that it is often possible to keep out of the way of active operations. Some mention must be made of the fine rock dust, particularly that from friable rocks such as limestone, which is produced by blasting and insinuates itself into woollens and other loosely woven garments. Therefore, it is advisable to wear some kind of smooth overall, impervious to dust.

WHERE TO LOOK

Even if the rock is of the right kind not all parts of it will be equally useful from our point of view.

In igneous formations we will, obviously, be looking for pegmatites, masses affected by pneumatolysis, thermal veins, cavities, junctions between rocks of different age, type and composition, ' rafts ' (p 25) etc. Unusual colour or structure also deserve attention, as well as eroded portions, for fresh ' live ' rock is difficult to deal with.

These rules are largely applicable to metamorphic and sedimentary rocks which also may be affected by pneumatolysis and contain thermal veins and mineral lodes with their attendant gangue minerals. Veins of quartz, calcite and fluorite, occasionally including other crystallites, are not infrequent in limestone and sandstone. In schists and other metamorphic rocks rare components have often been sorted out into quartz veins, winding white across the hill and moor. The quartzes themselves may contain clear coloured or uncoloured crystals.

A conglomerate or breccia may be barren or fruitful, depending on what stones make up the ' pudding '. Agates, opal and zeolites are deposited from solutions in the gas cavities or *amygdales* of the cooling lavas, weather out of these and may become embedded in conglomerate. If the conglomerate has been metamorphically indurated its contents will be very difficult to extract, but a loose sandy or limey groundmass will yield to hammer and chisel and in hand specimens can be dissolved or weakened by acetic and/or oxalic acid (p 20).

A lava may be hard and glassy, spongy, or soft and soapy to the touch, and it is mostly the latter kind that harbours mineral inclusions.

Characteristically, however, the parent rock is too hard and resistant to the tools at the rockhound's command, and he or she will have to look for weaknesses in its defences. Screes at the foot of the crags with promising veins are always worth a look. Especially worthwhile are small scree and gravel shoots abutting at a vein or chain of cavities, as fine crystals can be dug out of them with little effort. A hidden druse may be discovered by tapping a likely rock patch with the hammer and listening for a hollow sound.

Stream beds in gem-bearing localities provide a natural repository for the crystals weathered out of the rocks. The additional advantage is that only sound specimens, free from flaws and fractures, survive the fret of the elements, so that waterworn gemstones are usually of a high quality. However, having lost their sharp crystal points and edges, they do not look so good in a collection as stones eased out of a decaying druse. Similarly, grains of gold from the acid and of the metals of the platinum group from the basic igneous formations become concentrated in the river grits and sands, which can be panned for them. Such placer deposits may be found at considerable distances from the place of origin, and may in due course be incorporated in sandstone or siltstone.

All this is true of sea beaches as well, except that their stones need not necessarily originate in the nearby cliffs and may have come from under the sea. This is particularly true of the light species, such as jet and amber, which can be carried a long way by storms and powerful currents.

The time following a period of stormy weather is the most opportune for beachcombing, as new layers of sand and shingle are then exposed to view. The best part of the beach to search is the wet strip in the wake of the ebbing tide, because wet stones show their colour so much better than dry ones.

For the same reason a dull wet day is better than a dry sunny one for scanning screes and gravels inland where the stones are often additionally disguised by a thin overlay of dust.

8

EQUIPMENT, CLOTHING AND LEGAL POSITION

Fossicking may involve anything from a gentle stroll along a friendly beach to a full-scale expedition into a wild roadless land, infested with poisonous snakes, scorpions and spiders, crocodiles and man-eating tigers (if there are any such left), not to mention bandits, if perhaps not cannibals. The hazards may embrace anything from tropical heat in a waterless desert to numbing cold, snow, wind and rain. It is impossible to cover here so wide a range of alternatives, each of which demands special items of equipment. The reader planning an exotic or dangerous expedition should seek advice from a geographical society and specialist outfitters.

A beach stroll may need little more than a pair of sharp eyes. But a small *spade* or a gardening *trowel* may come in handy for digging up a promising bank of sand or pebbles.

A *geological*, or at least a *chipping*, *hammer* is a universally useful item of prospecting ironmongery.

A geological hammer has a square head on the one side and a point, adze, or an elongated spur with a slight inward curvature on the other (prospector's pick). The latter serves as a digging, prising and levering tool. The weight may vary, but is usually about 1 to 1½lb (say, ½kg). The handle is a foot

81

(30cm) or so long, to give the hammer a good striking moment. It should sit comfortably in the hand, which is protected against shock by a tight sleeve of perforated rubber or a helical winding of surgical dressing (like a tennis racket or a hockey stick).

The hammer is worn round the neck on a nylon cord, leather strap or the like, forming a continuous double loop and passed through a hole bored in the shank an inch or so from the end, or a metal eye at the end. The shank may be wood or metal. The advantage of this double-loop arrangement is that by slipping one loop off the neck, and so lengthening the cord, the hammer is freed for use without taking it off its cord. Otherwise it is quite easy to lose it in a deep crack in the rocks, between boulders, or to hear it tinkling down a 10,000ft mountain-side. To prevent the hammer from knocking against the body in walking or climbing, it may advantageously be tucked up behind the belt on the side and somewhat to the front, roughly in the position of a car seat-belt buckle.

A *chipping hammer*, used by stone masons, has a head some 5in (7½cm) long, an inch wide both ways and tapering at the two ends into a blunt adze, the two adzes standing at right angles to each other. This may seem a little awkward for hammering, but most geological hammering is in the nature of chipping, so that the two-adze shape presents considerable advantages. A blunt blow can be delivered with the flat central portion of the head, eg for striking a chisel.

A heavy-headed 2lb *rock* or *crack hammer* is sometimes used for breaking stones.

For fossicking purposes the suspension and grip-dressing is the same as in the previous case.

If most of the journey is done by car – say in visiting a quarry – a heavier hammer, even a sledge-hammer, a crowbar and a pickaxe may be taken along; but the usefulness of such heavy tools is much less than might at first sight seem.

A *mattock*, a kind of small garden hoe having an adze on the

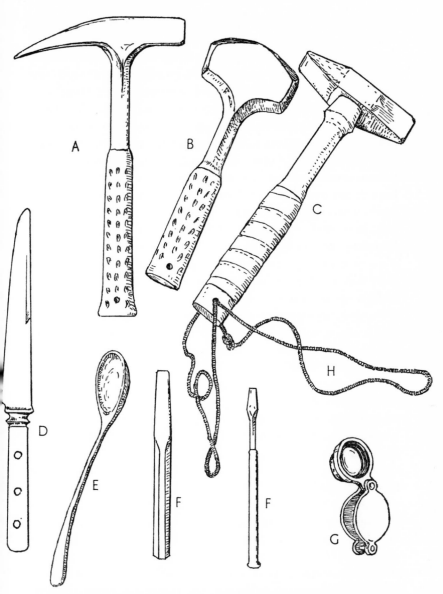

FIG 17   Rockhound's tools: A=geological hammer (prospector's pick;)
B=rock or crack hammer; C=chipping hammer; D=long blunt kitchen
knife; E=horn spoon; F=chisels; G=foldable pocket magnifier; H=
hanging cord for the hammer.

one side and a pick on the other, may be useful for small boulders or boulder-clay. A two- or three-pronged *grapple* is better adapted for turning over large stones.

Of more universal application for delicate rock work are two or three *stone-mason's chisels* of assorted sizes. These, too, may be provided with a protective sleeve. A hammer alone, however skilfully wielded, is a somewhat crude implement and many a good specimen has been ruined by hammering. In any case hammer blows should be carefully placed some distance from the part to be extracted, along the jointing or cleavage lines of the rock where it is most likely to part. A chisel driven into a crack greatly expedites the job. Big whacks have surprisingly little effect on the rock; lighter frequent knocks if well aimed are far more efficacious.

In hammering small stone chips are ejected with considerable force and goggles may be useful to protect the eyes.

Most good crystals are found in druses (p 16), which are often deep, narrow and filled with mud or clay from decaying felspar, in which the crystals released by the weathering of the cavity walls lie concealed like loose teeth dropping out of an ancient jaw. If the access opening is small neither hammer nor chisel can be used to great advantage. In any event, extracting the contents requires reach rather than force. A *long blunt knife* and a *long-handled* (runcible?) *spoon*, preferably made of horn to avoid damage to the crystal points and edges, are much more suitable for this purpose. The hammer and chisels may still be used to enlarge the entrance or remove awkward rock salients, but if the rock has been softened by decay the crystals can be eased out of it quite effectively with the knife.

Rockhounds have been known to use small explosive charges to break up rocks or boulders, but this is generally frowned upon.

If we are bent on looking for stream gold, a *frying pan* will do. If we find none we can at least use the pan for our eggs and bacon, although these can be fried quite nicely on a clean spade.

OTHER EQUIPMENT, CLOTHING ETC.

The collected specimens have to be reduced to manageable size and if possible identified, labelled and safely stowed away.

The time on a field trip is often limited. Chipping away superfluous parts of a find takes time and is a job of some precision which is better left till we return home or to the base. It is all too easy to ruin a specimen by an injudicious hammer blow. Moreover, a piece of vein rock or druse with crystals may make a fine collection item when intact but in being broken up to extract some often insignificant crystal, it will lose all its original interest. Thus, while it is difficult to take along big chunks of rock, unless we have some transport (a helicopter?) near at hand we must beware of 'overdressing' our finds.

A carrier of some kind will obviously be needed for these – a rucksack, or at least a shoulder bag, which will also be required for food, spare clothing, maps and tools. The longer and the more complicated the trip the roomier this carrier will have to be.

If stones and angular rock pieces are tumbled indiscriminately into a bag they will jar against each other. Crystals are easily damaged, and some minerals are very fragile and must be handled with care. It is usually enough to wrap up rough stones and rock samples individually in newspaper, but the delicate specimens are best protected with lint, cotton-wool, foam-rubber sheeting or similar soft material and placed in tins, canisters or boxes. A supply of polythene bags will be useful, and the place of origin of the finds should be clearly marked; the date of finding is less important, but can do no harm.

Some minerals can readily be identified on the spot by reference to a handbook such as this, which should be taken along together with maps, tide tables and other essential aids.

A *pocket magnifier* or *loupe* will be helpful in studying crystal structure, streaks, scratches etc.

Hardness pencils, or chips of materials of standard hardness (p 48), are employed to test hardness.

A *streak plate*, which is usually a rough-surfaced plate of hard ceramic, a *silicon-carbide* or an *emery cloth*, is another standard item of equipment for examining the streak.

A small narrow-beam electric torch may be useful for peering into cracks and hollows.

On the whole, however, it is desirable to keep the carried weight down to a minimum and not to complicate the field work beyond necessity, especially if all of it has to be done hurriedly in the open, perhaps in inclement conditions, with tired hands and brain.

The specimens may require cleaning. The stones picked up from the sea are often coated with brightly coloured organic matter which bears no relation to their true colouring. Such coatings can be removed with hot water and *washing soda*, or else by immersion in a solution of *oxalic acid*, used to eliminate incrustations of haematite or limonite which often envelop vein minerals. Oxalic acid is a corrosive substance and must be treated with respect. The specimens should be left immersed overnight, or longer if the incrustation is thick. *Acetic acid* is similarly used to remove calcareous overlays (p 20).

While some fossicking grounds can be reached by road, most are difficult of access and involve some foot-slogging, scrambling or even climbing. Conditions will vary and dictate their own requirements. One thing, however, is certain: wherever we go, we shall need stout *boots*, preferably with cleated rubber soles for good purchase. Waterproof and other reserve clothing will generally be necessary, and in changeable climates a general knowledge of the weather situation will help.

Binoculars will be found useful for spying out promising rock formations and examining the lie of the land ahead, especially in the hills or mountains.

The necessity of an adequate food supply is obvious. But on a strenuous excursion, where exhaustion may supervene, it is advisable to have some readily ingestible energising food-stuffs, such as glucose tablets, or less medically, lump sugar, boiled sweets, maple sugar, chocolate or dried fruit. Stale sandwiches are definitely not in this category. In cold countries or at high altitudes a thermos flask with some hot drink is recommended. In hot countries it may be dangerous to drink unboiled water from streams, and a water filter may have to be added to our outfit. The need for a handy supply of potable water in a *water-flask* hardly deserves mentioning. Alcoholic beverages are to be avoided, as after a brief euphoria they only serve to increase the weariness.

A rockhound venturing into high hills should become acquainted with at least the rudiments of mountain craft, and will do well to remember that it is easier to climb up a crag or rock face than to come down again.

NINE POINTS OF THE LAW

Property in all land and what lies beneath its surface is vested in somebody: the state, a corporation or an individual. Thus in principle the rockhound's finds are his on sufferance only. As a rule no objections are raised, but this practice varies greatly from case to case, place to place, and country to country. A fossicker seeking to explore unfamiliar foreign grounds will do well to acquaint himself with the legal position there.

The situation in active mines, quarries and excavations has already been considered (pp 76–78). Here the issue is not so much the removal of minerals as possible interference with the normal course of operations. However, there are areas, including some nature reserves, where any collecting is prohibited. Other areas may be out of bounds to unauthorised persons for one reason or another, such as military secrecy, which again should be ascertained in advance.

It is at least courteous to seek authorisation before entering fenced private land, although in some countries such minatory notices as ' trespassers will be prosecuted ' may be devoid of legal meaning.

Fortunately, the most likely fossicking grounds are either downright wasteland or land of low agricultural value, such as sheep grazings, so that at least the problem of damage to crops does not often arise. In Great Britain and Ireland access to mountain land and the seashore below the high-water mark is generally free and no questions are asked, although unauthorised camping may not be viewed with favour. Australia, being vast and underpopulated as well as the homeland of ' diggers ', is very liberal to fossickers; nor will they usually meet any obstruction in out-of-the-way places in Canada, New Zealand, the USA or Scandinavia. On the other hand, in some African countries ' unauthorised prospecting ' may result in summary incarceration. The distinction between fossicking and prospecting may not be immediately apparent, and trying to explain the differences to a poorly educated sergeant at a bush outpost may present its difficulties. In South Africa even a *blanke* would be ill advised to fall foul of the police, and only a fool or a hero would risk as much in the USSR. Still, an official permit could probably be obtained on application.

9

METALLIC MINERALS

There is no clear-cut system according to which the minerals can be arranged that would be both logically consistent and satisfactory from the rockhound's practical point of view: for what is required is the quickest way of identifying a find, combined with some indication of where it can be made. Therefore, we shall have to chop and change according to circumstances.

There is a group of minerals of metallic appearance, ie they are opaque and have a metallic lustre. Such minerals are either native metals or metal ores, most probably sulphides, and it is useful to be able to distinguish between the two without too much ado.

One quick way of doing so is examining the streak, eg by scratching the mineral with a penknife. All native metals have more or less shiny metallic streaks even when superficially discoloured by oxidation, carbonation or an alien coating, most frequently a brown one of iron oxides. The streaks of metallic ores, on the other hand, are usually dull and sometimes coloured. They are much harder than most native metals and characteristically brittle, whereas the metals, with the exception of the brittle *antimony, arsenic, bismuth* and *tellurium* and the hard native *iridium* and *osmiridium* alloy, are relatively

89

soft and malleable. They will yield to the penknife which, for instance, iron pyrite will not do.

Metallic ores are often well crystallised. Good crystals of native metals are comparatively rare: they are usually found in grains, lumps (nuggets), massive or arborescent (branched) structures, thin sheets or wires (silver).

Except for the platinum group, which has high melting points, native metals will fuse in the blowpipe flame (p 71) and on glowing charcoal; so, too, will some of the metallic ores. The arsenic group volatilises readily and poisonously – arsenic itself with the characteristic smell of garlic – and should not be exposed to heat without due caution. These are brittle metals.

The brittle metals have a further feature in common: they belong to the hexagonal crystal system. The malleable metals are all cubic.

The following metals occur in native form: *amalgam*, which is an alloy of silver and mercury: *antimony*; *arsenic*; *bismuth*; *copper*; *gold*; *iron*; *lead*; *mercury*; *palladium*; the *platinum* group; *silver*; and *tellurium*.

ABBREVIATIONS AND LOCALITIES

It is our intention to make the information given in this and the following chapters as comprehensive as possible. Too much abbreviation can be confusing. On the other hand, a great deal of valuable space can be wasted on spelling out recurrent terms in full. Therefore, the following abbreviations are introduced:

H, hardness; LR, lustre; RI, refractive index; SG, specific gravity; STR, streak; op, opaque; trl, transluscent; trp, transparent; xl, crystal.

With regard to localities, only the most important ones, more particularly those where the mineral is mined, are listed; but this does not necessarily mean that the mineral is found nowhere else. Where only a country of occurrence is noted its name is generally given in full. If there are further particulars, the names of the most important countries which frequently recur are shortened thus:

Ausl	Australia	Jap	Japan
Ausr	Austria	NI	Northern Ireland
Braz	Brazil	Nor	Norway
Can	Canada	NZ	New Zealand
Czsl	Czechoslovakia	Pol	Poland
Den	Denmark	Rum	Rumania
Eir	Irish Republic (Eire)	SA	South Africa
Eng	England	Scot	Scotland
Fin	Finland	Spn	Spain
Fra	France	Swd	Sweden
Ger	Germany	Swz	Switzerland
Grc	Greece	Tur	Turkey
Hun	Hungary	Wal	Wales
Ita	Italy	Yug	Yugoslavia

Co stands for county, but the names of counties are not abbreviated. The customary abbreviations are used for the Australian and USA states and Canadian provinces. The definite article before the names of mountains, rivers and like geographical features is omitted.

Further information, not included in the description, will be found in Table 5.

ANTIMONY, ARSENIC, BISMUTH AND TELLURIUM

As already stated, these four metals have many properties in common.

Native antimony is greyish white with a lead-grey STR, usually massive, laminar (like mica), botryoidal or granular; xls rare – hexagonal, pseudo-cubic or tabular, frequently twinned in foursomes or sixsomes; H $3-3\frac{1}{2}$; SG $6\cdot61-6\cdot72$; fuses readily; bluish green in reducing flame.

It is associated with stibnite, silver and arsenic minerals in lodes. Main localities: NSW and Queensl (Ausl); NB (Can); Kern Co and Riverside Co, Calif (USA); Bohemia (Czsl); Isère (Fra); Harz Mts (Ger); Sala (Swd); Kalimantan, Chile and Sardinia.

Native arsenic is black and non-metallic in appearance, but looks leaden grey on a fresh fracture, and its STR is tin white; H $3\frac{1}{2}$; SG 5·6–5·9. Its common form is massive, concentrically layered, or granular; xls, when present, are usually acicular.

It keeps company with cobalt and silver ores in Kalgoorlie, WA (Ausl); Lake Superior district, Ont and Montreal, Que (Can); Santa Cruz Co, Ariz and Winnfield Salt Dome, La (USA); Bohemia (Czsl); Alsace (Fra); Saxony (Ger); Ita, Rum, Chile and Jap.

Native bismuth is silvery with a reddish tinge, has a leaden metallic STR, and tarnishes readily; crystalline, massive, arborescent, foliated, feathery or granular. Xls often look like hollow cubes, and resemble type letters. The metal is brittle when cold, but malleable when heated; H 2–2$\frac{1}{2}$; SG 9·7–9·8; fuses and volatilises on charcoal, forming an orange-red incrustation; dissolves in concentrated nitric acid (HNO_3); the solution turns milky on addition of water.

It is found together with bismuthinite, cobaltite, cassiterite, nickel and silver ores in lodes and intrusive rocks. Chief localities: Cornwall and Devon (Eng); NSW, Queensl (Ausl); Cobalt Co, Ont (Can); Col, Conn, SC (USA); Saxony (Ger); Bolivia.

Native tellurium is tin white; STR leaden grey; H 2–2$\frac{1}{2}$; SG 6·1–6·3. Is easily fusible in the blowpipe and soluble in hot sulphuric acid (H_2SO_4). Mainly massive, it is also found in prismatic and acicular xls and columnar masses, in association with gold, seleno-tellurium, sulphur and pyrite, and in metalliferous lodes in Kalgoorlie, WA (Ausl); Cripple Creek, Teller Co, Colo and Delamar, Linnah Co, Nev (USA); and Transylvania (Rum).

92

SILVER AND SILVERY ORES

Native silver is silvery or yellowish, brown or black when tarnished; forms distorted cubes and octahedra, but commonly massive, platy, stringy or arborescent – like frost etchings on a window pane; STR brilliant; H $2\frac{1}{2}$–3; SG $9 \cdot 6$–$12 \cdot 0$; fuses easily in the blowpipe; dissolves in HNO_3.

It is found in cobalt-nickel veins, and with silver sulphides in their upper parts; keeps company with galena, silver glance and cerussite. Argentiferous galena looks silvery and contains a high proportion of silver. Occurrence: Broken Hill, NSW (Ausl); Cobalt Co, Ont (Can); Silver King Mine, Pinal Co, Ariz; Silver City, Owyhee Co, Idaho and Butte, Mont (USA); Annaberg, Saxony (Ger); Kongsberg (Nor); Mexico and Peru.

Native amalgam, which comes next in the order of increasing hardness, is a solution of silver in mercury (HgAg) in variable proportions and may also contain gold; silver-white with a silvery STR; cubic xls, also massive, platy or moss-like; H 3–$3\frac{1}{2}$; SG $10 \cdot 5$–$14 \cdot 8$. Mercury evaporates when heated, leaving a globule of molten silver. Amalgam is found in grains in cinnabar deposits and in the oxidation zone of some silver deposits in Chile, Hun, Spn and Swd.

Native mercury is of similar occurrence, in liquid globules; solidifies below $-39\,°C$ in rhombohedral xls; found in Santa Clara Co, Calif and Terlingua, Tex (USA); Idria (Ita); Almaden (Spn); and Peru – rare.

Dyscrasite, silver antimonite (Ag_3Sb), crystallises in orthorhombic bipyramids, also massive, granular or platy, striated; silver-white to pale yellow, tarnishes dark grey; STR silvery; H $3\frac{1}{2}$–4; SG $9 \cdot 4$–$10 \cdot 0$; fuses readily; decomposes in HNO_3, leaving a deposit of antimony oxide. Dys. occurs in association with silver ores, galena, arsenic and antimony minerals in Broken Hill, NSW (Ausl); Cobalt Co, Ont (Can); Reese River, Nev (USA); Harz Mts and Black Forest (Ger); Alsace (Fra); Spn and Chile.

Native palladium is a hard silver-white metal of the platinum group; H $4\frac{1}{2}$–5; SG $11\cdot3$–$12\cdot0$; melts at $1,546\,°C$; cubic; usually found in grains in crude platinum and in copper pyrite – rare. The chief sources of pal. are Sudbury, Ont (Can); Urals (USSR); Braz and San Domingo.

Smaltite is another holo-metallic compound, $CoAs_{3-2}$, tin white to pale grey; STR greyish black; H $5\frac{1}{2}$; SG $6\cdot4$–$6\cdot6$; belongs to the cubic system (modified octahedra and rhombo-dodecahedra); also massive, granular or reniform; fuses to a black globule; forms a red solution in HNO_3. Occurrence: Cornwall and Lancashire (Eng); Kirkcudbrightshire (Scot); Cobalt Co, Ont (Can); Bohemia (Czsl); Dauphiné (Fra); Saxony, Hesse, Black Forest (Ger); Morocco.

Linnaeite, a cobalt sulphide (Co_3S_4) – H $5\frac{1}{2}$, SG $4\cdot8$–$5\cdot0$, is silvery white with a reddish tinge to steel grey in colour and a greyish black STR, which it shares with *cobaltite* (CoAsS) – H $5\frac{1}{2}$, SG $6\cdot0$–$6\cdot3$. Both minerals occur in hydrothermal veins together with pyrite, chalcopyrite, millerite, siderite and pyrrhotite, especially in gneiss. Both form good xls of the cubic system: lin. usually octahedral, like spinel; cobaltite-cubes and pentagon dodecahedra, striated; both may also be massive or granular. Cob. is found in Cornwall (Eng); Ravensthorpe, WA (Ausl); Cobalt Co, Ont (Can); Bohemia (Czsl); Saxony and Westphalia (Ger); Pol, Scandinavia, India; lin. at Mine le Motte, Mo and Mineral Hill, Md (USA); Riddarhyttan (Swd); Zambia and Katanga (Zaire).

Arsenopyrite or *mispickel* (FeAsS) is a silver white to greyish metallic mineral with a blackish STR; H $5\frac{1}{2}$–6; SG $5\cdot9$–$6\cdot2$; orthorhombic – short, horizontally lined, prismatic xls; also in radial aggregates, massive, reniform or granular. When heated in a closed tube, it yields a sublimate of arsenic in grey xls and a black amorphous deposit; when struck with steel gives sparks and emits a garlic smell. It is common in Cornwall and Devon (Eng); Hastings Co, Ont (Can); Saxony and Harz Mts (Ger); Silesia (Pol) and Swd; but is of widespread occurrence.

Sperrylite, platinum diarsenide ($PtAs_2$), is tin white with a black STR; H 6–7; SG 10·6; cubic – tiny cubes or combinations of cube and octahedron; found at Sudbury, Ont (Can); Franklin, Macon Co, NC and Rambler Mine, Wyo (USA); Bushveld (SA).

Native iridium hobnobs with platinum, osmium and gold. It is silver white, hard (6–7), and very heavy (22·6–22·8).

Osmiridium or *iridosmine*, an alloy of osmium and iridium, whose proportions vary, is tin white to steel grey; H 6–7; SG 19·3–21·1; melting point 2,290°C; occurs in rhombohedral xls of hexagonal system and flattened grains. Both metals are found in gold washings at Bingera, NSW (Ausl); Sudbury, Ont (Can); Orepuki, Wallace Co (NZ); Braz, SA, Tasmania and Urals (USSR).

COPPER, GOLD AND BRASSY ORES

Native copper, unless tarnished, which it usually is, is of the familiar copper-red colour with the like STR; but tarnishes to dull red, green, blue or black and is often coated with iron oxides which give it a rusty look. It belongs to the cubic system (octahedra and tetrahedra); more usually massive, arborescent, in thin sheets or incrustations; H 2½–3; SG 8·5–9·0; fuses readily; associated with basic rocks and hydrothermal deposits, with cuprite, calcite and quartz. The main localities are: Cornwall (Eng); Stirlingshire (Scot); Broken Hill, NSW (Ausl); Cap d'Or, NS (Can); Ariz, Utah and near Lake Superior (USA); Hesse-Nassau (Ger); Katanga (Zaire); Tuscany (Ita); Spn, Bolivia, Chile, Mexico, USSR.

The hexagonal *pyrargyrite*, Ag_3SbS_3, may superficially resemble copper in colour when tarnished, ranging from dark red through blue–grey to black, but its STR is carmine and although of the same hardness, it is much lighter – SG 5·85; when heated in an open tube yields sulphurous fumes and an antimony-oxide sublimate; fuses readily to an AgS globule; decomposes in HNO_3. Pyr. is found in hydrothermal deposits

95

in Cobalt Co, Ont (Can); Comstock Lode, Nev (USA); Pribram (Czsl); Spn, Bolivia, Chile, Mexico and Peru.

Another similar hydrothermal mineral is *niccolite* or *kupfernickel* (copper-nickel), NiAs, but it is much harder – 5–5½ – and has a brownish black STR; SG 7·3–7·8. It fuses in the blowpipe, and forms a red solution in concentrated acids; occurs with nickel, copper and silver ores, barite, galena and chromite, in Cornwall (Eng); Sudbury, Ont (Can); Silver Cliff, Custer Co, Colo and Franklin, NJ (USA); Black Forest and Saxony (Ger); Spn and Argentina.

Native gold is soft (2½–3) and heavy (SG 15·5–19·3), untarnishable, but may be reddish or pale (electrum) when impure and give a greenish cast to the enclosing quartz. Unlike the ' false golds ', it is easily marked with a penknife; STR silvery yellow to reddish golden; belongs to the cubic system, but good xls are rare – cubes with rounded edges; more often massive, in thin foils, flakes etc; fuses readily and is soluble in *aqua regia*. It is of worldwide distribution in acid rocks and products of their decay, quartz veins (reefs), placers, alluvial deposits; also in the form of *amalgam* with mercury and of *tellurides* with silver and tellurium. Small quantities are found in Cornwall (Eng); North Wales; Leadhills and Sutherland (Scot); but the main suppliers are Ausl, Can, western USA, Alaska, SA, western Africa, South America and USSR.

The ' false golds ' are all pyrites of some kind or other, from brass yellow to bronze in colour with greenish or blackish STR, rather hard and brittle so that they are not difficult to distinguish from real gold. An attempted scratch with a penknife will soon reveal their ' pretence '. They are arranged below in the order of increasing hardness.

Chalcopyrite or *copper pyrites*, $CuFeS_2$, is the most golden of them all, although it may be tarnished and assume iridescent hues, which gold does not; STR greenish black; H 3½–4; SG 4·1–4·3; forms handsome tetragonal xls – typically bisphenoids; also amorphous or reniform; fusible into black magnetic grains; blue flame; dissolves in HNO_3 with separation of sulphur. Ch. is found in pneumatolytic and hydrothermal veins, especially at limestone-igneous contacts; is of widespread occurrence in company with other pyrites, ores of zinc, copper and iron.

Millerite or *nickel pyrites*, NiS; H $3–3\frac{1}{2}$; SG $5\cdot3–5\cdot6$; shares colour and STR with chalcopyrite, but may be darker – to bronze; crystallises hexagonally in needles and fibrous bushes, occasionally massive; fuses readily to a magnetic bead; forms a green solution in HNO_3. It is relatively rare, found in lodes with other nickel minerals and sulphides, sometimes in coal, in Cornwall (Eng); Merthyr Tydfil (Wal); Sudbury, Ont (Can); Sterling Mine, NY and Gap Mine, Pa (USA); Saxony (Ger).

Pyrrhotite or *magnetic pyrites*, FeS with Ni, is bronze-yellow to brown; STR dark grey; H $3\frac{1}{2}–4\frac{1}{2}$; SG $4\cdot6$; hexagonal tabular xls, often in rosettes; massive, granular or foliaceous; fuses to a back magnetic globule; decomposes in HCl with release of H_2S (rotten-egg smell). It is associated with basic rocks, especially norites, in Cornwall and Devon (Eng); Dolgelly (Wal); Sudbury, Ont (Can); Standish Mine, Conn and Ducktown, Tenn (USA); Saxony, Black Forest and Harz (Ger); Nor and SA.

Pyrite or *iron pyrites*, FeS_2, is ' the Fool's Gold ' proper, pale brass to bronze-yellow; STR greenish black; H $6–6\frac{1}{2}$; SG $5\cdot0–5\cdot2$; cubic, striated xls in at least sixty variants, but often cubes or cubo-octahedra; also massive, nodular or reniform; often forms substitute material in fossils; fuses to a black magnetic residue and gives off sulphurous fumes; borax bead, yellow in oxidising flame, bottle green in reducing flame; soluble in HNO_3, not in HCl; may contain traces of gold and silver. Py. is sometimes used in jewellery under the incorrect name of marcasite, qv; common, of worldwide occurrence in sedimentary, metamorphic and igneous rocks, sometimes with gold, haematite and other pyrites; main producers: Spn, Jap, Ita and USA.

Marcasite or *white iron pyrites*, FeS_2; colour, like pyrite, but paler with a greenish cast; STR greyish; H $6-6\frac{1}{2}$; SG $4\cdot8-4\cdot9$; orthorhombic, forms short prisms, and is much given to twinning, yielding various shapes, such as ' cockscomb ', ' spear ', branched and radial aggregates, and nodules; chemical tests as for pyrite. Mar. is found in chalk and limestone as a secondary, concretional and replacement mineral, with chalcopyrite, pyrite, galena and zinc blende, especially in the English chalk; Bohemia (Czsl); Bolivia; is used in jewellery.

Bornite and *pentlandite* make less likely ' golds ', both cubic, but usually granular or massive; xls rare. They are bronze rather than brassy, reddish and yellowish respectively. *Bornite, erubescite* or *peacock ore*, Cu_5FeS_4, with a greyish black STR, tarnishes to rainbow hues; H 3; SG $4\cdot9-5\cdot3$; fuses to a grey magnetic globule; soluble in HNO_3, forming a whitish sulphur deposit. Bor. occurs in copper lodes and pneumatolytic deposits, together with chalcopyrite, chalcocite, blende, galena and magnetite in Cornwall (Eng); BC and Que (Can); Ausl, USA, Ausr, Ger, Ita, Swd, Chile, Peru and SA.

Pentlandite, $(Fe,Ni)_9S_8$; H $3-3\frac{1}{2}$; SG $4\cdot6-5\cdot0$; is soluble in HNO_3, insoluble in HCl; is found in basic and ultrabasic rocks with pyrrhotite, niccolite and chalcopyrite, in Yale Mine, BC and Sudbury, Ont (Can); Key West, Alas (USA); Transvaal (SA); Ger, Nor, Swd, USSR.

GREY METALLIC MINERALS

Native platinum is steel grey to silvery, with the same STR, cubic, but usually in irregular grains, occasionally in larger quantities through magmatic segregation, and in placers: it is to the basic rocks what gold is to the acid; H $4-4\frac{1}{2}$; SG $21\cdot46$; melting point $1,760\,°C$; dissolves in hot *aqua regia*; occurs with platinum minerals, olivine and chromite in quartz veins – similar to osmiridium (p 89). Occurrence: Wicklow (Eir); Sudbury, Ont (Can); Orepuki, Wallace Co (NZ); Alas, Oroville,

Butte Co, Calif and Rutherford Co, NC (USA); Bushveld (SA); USSR (Urals); Ethiopia, Kalimantan, Colombia and Zaire.

Native iron, steel grey to black, grey metallic STR; cubic, but no xls, only scales, plates or grains; H 4–5; SG 7·3–7·9; blowpipe infusible; soluble in acids; occurs in meteorites with nickel and in basic rocks with magnetite, olivine, enstatite, augite and anorthite. Localities: Giant's Causeway (NI); St Josephs Isl on Lake Huron, Ont and BC (Can); Cameron, Clinton Co, Mo (USA); Disko Isl (Greenland); NZ.

Native lead is very rare, grey to black, grey metallic STR; H 1½; SG 11·4; cubic with cubical xls up to 4cm high, but mainly capillary, wiry; fuses readily; found with manganese ores in NJ and Idaho (USA); Altai and Urals (USSR); Transylvania (Rum); Swd, Korea.

Molybdenite, MoS_2, is lead grey with a violet cast; STR dark grey; H 1–1½; SG 4·7–4·8; hexagonal, but its barrel-like xls rare; mainly foliaceous like mica, massive, flexible; infusible, green flame, decomposes in HNO_3. It is found in granite pegmatites and metamorphic aureoles; of widespread occurrence, including Loch Tayside (Scot); Can; Qun and NSW (Ausl); Colo and N Mex (USA); Nor, China, Morocco.

Bismuthinite or *bismuth glance*, Bi_2S_3, and *stibnite, antimonite* or *antimony glance*, Sb_2S_3, are very similar; both grey with a dark leaden STR, tarnishing with iridescence, though bis. may be tin white; both orthorhombic, forming needle-like prisms, or massive, but st. also fibrous and in radiating masses; H 2; SG 6·4–6·5 and 4·6–4·7 respectively. Both occur in quartz veins, in association with each other, silver, cobalt and other ores. Bis. fuses readily; heated on charcoal with potassium iodide and sulphur, gives yellow and bright red incrustations; St. fuses in a match flame; soluble in HCl. Localities: Bis – Cornwall, Devon and Cumberland (Eng); Colo, Conn, Minn, Pa, Utah (USA); Saxony (Ger); Swd and Bolivia; St – Cornwall (Eng); Que (Can); San Benito Co, Calif and Shoshone Co, Idaho

(USA); Haute-Loire (Fra); Saxony and Westphalia (Ger); Sardinia, Portugal, USSR, Bolivia, China, Jap.

Pyrolusite, MnO_2, is steel grey to dark grey, yellowish, with a blue–black STR, brittle, orthorhombic – xls rare; mainly, fibrous, massive, reniform; H $2-2\frac{1}{2}$; SG $4\cdot8$; infusible; soluble in HCl with evolution of Cl2; brightly coloured in bead tests. Py. is a common lake, bog and shallow marine deposit, found in Ark (USA); Transvaal (SA); Transcaucasia (USSR); Braz, India.

Argentite or *silver glance*, Ag_2S, is dark lead grey to iron black, with a dark grey metallic STR; cubic system poorly expressed, massive, platy or arborescent; H $2-2\frac{1}{2}$; SG $7\cdot0-7\cdot3$; fusible in blowpipe, soluble in concentrated HNO_3; found in veins with lead and silver ores and chalcopyrite, in igneous rocks: Liskeard, Cornwall (Eng); Ont and BC (Can); Leadville, Colo; Butte, Mon; Nev and Utah (USA); Saxony (Ger); Czsl; Nor, Bolivia, Chile, Mexico, Peru.

Galena, or *lead glance*, is lead grey, sometimes bluish and iridescent; PbS with AgS, when tin white as *argentiferous galena*, with corresponding STRs; cubic, often well crystallised in modified octahedra; also massive, platy or granular; H $2\frac{1}{2}$; SG $7\cdot2-7\cdot6$; fuses with sulphurous fumes, giving a lead globule with a yellowish-green incrustation; soluble in HNO_3; of worldwide occurrence in veins and lodes in limestones and dolomites – rarely sandstones – in the vicinity of igneous intrusions, with quartz, fluorite, calcite, blende, pyrite, chalcopyrite, barite and siderite.

Chalcocite, Cu_2S, is very similar to galena in colour; blackish lead-grey STR; but orthorhombic, forming thick plates or prisms, often in stellate aggregates; also massive, tabular; easily cleavable; H $2\frac{1}{2}-3$; SG $5\cdot7-5\cdot8$; in blowpipe boils and fuses into a copper globule, forms a blue solution in HNO_3 with a sulphur precipitate. Occurrence: Cornwall (Eng); Alas, Ariz, Conn, Mont, Nev, N Mex, Tenn, Utah (USA); Czsl, Ger, Sicily, Nor, Spn, S W Africa, Mexico, Peru, USSR –

mainly in the secondary enrichment zones of primary copper ores.

Bournonite, $2PbS.Cu_2S.Sb_2S_3$, is a lead-copper sulphantimo-nide, of a lead-grey to iron-black colour, grey STR: H $2\frac{1}{2}$-3; SG $5 \cdot 5$-$5 \cdot 9$; orthorhombic with twinned xls that look like cogwheels; also massive or granular; decomposes in HNO_3, giving a bluish-green solution clouded with precipitated lead and sulphur. Br. is found in hydrothermal veins, in association with tetrahedrite, galena, barite and siderite, in Cornwall (Eng); Broken Hill, NSW and Vic (Ausl); Ont (Can); Ariz, Ark, Calif, Colo, Mont, Nev, Utah (USA); Harz (Ger); Czsl; Fra, Hun, Ita, Rum, Spn, Bolivia, Chile, Mexico, Peru.

Tetrahedrite, *grey copper ore* or *fahlerz*, $(Cu,Fe)_{12}Sb_4S_{13}$, is steel grey to iron black, but often thinly coated with chal-copyrite and brassy; STR black, brown to cherry red; H 3-$4\frac{1}{2}$; SG $4 \cdot 4$-$5 \cdot 4$; cubic, tetrahedral xls with additional facets – triangular striations; also massive or granular; may contain Ag, As and Hg; fusible; decomposes in HNO_3 with separation of S and antimony oxide. Tr. is widespread in thermal veins, with chalcopyrite, pyrite, mispickel, galena, chalcocite, bournonite etc: Cornwall (Eng); Mont (USA); Harz and Saxony (Ger); Přibram (Czsl); Hun, Bolivia, Chile, Peru etc.

Stannine, *stannite*, *tin pyrites* or *bell metal ore*, Cu_2FeSnS_4, is steel grey to iron black, or ' bell-metal ' colour, tarnishing blue; STR black; H 4; SG $4 \cdot 3$-$4 \cdot 5$; tetragonal – rarely in small tetrahedra; mostly massive, finely disseminated, or in dense aggregates in cassiterite and tin lodes; fuses with difficulty; forms a blue solution in HNO_3. Localities: Cornwall (Eng); Zeehan (Tasmania); Erzgebirge (Ger); Bolivia.

Haematite, Fe_2O_3, is steel grey to iron black, red when weathered; STR cherry red to red–brown; H $5\frac{1}{2}$-$6\frac{1}{2}$; SG $5 \cdot 2$-$5 \cdot 3$; hexagonal xls – pyramidal or rhombohedral (specular iron); typically massive, reniform or botryoidal (kidney ore); also scaly (micaceous haem.); used in jewellery – polishes to a stainless-steel shine; infusible in blowpipe; dissolves in HCl. Haem. is of widespread occurrence as replacement in limestone and other sedimentary and metamorphic rocks, eg in North Lancashire, Cumberland, Forest of Dean (Eng); Lake Superior, Ala, eastern states (USA); Spn, Braz, Cuba.

Magnetite, magnetic iron ore, Fe_3O_4, iron black to brownish black; STR black; H $5\frac{1}{2}$–$6\frac{1}{2}$; SG $5\cdot0$–$5\cdot2$; cubic – octahedra, often striated, twinned and distorted; also massive or scaly; magnetic; fuses with difficulty; dissolves in HCl. Mag. occurs in igneous and metamorphic rocks with ilmenite, corundum, spinel, olivine, haematite, chalcopyrite, pyrite, garnet, lievrite and pyrrhotite; large deposits produced by magmatic segregation; of widespread occurrence, more particularly in the states of NY, Utah and Wyo (USA); Gällivare and Kiruna (Swd); Fin, Ger, Chile, Mexico, USSR.

Franklinite, $(Fe,Zn,Mn)(Mn,Fe)_2O_4$, a member of the spinel family, is iron black, STR dark brown to reddish brown; H 6–$6\frac{1}{2}$; SG $5\cdot0$–$5\cdot2$; cubic – octahedral xls, often rounded at edges; also in rounded grains and lenses; infusible; soluble in HCl; bottle green in reducing flame; colours borax bead amethyst in oxidising flame; found in metamorphosed, crystalline limestones at Franklin, Sterling Hill, NJ (USA).

MINERALS OF ACID ROCKS

MODES OF OCCURRENCE

The same minerals are often found under various conditions in different types of rock, so that in many cases one can speak at best of the typical mode of occurrence – and it is not always easy to decide how typical it is either. Clear-cut situations are comparatively rare. Nevertheless, in being confronted with some geological formation, say, rocks affected by regional metamorphism, it is useful to know, if only approximately, what can be expected of them.

The primary rocks on the Earth's surface are igneous, and in continental regions mainly acid, ie characterised by a content of silica of over 66 per cent. Some of this may be in the bound form of silicates – indeed, most rock-forming minerals are silicates – and some free as quartz. Quartz is always present in the acid granite clan, but scarce or absent in the predominantly felspathic (referring to felspars and similar minerals, or *felspathoids*) syenites and other intermediate rocks. It may show up sparsely in gabbro, but does not, in principle, occur in the basic division.

It will be recalled that in any igneous rock we must distinguish between the *essential minerals*, which define the rock species and so must inevitably be present if the rock is what it is supposed to be, and *accessory minerals*, which may or may not accompany the essential ones in variable but generally small amounts.

The most common acid plutonic rock is granite, and, as we know, its essential constituents are quartz, felspar and mica; but it may be subdivided into subspecies according to a predominant accessory mineral. Thus we have a hornblende granite or a diopside granite etc. The felspars and micas may also vary in composition and proportions of the different compositions (see Table 1). Most of the accessory minerals are silicates, but some, such as gold and fluorite, are not, and have been or will be described under other headings. The micas apart, most granite minerals either are or may occasionally be used as gemstones.

QUARTZ

Quartz is a ubiquitous mineral. It occurs not only in crystalline acid igneous rocks, but in metamorphic rocks, as a gangue mineral in metalliferous lodes, and in thermal veins and concretions in sedimentary rocks. Rare rock constituents, including gold, often become sorted out into quartz veins which, therefore, deserve inspection. Sand commonly consists of quartz grains, and so, of course, does sandstone which is metamorphosed by heat into tough quartzite or quartz rock. This can be white, yellow, brown, red or purple. The main ingredient of most conglomerates is quartz balls which may acquire various tints and greater transparency through exposure to magmatic heat.

Quartz is one of Mohs' scale (p 48) markers with H=7. Its SG is 2·64–2·66, and it belongs to the hexagonal xl system of incomplete trigonal symmetry (p 40), assuming various forms, most commonly prismatic, terminated at one or both ends by a pyramid or ' roof ', also bipyramidal, rarely pseudocubic. The xls are often, though not always, striated or lined across the prism, which provides one ready way of distinguishing them from the somewhat similar prisms of beryl or topaz, lined lengthwise, and the smooth ones of apatite. A greasy LR and conchoidal fracture provide further tests. The xls may be of any size, from minute incrustations giving a shark-skin effect to many feet long. Quartz is a crystalline form of silica, SiO_2, and what is known as 'massive quartz' consists of inchoately intergrown xls.

This is usually the case in veins, well-formed xls appearing only in hollows, where they may be clear, while the vein as a whole is op or trl, usually white. White quartz has occasionally been used for beads, but it is not reckoned a gemstone. The so-called 'milky quartz' is trl with a bluish undertone (the milk has been 'baptised'). Trp colourless quartz is *rock crystal*. It may, however, assume almost any colour of the rainbow, depending on minor impurities. *Citrine* is yellow, *cairngorm* ('false topaz') is brown, *smoky quartz* has an indeterminate smoky hue, *rose quartz* is carmine pink in contradistinction to the flesh-pink *ferruginous quartz*, *prase* is green, *sapphire* or *azure quartz* is blue, *amethyst* is violet to purple or wine red, and *morion* is peat brown to black. The yellow and brown hues are usually due to colloidal silicon, the violet colour is ascribed to colloidal iron, pink to titanium, green to actinolite, and blue to crocidolite inclusions. The two latter are fibrous and may give the stone a shimmer, producing a moving band of light when it is cut *en cabochon*. This effect is generically known as *cat's-eye*, but the azure quartz thus affected is called *pheasant's-eye* in the trade, the name *quartz cat's-eye* being reserved for the case where the crocidolite has been oxidised to brown. Actinolite yields a green *falcon's-eye*. There are also red and yellow *tiger-eyes*.

As mentioned, ferruginous quartz is flesh pink or red–brown, a colouring due to haematite which may also occur as specular flakes, or else the flakes are mica, giving the stone a sparkle. This is *aventurine quartz*. Tourmalinated and rutilated quartz is shot through by needles of tourmaline and rutile respectively. The latter are known fancifully as *flèches d'amour* (arrows of love), and when densely packed look like blonde or red hair encased in glass. Such quartz is known as *Venus' hairstone*.

Sometimes the xls have small internal fractures, causing iridescent reflections in *rainbow quartz.*

The pink, green and blue varieties are usually somewhat milky, but clear crystals of almost any colour with different pigmental ingredients occur.

Quartz is weakly birefringent, has low RIs of $1 \cdot 54$ and $1 \cdot 55$, and little fire, but its varied colorations and adequate hardness make it a popular gemstone.

FELSPARS

Felspars or *feldspars* are a group of minerals whose composition varies continuously within certain limits. They may be thought of as isomorphic (ie having the same shape) mixtures of four minerals: *orthoclase* or *potash* felspar, $KAlSi_3O_8$; *albite* or *soda* felspar, $NaAlSi_3O_8$, *anorthite* or *lime* felspar, $CaAl_2Si_2O_8$; and *celsian* or *barium* felspar, $BaAl_2Si_2O_8$.

Orthoclase is usually monoclinic, and so is the rare *celsian.* The remaining types, bracketed under the name of *plagioclase*, are triclinic. However, orthoclase can shade over more or less imperceptibly into albite through the partial substitution of sodium, Na, for potassium, K, yielding a soda-orthoclase which may become triclinic. There are other intermediate types.

Orthoclase is a characteristic mineral of acid rocks, and plagioclase of basic, although albite is frequently present in granites, and the rule is not absolute. For the sake of order, however, we will consider plagioclase under the basic heading and deal here with orthoclase, microcline, anorthoclase and celsian.

Orthoclase, H 6 of Mohs'; SG $2 \cdot 53 - 2 \cdot 56$. Is typically bone-like, often with a satin sheen, white, grey, greenish or flesh coloured, but may also be colourless and trp or trl. The latter variety is known as *adularia*, from the Adular Mts of Switzerland, but it is also found on Snowdon (Wal), in the Mourne Mts (NI), in Peru, and sporadically elsewhere. A subspecies of adularia with a blue chatoyancy is *moonstone* – a classical gemstone. But the yellow trp ortho., more particularly from

Madagascar, and green specimens with a cat's-eye shimmer also look fine cut. The mineral is normally crystalline (Fig 5), but may also be massive, and occurs throughout the world in granites, syenites, porphyries, trachytes, gneisses and crystalline schists. It fuses with difficulty at the edges and decomposes in HNO_3. A glassy, grey, pearly variety called *sanidine* occurs in volcanic rocks.

Microcline is triclinic orthoclase, white to pale yellow, occasionally red or green, the latter being a gemstone known as *amazonite* or *amazon stone*. It is op and may be somewhat harder than the monoclinic kind (up to $6\frac{1}{2}$). *Anorthoclase* resembles microcline, except that its proportion of Na is greater than of K. It may be found in Obsidian Cliff, Yellowstone National Park (USA); on Pantellaria (Ita); in southern Norway, and on Kilimanjaro (Kenya).

Celsian, H 6–$6\frac{1}{2}$; SG $3\cdot37$. Crystallises in short stout prisms, but may also be acicular or massive; commonly colourless, sometimes reddish brown or grey; gives a yellow–green flame; occurs in Benalf Mine, Caernarvonshire (Wal); Broken Hill, NSW (Ausl); Ita, Swd, Jap and SW Africa.

MICAS

Mica is flaky and flexible, sometimes in six-sided ' books ' readily splitting into ' pages ', and found in granite and many other igneous, metamorphic and sedimentary rocks, more particularly the silvery, glittering mica-schists. The system is monoclinic: H 2–3; SG $2\cdot5$–$3\cdot0$, depending on the somewhat complicated composition. The two main varieties are:

The pale, colourless, yellowish or brownish, generally more or less trp *muscovite*, $KAl_3S_3O_{10}(OH)_2$, with colourless STR and perfect laminar cleavage, fusing with difficulty into a yellowish bead.

The dark, black or green *biotite* with a metallic LR and white STR, fusible to black glass, is the more common. The dark colour is due to magnesium (Mg), iron (Fe) and manganese (Mn), which have a similar effect on other minerals. Both these micas are of worldwide distribution.

There are further minor varieties associated with these two main types: *paragonite*, the sodium mica, and *lepidolite*, the lithium-potassium mica, which are classed as ' muscovites '; and *phlogopite*, the magnesium mica, and *zinnwaldite* or lithium biotite, similarly regarded as subdivisions of the ' biotites '. Even this does not quite complete the list as there are other secondary micas arising from the alteration of various rock-forming minerals.

However, *paragonite* is yellowish or greenish, occurs mainly in metamorphic rocks with garnet, kyanite and staurolite, more particularly in Saxony (Ger) and Tessin (Swz). *Lepidolite* is rose red or lilac to magenta, has a pearly LR and white STR; reacts weakly to HCl; yields a red lithium flame; contains fluorine. It occurs in pegmatite and pneumatolytic veins in San Diego Co, Calif, Portland, Conn and Auburn, Me (USA); Zinnwald, Saxony (Ger); Varuträsk (Swd); Elba, Madagascar.

Phlogopite is another rare mica; it may be colourless, brown or copper red; has a pearly LR; shows asterism; occurs mainly in impure crystalline limestones – and so properly belongs in Chapter 13 – especially in Ont (Can).

Zinnwaldite takes its name from Zinnwald in Saxony (Ger), but is found also in Cornwall (Eng) together with cassiterite in granite affected by pneumatolysis. It may be violet, pale yellow or brown; has a pearly LR; is readily fusible, and colours the flame red.

ACCESSORY MINERALS OF GRANITE

The granite clan, and its pegmatites in particular, may contain a whole litany of minerals, many of which are gemstones: (1) allanite; (2) apatite; (3) beryl and chrysoberyl; (4) cassiterite; (5) corundum; (6) cryolite; (7) diopside; (8) fluorite; (9) garnet; (10) gold; (11) hornblende; (12) kyanite; (13)

molybdenite; (14) monazite; (15) phenakite; (16) sphene; (17) spodumene; (18) topaz; (19) tourmaline; (20) zircon; and this list is far from complete. Items (2), (5), (7), (8), (9) and (12), however, are more typical of metamorphic rocks; (10) and (13) have been dealt with in Chapter 9, and (11) will be considered in Chapter 11.

Allanite or *orthite* is not a recognised gemstone, but its H of $5\frac{1}{2}$–6 is adequate, RI is high, it is pleochroic, and its composition and appearance vary so much that some pieces may be worth cutting. It is a complex silicate of rare-earth elements; monoclinic – tabular or long slender xls; also massive or granular; the usual colour is black to brown; LR sub-metallic or vitreous; STR grey to greenish or brownish; SG $3 \cdot 5$–$4 \cdot 2$; brittle; fuses easily in borax bead to a dark magnetic glass; gelatinises in HCl; found in felspathic granite, gneiss, syenite and porphyry, in NY (USA); Scot, Can, Den, Greenland, Nor and Madagascar.

Beryl is a silicate of beryllium and aluminium, $Al_2Be_3(Si_2O_6)_3$; H $7\frac{1}{2}$–8; SG $2 \cdot 6$–$2 \cdot 8$; crystallises in the hexagonal system, typically in long six-, sometimes twelve-sided prisms with longitudinal striations and a flat, but sometimes faceted or pointed, top; also massive or granular; op to trp; LR vitreous; STR white. Ber. may be colourless, milky-white, grey, red, opalescent or iridescent, but is more usually green, blue, yellow or pink to mauve. More than one colour may be present in the same xl. Opalescence occurs in the yellow variety known as *golden beryl*. The blue to green–blue stones are called *aquamarines*, yellow–green – *heliodors*, pink to mauve – *morganites*, and colourless – *goshenites*.

Beryl is a gemstone, slightly dichroic (RI $1 \cdot 57$ and $1 \cdot 59$), of low dispersion and little fire. *Emerald*, a more precious variety of shamrock hue, differs from ordinary beryl in a partial replacement of aluminium by chromium, yielding a formula $Be_3AlCr_2(Si_2O_6)_3$; it is somewhat softer and heavier and gives in a dichroscope colours different from aquamarine (p 62).

Beryl is unaffected by acids, glows white and becomes clouded in the blowpipe; fuses with great difficulty to white glass.

Apart from the granite pegmatites, it is also found in metamorphic rocks, eg mica-schists. It occurs in the English, Scottish and Irish granites, including the emerald variety (in the Cairngorms, Scot); Calif, NC, SC, Carolina, New England, N Mex, S Dak (USA); Transvaal (SA); Urals (USSR); Braz, Colombia.

Chrysoberyl, although often bracketed with beryl, is beryllium aluminate, $BeAl_2O_4$, harder and heavier than beryl; H $8\frac{1}{2}$; SG $3 \cdot 71$–$3 \cdot 72$; with more fire – RI $1 \cdot 76$–$1 \cdot 75$; orthogonal, not hexagonal, with tabular xls, often arranged in stellate six-somes. The colour is green, greenish yellow or brown; STR colourless; LR vitreous. The green variety which looks red in artificial light is called *alexandrite*. There is also a chatoyant cat's-eye. The stone is trp, brittle, resistant to acids, but is decomposed by fusion with KOH. It is supposed to occur in the Mourne Mts (NI). Other localities are: Que (Can); W Ausl; Colo, Conn, Me, NH, NY (USA); Helsinki (Fin); Lake Como, Veltlin (Ita); Saetersdalen (Nor); St Gotthard (Swz); Urals (USSR); Katanga (Zaire); Burma, Ghana, Jap, Rhodesia (south of Gwelo).

Cassiterite, *stannite* or *tinstone*, SnO_2; H 6–7; SG $6 \cdot 8$–$7 \cdot 1$ – feels heavy in the hand; op to trp; strongly birefringent, RI $1 \cdot 99$ and $2 \cdot 09$ and dichroic; brown to brownish black; STR white to pale yellow; LR splendent or adamantine (diamond tin). Cas. may be massive, fibrous or granular, but when found in granite, porphyry or pegmatites, usually crystalline; tetragonal; the short striated prisms ending in pyramids are very variable. When trp cas. makes a beautiful gem, but even trl xls are not to be despised. It is infusible and insoluble in acids; widely distributed, eg in Cornwall (Eng); Bohemia (Czsl); Ausl, Malaysia etc.

Cryolite, $Na_3(AlF_6)$, is associated with cassiterite, galena and chalcopyrite in tin-bearing granites and pegmatite veins; H

$2\frac{1}{2}$-3; SG 2·95; trl, reddish or brownish; LR pearly; STR white; mostly massive; monoclinic xls rare, cuboidal. The mineral is no gem, and is important mainly in the electrolytic process of aluminium extraction. Main localities: Colo (USA); Urals (USSR); West Greenland.

Monazite is a complex silicate of thorium and rare earths, pale yellow to dark brown, op, white STR, resinous LR, brittle; H 5–5$\frac{1}{2}$; SG 4·8–5·3; monoclinic – thick tabular or beady xls, sometimes intergrown; keeps company with garnet, zircon, chromite, gold and diamond in granite and gneiss; decomposes slowly in HCl; of worldwide distribution, especially Travancore (India); Nor, Braz and Nigeria.

Phenakite or *phenacite*, silicate of beryllium, Be_2SiO_4, is a ' minor gemstone '; it is trp, colourless, pale yellow to pink, with vitreous LR and white STR; orthorhombic – xls similar to quartz, with which it is often confused, but unlined across and harder – H 7$\frac{1}{2}$–8; SG 3·0; infusible, insoluble in acids; found with emerald, chrysoberyl and apatite in granite veins and biotite schists. Localities: St Agnes, Cornwall (Eng); Topaz Butte, Colo and Bald Face Mt, NH (USA); Minas Geraes (Braz); Valais (Swz); Urals (USSR); Nor; Tanganyika.

Sphene or *titanite*, $CaTi(O/SiO_4)$, rivals diamond in adamantine LR and fire, being highly dispersive and birefringent – RI 1·91 and 2·09; but is comparatively soft – H 5–5$\frac{1}{2}$; SG 3·45–3·53; may be yellow, green, brown, red–brown or black, sub-trp to op; STR white; monoclinic, but good xls rare and even these incline to cloudiness – wedge-shaped or prismatic; also massive; fuses with difficulty; decomposes in H_2SO_4. Sp. keeps company with chlorite, albite, adularia and hornblende in acid rocks rich in lime, and at contact with limestones. Occurrence: nr Tavistock, Devon (Eng); Craig na Cailleach, Perthshire (Scot); Crow Hill, Newry granite (NI); Sandford, Me and Pitcairn, St Lawrence Co, NY (USA); Saxony (Ger); Arendal (Nor); Kola Peninsula (USSR); Can, Austr and Swiss Alps.

Spodumene, $AlLi.Si_2O_6$, has a wide range of colours; amethystine, dark lilac, pink, yellow and emerald green (lithia emerald). The pink to violet variety is known as *kunzite* and green as *hiddenite*. The striated xls with a vitreous LR and white STR resemble those of quartz and diopside, but are monoclinic, mostly eight-sided prisms, usually trp, often large; H $6\frac{1}{2}$–7; SG $3 \cdot 1$–$3 \cdot 2$; resembles diopside, *qv*; dichroic, birefringent; fuses in blowpipe with red flame. It is found in granite and gneiss pegmatites with beryl, cassiterite and tourmaline nr Peterhead, Aberdeenshire (Scot); Killiney Bay and west side of Leinster granite (Eir); Man (Can); Windham, Me; Chester, Mass; Stone Point, Alexander Co, NC and S Dak (USA); Braz and Madagascar.

Topaz, hydrous fluoro-silicate of aluminium, $Al_2[(F,OH)_2 SiO_4]$, marks 8 on Mohs' scale; SG $3 \cdot 4$–$3 \cdot 6$; orthorhombic, forms short and long, often flawless prisms, usually eight-sided, variously terminated and lined lengthwise; brittle across the long axis; also massive; trp to op; when pure colourless, but may be variously tinted: yellowish red, wine yellow, brown, sky blue or green, with a vitreous LR and colourless STR; is partially attacked by H_2SO_4. It is found in granite pegmatites, and more particularly in greisen (p 27), also as a gangue mineral in tin lodes, and contact-metamorphosed rocks around granite plutons, with cassiterite, fluorite and tourmaline, in Cornwall and Lundy (Eng); Arran, Kintyre, Cairngorms and Sutherland (Scot); Mourne Mts (NI); Mt Bischoff (Tasmania); Pikes Peak, Colo; Trumbull, Conn; Stoneham, Me and Calif (USA); Fossum (Nor); Finbo (Swd); Urals (USSR); Asia Minor, Braz, Jap and Rhodesia. *Brazilian ruby* is a salmon-pink to purple-red topaz, obtained by heating yellowish xls to 450°C. T. is pyro-electric and becomes charged when heated, a property it shares with tourmaline.

Tourmaline is a highly complex silicate of boron and aluminium, containing variable proportions of iron, magnesium and light alkali metals, which affect its colouring and physical properties; H 7–7½; SG 3·0–3·2; hexagonal system of trigonal habit – usually long, roughly triangular prisms with rounded corners and deeply grooved lengthwise, the sixsome pattern appearing only in the ending, in facets that often fail to match; LR vitreous; STR colourless. The colour ranges from black in the non-gem variety of *schorl* through brown in *dravite*, indigo-blue in *indicolite*, red in *rubelite* to green in *verdelite* or fancifully ' Brazilian emerald '. But *achroite* is colourless, and yellow and orange stones likewise occur, some xls being zoned in different colours; all tourmalines are strongly dichroic; infusible and unaffected by acids. Their distribution is worldwide, in granite, greisen, gneiss and crystalline limestones, eg Cornish and Scottish granites and schists, also nr Okehampton, Devon (Eng) and the English Lake District; in the Donegal and Leinster granites and Ox Mts (Eire); NT and Vic (Ausl); NH; Mason Co, Tex; Pikes Peak, Colo and Juab Co, Utah (USA); Harz Mts (Ger); Bolivia, Braz, Chile, Madagascar, USSR.

Zircon, silicate of zirconium, $ZrSiO_4$, is found in tetragonal xls, usually simple prism-cum-pyramids, sometimes twinned, never massive; op to trp; in a number of colours: grey, pale yellow (*jargoon*), red or brown (*hyacinth* or *jacinth*), green, purple, as well as uncoloured, although most colourless stones, known fancifully as ' Matura diamonds ', and the blue ones are obtained by heat treatment. Zr. is birefringent – RI 1·99 and 1·92, has a dispersion of 0·038 and considerable fire which enables it to be passed off for diamond. It is, however, much softer and heavier: H 7–7½; SG 3·9–4·8. These differences reflect a variability of composition, including the radioactive elements, uranium and thorium. The ' low-type ' zrs. are greenish, less well crystallised, softer and less refractive; the ' high-type ' ones usually red or brown; but the low type can be converted into the high by heating, which also makes the stone dichroic, a property lacking in natural zr. Zr. is infusible and insoluble in acids. It is of widespread occurrence in acid

113

and metamorphic, as well as detrital rocks, including ' black sands' with rutile and ilmenite, and some sandstones. NSW (Ausl); Urals (USSR); USA, Nor, Sri Lanka, India, Madagascar and W Africa are the main sources of gem-quality material.

INTERMEDIATE TO ULTRABASIC ROCKS

INTERMEDIATE ROCKS

It will be recalled that intermediate rocks, containing 55-65 per cent of silica, such as syenites, trachyte, diorite and andesite, are transitional between the acid and the basic division and so share many of their minerals with the granites at the one end and with the gabbro clan at the other. There are, however, four minerals which characteristically belong to this type: aegirine, hornblende, nepheline and sodalite; we might add diopside, which occurs in granites as well, but it is mainly found in metamorphic rocks.

Aegerine is one of the *pyroxenes*, a group of magnesium-calcium silicates, which may also contain aluminium, sodium and lithium: diopside and spodumene are likewise members of this group, and accordingly may accompany aegerine. Once again, as in the case of felspars, the composition varies almost continuously. Pyroxenes are typical of soda-rich rocks and crystallise in the orthorhombic or monoclinic system.

Aegerine is mainly a sodium-iron silicate of fluid composition, $NaFe \ldots (Si_2O_6)$; H 6–6½; SG 3·4–3·5; monoclinic, forms prismatic xls with pointed or blunt endings, long and short; also acicular or fibrous – in druses, with soda-felspars, augite and hornblende, in syenite pegmatites and like rocks. It is op, trl at the edges, brown, reddish brown, black or green; LR vitreous; STR yellowish to dark green; fuses readily to a shiny, black, magnetic bead, colours the flame yellow. Occurrence: nr Montreal (Can); Ozark Mts, Ark; Colorado Springs, Colo and Beemervilla, NJ (USA); Kangerdluarsuk (Greenland); Langesund Fjord (Nor); Kola (USSR); Portugal, Rum, Swd, Braz.

Hornblende is similar in being a highly complex silicate of the amphibole family. These are (mainly) magnesium, iron and calcium, sometimes sodium, silicates of the general formula $X_{7-8}(Si_4O_{11})_2(OH)_2$, where X stands for a variable combination of the above-mentioned metals with aluminium; orthorhombic, monoclinic or triclinic; dark-coloured. Hrn. itself is monoclinic of prismatic habit, but may also be blade-like, fibrous, massive or granular; H 5–6; SG 2·9–3·4; grey-, greenish- or brownish-black in colour and STR; LR vitreous; readily fusible; decomposes in HCl. It is a primary mineral in some acid and intermediate rocks, schists and gneisses; predominant in amphibolites (metamorphic). Of worldwide distribution.

Nepheline, nephelite or *eleolite* is a felspathoid, $Na_3K(AlSiO_4)_4$, and a gemstone of sorts, trp or trl; white, colourless or pale grey; STR white; LR greasy or vitreous; hexagonal system, xls similar to beryl, but usually short, twinned or aggregated; also columnar; H $5\frac{1}{2}$–6; SG 2·55–2·65; fusible; gelatinises in HCl; of worldwide occurrence with garnet, hornblende and sanidine in soda-rich, silica-poor rocks, eg syenites, nepheline basalts etc.

Sodalite, $Na_8[Cl_2/(AlSiO_4)_6]$, is typical of soda-rich syenites; H 5–6; SG 2·2–2·4; trp or trl; blue, colourless, grey, yellowish, greenish or red, with a vitreous or fatty LR, and colourless STR; cubic – dodecahedral xls, or massive; qualifies as a minor gemstone; fuses with difficulty, and decomposes in HCl with separation of gelatinous silica. It may be found at Salem, Mass and in Crazy Mts, Mont (USA); Monte Somma and Vesuvius

(Ita); Langesund Fjord (Nor); Kola (USSR); Bolivia, Ger, Greenland and Portugal.

BASIC AND ULTRABASIC ROCKS

In basic rocks the silica content sinks to between 55 and 45 per cent and in ultrabasic below 45 per cent. Quartz does not occur in the latter at all, and in the basic division only occasionally as an accessory mineral. The orthoclase felspar of the acid clan is replaced by plagioclase, and this too fades away in the ultrabasic division. All these rocks are dark and heavy, which is due to the increasing proportion of ferro-magnesian minerals such as pyroxenes and amphiboles (pp 18, 115f). These are generally less transparent and gem-like than the silicates of lighter metals, found mainly in the more siliceous formations.

Gabbro is the ' granite ' of the basic rocks. Its essential minerals (Table 1) are plagioclase, augite and diallage, olivine and sometimes hornblende, with leucite, apatite, ilmenite, spinel and magnetite as the most usual accessories. Biotite, nepheline and analcite are essential in some varieties. Anorthosites are purely felspathic. Gabbros have their aplites and pegmatites with the corresponding assortments of rarer minerals. Basalt is a microcrystalline or glassy rock of the same composition.

In the ultrabasic division olivine is essential and felspar accessory only, with hornblende, enstatite and augite for picrites. Perknites are made up mainly of pyroxenes. Peridotite and dunite are predominantly olivine rocks.

As in other cases there are extensive overlaps in occurrence between the basic, acid and metamorphic rocks, but in addition to those listed the following minerals may be expected in the basic division: (1) bronzite, (2) chromite, (3) datolite, (4) diamond; (5) garnet; (6) iron (native); (7) jadeite; (8) platinum-group metals; (9) pyrrhotite; (10) rutile; (11) uvarovite in association with (2); (12) zeolites.

However (5) is typically a metamorphic mineral and will

be dealt with under this heading; (6), (8) and (9) have already been described (Chapter 9). The mode of occurrence of (7) is somewhat uncertain: according to H. H. Read it may be a metamorphic mineral, but it may be a secondary basic one as well, which also applies to zeolites, found in the cavities of basic lavas. Fluorite and opal may occur in similar situations, as may epidote and some other minerals. Leucite is typical of volcanic rocks.

ESSENTIAL BASIC MINERALS

Analcite is one of the zeolites, which are hydrated alumino-silicates of alkali metals and alkaline earths. While it forms a secondary filling in the basalt cavities, it is also a primary mineral in some rocks of the gabbro clan. It is an alumino-silicate of sodium, $Na(AlSi_2O_6).H_2O$, trp to trl, colourless or white, occasionally greenish, yellowish or reddish; LR vitreous; STR white; H $5-5\frac{1}{2}$; SG $2\cdot2-2\cdot3$; of the cubic system – usually in small 'beady' (icositetrahedral) xls; but also massive, granular or earthy; readily fusible to colourless glass; gelatinises in HCl. It occurs in company with magnetite and nepheline in Dunbartonshire and Stirlingshire (Scot); Antrim (NI); NS (Can); NJ (USA); Bohemia (Czsl); Harz Mts (Ger); Greenland, Iceland, Ita and the islands of the Indian Ocean.

Augite is a pyroxene of variable composition, $Ca_{8-10}(MgFeAl)_2(AlSi)_2O_6$, shading over into other pyroxenes (p 115); H 5-6; SG $3\cdot3-3\cdot5$; op, black to greenish black; LR dull vitreous; STR grey–green; monoclinic of prismatic habit, forming short eight-sided xls with roof-like endings; brittle, fusible, insoluble in acids. Aug. is of widespread occurrence in gabbros and metamorphic rocks, and keeps company with diopside, hornblende, epidote, biotite, chlorite and limonite.

Diallage is halfway between augite and diopside in composition, $Ca(MgFe)Si_2O_6$; monoclinic, usually lamellar or folia-ceous, sometimes fibrous; H 5-6; SG $3\cdot3-3\cdot4$; greyish green to dark or deep green, also black or brown, op; LR pearly, sometimes with a schiller, or sub-metallic, brassy; STR greyish white; infusible, insoluble in acids. D. is of worldwide occurrence in the gabbro clan with augite, diopside, chlorite and serpentine; also in the ultrabasic *diallogite*, where it is the principal constituent together with hornblende, garnet, pyroxenes, olivine, plagioclase and pyrite as accessories.

Olivine is to the basic rocks what quartz is to the acid; $(Mg,Fe)_2(SiO_4)_3$; H $6\frac{1}{2}$–7; SG 3·3; olive green, yellowish green, dark green, brown, red; trp to trl; LR vitreous; STR white; orthorhombic, of prismatic habit, with domical or pyramidal endings, also tabular; in rounded grains in volcanic rocks (basalts); infusible, gelatinises in HCl. Ol. seldom attains gem quality: the yellowish-green variety is known as *chrysotile* and the dark green as *peridot*. The best peridot comes from St John's Island in the Red Sea, Brazil and Burma, but it is also found in Arizona (USA); chrysotile gems stem mostly from Sri Lanka. The red variety is found in druses on Island Magee (Northern Ireland). Common ol. is the main constituent of dunite and peridotite, it is of worldwide occurrence; decays to serpentine.

Sinhalite is often confused with olivine, and indeed the two are difficult to distinguish in hand specimens. Sn., however, is the alumino-borate of magnesium, $Mg.AlBO_4$, of a pale-yellow to deep-brown colour; vitreous to adamantine LR, and white STR. Its orthorhombic xls closely resemble olivine, but are a little heavier – SG 3·47–3·60, softer – H $6\frac{1}{2}$, and have higher RIs: 1·67 and 1·71; dichroic. It is a fine gem, found in Warren Co, NY (USA); and in the gem gravels of Burma and Sri Lanka.

It will be recalled (p 106) that *plagioclases* are a series of felspars varying continuously from *albite*, $Na(AlSi_3O_8)$, to *anorthite*, $Ca(Al_2Si_2O_8)$, or isomorphous mixtures of these. They are generally crystalline, triclinic of tabular or lath habit, often twinned or intergrown; H 6–$6\frac{1}{2}$; SG 2·51–2·77; usually op, but occasionally trp or trl; LR vitreous to pearly; STR white.

The colouring is very variable: white, green, red, yellow and grey. Albite fuses with difficulty and colours the flame yellow (Na); anorthite is fusible and is decomposed by acids.

Mineralogical *albite* contains less than 10 per cent of anorthite; is most often white, but may be bluish, grey, reddish, greenish or green. It is of worldwide occurrence.

In *oligoclase* the proportion of anorthite is 10–30 per cent. It is white, green or red; a trl variety spangled with little flakes of haematite is a gemstone, known as *sunstone* or *aventurine felspar*.

In *andesine*, which runs through the full gamut of plagioclase colorations, this proportion rises to 30–50 per cent, and becomes 50–70 per cent in *labradorite*. This is usually of a greyish-brown colour with a vitreous LR and colourless STR, but occasionally trp and cut as a gem. Labr. is further characterised by iridescence (p 33), mainly in green, pale and dark blue, but also red and yellow, which is brought out by appropriately slanted cutting. Labr. is used as an ornamental stone. It is found in Labrador; Adirondack Mts, NY (USA); Transylvania (Rum); Scandinavia; and in small amounts in the English Lake District and the Mts of Mourne (NI).

Bytownite contains 70–90 per cent of anorthite, and mineralogical *anorthite* is not less than 90 per cent pure. Bt. is grey, dark grey or bluish, but occasionally of a clear pale-yellow colour and suitable for cutting as a gem. It is found in ultrabasic rocks. An. may be colourless, white, grey or greenish, with a vitreous or pearly LR and white STR; it decomposes in HCl with separation of silica gel; occurs in basic volcanics and crystalline limestones, eg nr Franklin, NJ (USA).

ACCESSORIES

Bronzite and *enstatite* are variations on the same theme, being a magnesium-iron and magnesium silicate with formulae, $(Mg,Fe)_2Si_2O_6$ and $MgSiO_3$ respectively. The xls of both belong to the orthorhombic system, are seldom well developed, greyish, greenish, yellowish or bronze brown to near-black; with a vitreous, metallic or silky LR, and a greyish or colourless STR. In bronzite, which is a gemstone usually cut *en cabochon*, they are trl to op with a bronze sheen due to minute inclusions of ilmenite. A green trp variety occurs in Transvaal (SA). The properties fluctuate with composition: H $5\frac{1}{2}$–6; SG 3·2–3·9. The xls are fusible at the edges, unaffected by HCl. Br. hobnobs with olivine and serpentine. It is of widespread occurrence; eg at The Lizard, Cornwall (Eng); Colo, Md, Brewster, NY and Pa (USA); Bavaria, Eifel, Harz (Ger); Kjörrestad (Nor); Mogok (Burma); Ausr, Czsl, SA; also found in meteorites.

Chromite, iron chromate, $FeCr_2O_4$, with traces of aluminium and magnesium, iron black to blackish brown, with a sub-metallic LR and brown STR; H $5\frac{1}{2}$; SG 4·5–4·8; belongs to the cubic system with octahedral habit, but good xls are rare; usually granular, massive or compact. Cr. is a primary mineral in peridotites and other ultrabasic rocks, where it is associated with serpentine, nickel ores, platinum, sometimes uvarovite; infusible, insoluble in acids. Occurrence: Balta Sound and Unst, Shetlands (Scot); NSW and New Caledonia (Ausl); Que (Can); Calif, Md, NC, Oreg, Pa, Tex, Wyo (USA); Var (Fra); Ramberget (Nor); Antioch, Izmir (Turkey); Uskub (Yug); Gt Dyke (Rhodesia); Ausr, Bulgaria, Cuba, Grc, India, Philippines and SA.

Datolite, $Ca(OH/BSiO_4)$; H 5–$5\frac{1}{2}$; SG 2·9–3·2; may be colourless, white, or variously tinted: pink, red, magenta, pale green, olive green, yellow or brown; trp or trl; LR vitreous; STR white; monoclinic, forms short prisms; also massive, reniform or granular; fuses to black glass; gives green flame; used as a gemstone. It is found in Cornwall (Eng); Dunbarton-shire, Kilpatrick Hills, Stirlingshire and Salisbury Craigs, Perthshire (Scot); Calif, Conn, Lake Superior district, Mass, Minn, NJ, NY (USA); Tyrol (Ausr); nr Prague (Czsl); Bavaria, Harz, Thuringia (Ger); Arendal (Nor); Utö (Swd); Italian Alps; and Tasmania.

Diamond is a high-temperature and high-pressure allomorph of graphite and the element carbon, C, gr. being sometimes transformed into dia. by contact metamorphism, eg at New Cumnock, Ayrshire (Scot). Dia. is a primary mineral in basic and ultrabasic rocks, but is more usually found in volcanic pipe fillings (blue ground) and detrital deposits, such as river gravels and conglomerates. Unless waterworn, it is clearly crystallised in cubes, cubo-octahedra and more developed forms of the cubic system, with bulging and often distorted faces, which are striated or etched; colourless, though commonly tinged lightly with blue or yellow; sometimes pink, mauve, green, blue, red or black (*carbonado*); trp to trl; LR adamantine to greasy; STR normally unobtainable, but ash grey when crushed; H 10; SG 3·5; infusible, but burns in small splinters. Good specimens are used as gems, poor-quality ones as abrasive; crude varieties are known as bort (boart). Occurrence: Queensl, NSW, Vic (Ausl); Ark, Calif, Colo, Ga, NC, Oreg, Va, Wis (USA); Minas Geraes (Braz), Bolivia, China, Ghana, Guiana, India, Indonesia, S and SW Africa, USSR, Venezuela.

Ilmenite, menaccanite or *columbite* is a titanium-iron oxide, $FeTiO_3$; H 5–6; SG 4·5–5·0; iron black to blackish brown; op or trl; hexagonal system, tri-rhombohedral habit, in rosettes and twins; also thin plates or scales, and in sand grains; infusible, soluble in acids with great difficulty. Ilmenite is of widespread occurrence in the gabbros, especially pegmatites and dykes, eg in Adirondacks (USA); Can, Alps, Scandinavia etc.

Jadeite, a much-prized ornamental stone, is a sodium-aluminium silicate, $Na(AlSi_2O_6)$, of the pyroxene family, with variable proportions of calcium, magnesium, chromium and manganese, to which the variations in colour and other properties are due. Jd. is usually green or whitish with emerald-green patches, but may be off-white or mauve; op to trl; LR sub-vitreous to pearly; STR colourless; H 6½–7; SG 3·2–3·5; monoclinic, but xls extremely rare; usually massive, when it is known as *jade* (see also *nephrite*, p 136); fusible, gives a yellow flame. Jd. has been recorded at the Lizard, Cornwall (Eng); and in Sutherland (Scot); of widespread occurrence in BC (Can) and Eastern Asia.

Rutile is one of the three allomorphs of titania or titanium oxide, TiO_2, with which it shares very high RIs, exceeding those of diamond; synthetic rutile makes a beautiful gem. In nature it is trl to op, brown, black, reddish brown to blood red; with a metallic LR and pale-yellow to green STR; feels heavy in the hand – SG 4·2–4·3; H 6–6½; occurs in compact masses, grains and needles – *flèches d'amour* in quartz (p 105); also xls of the tetragonal system, as a rule longitudinally lined, short prisms terminating in four-sided pyramids, often twinned and in multiple stellate aggregates; infusible, insoluble in acids. Rt. is of worldwide occurrence in gabbros and gabbro pegmatites, some gneisses, apatite veins and detrital deposits, with apatite, quartz, kyanite and other titanium minerals.

Anatase is likewise tetragonal, occurs in sharp pyramids, tabular slabs and bipyramids; somewhat softer and lighter than rutile: H 5½–6; SG 3·8–3·9. The colour varies from honey brown and hyacinth red to indigo-blue and black, but may also be greenish, blue–green, pale lilac or slate grey; sub-trp or trl; highly birefringent: RI 2·48 and 2·56; LR adamantine, resinous or metallic; STR colourless to pale yellow; occasionally used as a gemstone; infusible, insoluble; keeps company with quartz and rutile, chiefly in thermal veins; also found in gneiss and schist. Localities: Liskeard and Tintagel, Cornwall and Tavistock, Devon (Eng); Sherbrooke, NS (Can); Gunnison Co, Colo and Sommerville, Mass (USA); Urals (USSR); Ger, Braz.

Brookite is of the same hardness, but heavier – SG 4·2–4·9, and orthorhombic, forming vertically lined tabular xls; yellowish brown, red–brown, occasionally black; trp or trl; LR adamantine or metallic; STR colourless, yellowish to brown; infusible; brittle. Xls may be large and occur singly, in druses – on

Dartmoor and in Yorkshire (Eng); at Tremadoc (Wal); Magnet Cove, Ozark Mts, Ark (USA); Minas Geraes (Braz); Urals (USSR); Alps, Czsl, Ita.

Rutile is a primary mineral; anatase and brookite are secondary products of alteration of it and other titanium minerals; but they tend to occur together, especially in rocks affected by pneumatolysis.

Spinel, $MgAl_2O_4$; H $7\frac{1}{2}$–8; SG $3 \cdot 5$–$4 \cdot 1$; is a gemstone; belongs to the cubic system and forms well-developed octahedra and twins; also found in small scattered grains; may be of almost any colour – most commonly red, blue or black; trp or trl; LR vitreous; STR white. The variability of colour and other properties reflects a continuous variation in composition, magnesium and aluminium being partly or wholly replaced by other metals so that we have here a whole family of minerals. Sp. is singly refracting with RI $1 \cdot 72$, but up to $1 \cdot 75$ in blue zinc spinels (*ghanospinels*). Red stones are referred to as *ruby spinels* or *balas rubies*, purple as *almandine spinels*, orange and yellow as *rubicelles*, blue as *sapphire spinels*, and green-to-black ones as *pleonases* or *ceylonites*. Sps. are of worldwide occurrence in basic igneous and contact metamorphic rocks; most of the high-quality stones come from Afghanistan, Burma, Sri Lanka and Thailand; but some hail from the USA, Brazil and Sweden.

Apart from analcite, which is a primary mineral, *zeolites* are secondary, deposited in the gas cavities and veins of basic lavas, and so will be dealt with in Chapter 12. Uvarovite is considered with the other garnets.

12

VOLCANICS

THE LEGACY OF VOLCANOES

Volcanic or extrusive igneous rocks are made up of the same magma as the corresponding plutonic or intrusive ones. Nevertheless, their different history is reflected in their mineralogical composition. Pneumatolytic, thermal and chemical action on the cooling melt is involved, and is much more rapid and of shorter duration than in underground intrusions; it is as it were open-ended, and may be frequently renewed.

Thus certain minerals are particularly characteristic of volcanics. Such minerals may be primary or secondary, crystalline, cryptocrystalline or amorphous, being precipitated from hot solutions in the cracks and cavities (amygdales) of the lavas, which may retain their internal heat under a hard crust for months after the eruption. Zeolites, opal and various forms of chalcedonic silica, such as jasper, agate etc, are in this class. Other minerals are deposited from hot springs or volcanic vapours, and others still are the products of alteration of primary minerals already formed.

It will be understood that, except in the latter case, it makes little difference whether the volcanics are recent or ancient. western Scotland, the English Lake District, Nordmarka in Norway, Alvernia in France or the Eifel district of Germany, were once as volcanic as Iceland or Mexico are today, and preserve at least some of the rocks and minerals formed at that time.

125

As in other cases, some minerals present in the volcanics occur in other rocks as well and may, in fact, be more typical of these; for instance, garnet and idocrase, which goes under the alternative name of vesuvianite, are characteristic of non-volcanic metamorphic rocks. Contact metamorphism and thermal veins are unquestionable features of volcanic activity, but they are also generated by underground plutons – indeed, more effectively, as these usually carry more heat and the escape of volatiles into the air is more or less completely blocked. Therefore, their products are listed in Chapters 9, 10, 11 and 13.

The selection given below is not exhaustive, but it is representative and includes the following minerals: alunite; aragonite; chalcedony; cinnabar; haüyne; leucite; nosean; opal; orpiment; realgar; tridymite and cristobalite; and zeolites. Sanidine is a volcanic variety of felspar and ought to appear in the above list, but has already been dealt with in connection with other orthoclases (p 107). These volcanic minerals can be variously grouped; thus chalcedony, jasper, agate etc and opal are all forms of silica and constitute a natural group; zeolites are another example.

PRECIPITATES AND INCRUSTATIONS

Aragonite, orpiment and realgar are principally hot-spring precipitates, and sulphur is usually a sublimate from volcanic exhalations.

Aragonite is calcium carbonate, $CaCO_3$, with traces of strontium, lead and zinc, but it is harder and heavier than calcite, a more common form of $CaCO_3$, with H $3\frac{1}{2}$–4, SG $2\cdot9$–$3\cdot0$ and orthorhombic, whereas the latter is hexagonal. The xls may be long, needle-like or short prisms; repeated twinning may give them a pseudo-hexagonal appearance; but ar. may also be massive, columnar, fibrous or form radial aggregates. It is trp, trl or op; colourless, white or variously tinted; has a vitreous or resinous LR, and a colourless, white or yellowish STR; infusible; dissolves with effervescence in cold

126

HCl; of worldwide occurrence with calcite, siderite, clay, gypsum and sulphur, in hot springs, volcanic rock cavities and upper parts of coral reefs.

Orpiment, As_2S_3, is a soft – H $1\frac{1}{2}$–2, moderately heavy – SG 3·4–3·5, lemon-yellow mineral, trl, with a fatty or pearly LR and yellow STR, formed as a volcanic sublimate, hot-spring deposit or by weathering of arsenical minerals. Good xls are rare, short monoclinic prisms; orp. usually takes the form of lenticular or rounded aggregates and incrustations; on heating yields a reddish sublimate; readily fusible; bluish-white flame; soluble in H_2SO_4. It keeps company with realgar and other arsenic compounds in Manhattan, Nye Co, Nev, and Mercur, Toole Co, Utah (USA); Maritime Alps (Fra); Macedonia (Grc); Saxony (Ger); Caucasus (USSR); Ita, Turkey.

Realgar, As_4S_4, is a related compound of similar occurrence, chiefly as a hot-spring deposit and in lodes in volcanics; H $1\frac{1}{2}$–2; SG 3·5–3·6. It may be massive, granular, or form short or long monoclinic prisms and needles; trl with an adamantine LR, red to orange; STR orange–yellow; fusible; bluish-white flame; decomposes in HNO_3. Rl. has the same American distribution as orp., but is also found in the Norris Geyser Basin, Yellowstone Park; Bosnia (Yug); Macedonia (Grc); Ita, Ger, Hun, China and Iran; may be accompanied by stibnite, lead-arsenic, silver and gold ores.

Cinnabar, HgS, is not unlike realgar – typically red, carmine, grey or steel coloured; LR adamantine to metallic; STR carmine; the same mode of occurrence. But it is very heavy– SG 8·0–8·2, and a shade harder – H 2–2$\frac{1}{2}$; hexagonal, forming thick tabular prisms and rhombohedra; mostly massive, granular or fibrous, as a vein impregnation; yields a sublimate of mercury in blowpipe, or closed tube with carbonate of sodium. Cn. is found with pyrite, stibnite, quartz, chalcedony and carbonates, in Ark, Calif, Nev, Oreg, Tex and Utah (USA); Gorizia and Tuscany (Ita); Almaden (Spn); Mexico, Peru, Surinam and USSR. It may be confused with *proustite*, the

127

'light-red silver ore', Ag_3AsS_3, which is similar in colour, crystalline habit and H, but much lighter (SG 5·57).

Sulphur, S, is a common volcanic incrustation along vents and crevices. It is trp to trl, yellow to brown, with a pale-yellow STR, a resinous to greasy LR; forms simple orthorhombic bipyramids, sometimes of considerable size; also granular, fibrous or nodular; bedded in old volcanic deposits; H 2; SG 1·9–2·1; fuses and volatilises readily; burns with a violet-blue flame. It is found among lavas, tuffs and ashes at Rotorua and other places in NI (NZ); La, Tex and Wyo (USA); on Vesuvius (Ita); and Etna (Sicily); nr Cadiz (Spn); in Jap, and other volcanic countries.

OTHER VOLCANIC MINERALS

Alunite or alumstone, $KAl_3[(OH)_6/(SO_4)_2]$, is a product of alteration of acid lavas (trachytes, rhyolites), forming pockets and seams; H $3\frac{1}{2}$–4; SG 2·6–2·8; hexagonal (rhombohedra and pseudo-cubes), also massive or earthy; op, with a vitreous LR and white STR; white, reddish, yellowish; in blowpipe crackles and gives off sulphurous fumes; soluble in HCl and hot H_2SO_4; occurs in NSW (Ausl); Colo and Nev (USA); Grc, Hun, Ita, Spn.

Haüyne or *haüyinite* has a complicated and variable chemistry – basically $3NaAlSiO_4.CaSO_4$; is trp or trl, and occurs in a variety of colours – most commonly bright blue, also grey, green, red and yellow; STR colourless, white to pale blue; H $5\frac{1}{2}$–6; SG 2·3–2·4; forms neat, multifaced beads in the cubic system, rather like those of garnet; also granular aggregates and isolated xls in fine-grained rocks, especially recent volcanics rich in alkali; may qualify as a gem. Hu. is of widespread occurrence, eg Monte Somma, Vesuvius and Alban Mts nr Rome (Ita); Eifel district (Ger).

Leucite, $KAlSi_2O_6$, is similar in appearance and occurrence; but it is a primary mineral in silica-poor basic lavas of recent origin; usually op, white or grey, but also clear, colourless; with a glassy or greasy LR; white STR; H $5\frac{1}{2}$–6; SG 2·4–2·6; barely fusible; decomposes in HCl; keeps company with nepheline, analcite and muscovite in BC (Can); Ozark Mts, Ark and Leucite Hill, Wyo (USA); Vesuvius (Ita); Ausr, Ger, Braz. *Nosean* or *noselite*, $Na_8Al_6O_{24}SO_4$, is another mineral found in alkaline (basic) volcanics, of the cubic system with very similar xls; also granular; H $5\frac{1}{2}$; SG 2·2–2·4. The colouring is grey, blue or brown, with a variable STR and subvitreous LR; it gelatinises in HCl. Nos. is a felspathoid of worldwide distribution.

Tridymite and *cristobalite* are high-temperature allomorphs of quartz, SiO_2; they are softer and lighter than it, and occur in acid volcanics, eg rhyolite and trachyte; tr. in hexagonal plates, often bevelled and repeatedly twinned. It is trp or trl, colourless, clear or milky; vitreous LR; white STR; H $6\frac{1}{2}$–7; SG 2·27; may also be found in meteorites and at contact in metamorphosed sandstones: Main localities: Antrim (NI); Washington (USA); Transylvania (Rum); Ger, Hun, Mexico, SA. Tr. may be accompanied by the dull, white, sometimes tinted, cubic xls of *cristobalite*; H 6–7; SG 2·27–2·34; doubly refractive; in andesite cavities, more particularly in the San Cristobal Mts, nr Pachuca (Mexico), also in California. Tr. and cr. are infusible in blowpipe, soluble in HF.

CHALCEDONY AND ITS KIN

Chalcedony is cryptocrystalline silica usually deposited from alkalised solutions in lava cavities and thermal veins; but it also occurs in flint and as a replacement mineral in fossils. Chal. provides a number of gemstones, has a characteristic waxy LR and white STR regardless of surface colour; may be trl to op, grading over imperceptibly into quartz, opal, jasper and flint; H $6\frac{1}{2}$–7; SG 2·59–2·61; RI, when measurable, 1·54–1·55. The xls are too fine to be seen individually without magnification, but are often ranged at right angles to the base surface, yielding a structure rather like the bristles in a very dense brush. Being formed by deposition from solution, chal. tends to assume botryoidal or stalactitic structure and is often layered. The layers may be of the same or different colours. Such banded chalcedony is called *agate*, and if the bands run more or less flat and parallel to each other – *onyx*.

The jewellers and gemmologists reserve the name *chalcedony* for the grey or blue variety; the trl yellow to brown stones are called *sard*; flesh pink to red, coloured by ferric oxide, are known as *carnelians, cornelians* or *carneols*; nickel hydroxide may produce an apple-green hue in *chrysoprase*; ferrous oxide or hydroxide is responsible for the darker green of *plasma*.

Hornstone, which closely resembles horn, is a coarser variety, halfway between trl chalcedony and *flint*, which is still essentially the same substance, contaminated with chalk and clay. It is non-volcanic and occurs as *concretions* or fillings in the hollows in chalk and limestone, more particularly in south England and Western Europe. Flint may enclose fossils (sponges, bryozoa etc) and be partly opalised. The flints embedded in lava in Northern Ireland have been converted to opal. Fl. is usually grey to brown, but may be variously tinted, eg red by ferric oxide, and shade over into jasper. It may also be coarsely banded, like agate: Cornish agates are rather ' flinty '.

Jasper proper is op chalcedony, mixed with clayey or ferruginous matter. It forms inclusions, seams and even dykes in volcanic rocks, and may arise through metamorphism in clay or shale. The prevalent colour is red, but it may be brown, yellow, purple, green, blue or black. An attractive variegated variety comes from Windhoek in SW Africa. The main sources of jasper are India and Egypt, but it is not uncommon and of worldwide occurrence.

Green plasma spotted with red jasper is called *bloodstone* or *heliotrope* (the best material comes from India).

When siliceous solutions diffuse through the silica gel filling a hollow in lava their contents are precipitated ripple-wise in so-called Liesegang rings, and so an *agate* is born. Agates are often artificially stained and those found in nature may not be quite so colourful. But they can assume any colouring or combination of colourings to which chalcedony is prone, including the violet hues of amethyst, with very pleasing results. The bands may be trp or op, of the same or different colours in the same stone, sharp and narrow, or wide and diffuse, in any manner of combinations. There are *jasper agates* and *carnelian agates*. The bands generally tend to follow the outlines of the enclosing cavity, especially in the outer part, but may change orientation towards the middle. This gives rise to various patterns, described by such terms as *eye agate*, *landscape agate*, *fortification agate*. The core of an agate is often hollow and lined with quartz xls, or else filled with a crystalline mass.

Large hollow stones of this kind are known as *potato stones*, and their internal cavities as *geodes*. These may harbour fine xls of amethyst or other varieties of quartz, calcite and occasionally other minerals. The lava cavities are usually lined with a bluish-green substance, called *delessite* – a hydrated magnesium silicate containing ferric and ferrous oxides of a very complicated composition. When an agate or a potato stone weathers out of its matrix it takes this coating with it, which is one way of recognising it among other pebbles. In time, however, the delessite wears off, exposing a pitted or knobbly structure, which with a little imagination may be described as a ' fossil blancmange with a thimble surface ', and sometimes like a kind of 'petrified white of egg'; the agate laminations may be exposed at the edges.

Delessite may penetrate the silica gel in dendritic growths, which look like moss, producing a *moss agate*. In a *mocha stone* the dendrites are of brown manganese oxide.

Opal is hydrated chalcedony, SiO_2nH_2O, which means that n molecules of water are attached to one of silica; and since n may be any whole number (you cannot have half a molecule), the degree of hydration varies so that the silica may be more or less ' opalised '. Opal is particularly associated with recent volcanics and fills cavities in basalt or sandstone. It also occurs as a replacement mineral in petrified wood – *wood opal*. Opal is somewhat softer – H $5\frac{1}{2}$, and lighter – SG $1\cdot8$–$2\cdot2$, than chalcedony and has a lower RI of $1\cdot44$–$1\cdot46$. It is amorphous, reniform or stalactitic and may be of any ground colour, except violet. Most opals have a milky sheen, tending to an iridescent glimmer, due to reflections from filmy surfaces within the stone, and in *precious opal* this becomes a brilliant display of rainbow hues varying with the viewing angle. In *harlequin opal* the colours are scattered in patches; in *flash opal* there is a large area of colour. The background is usually white, greyish blue or black. But *fire opal*, which is a development of carnelian, is red to yellow, trl or nearly trp, and is sometimes faceted, although the cabochon cut is the rule for opals. *Jasp opal* is hydrated trl jasper. *Girasol* has a blue sheen.

Milk, wax, resin and *ferruginous opal* are varieties of *common opal*, or *semi-opal*, with little or no iridescence. *Hyalite* is glassy, colourless and trp. Hydrophane is more or less op when dry, but becomes trp when immersed in liquid. *Cachalong* is an op, white or cream-coloured variety.

Chalcedony and opal are of worldwide distribution. Some very fine agates have come from Queensland (Ausl), Minas Geraes (Braz) and Mexico; but they occur commonly in many Scottish lavas and conglomerates, and are locally known as *Scotch pebbles*; agates and potato stones are also known from south-west England (Somerset and Bristol area). Some of the best precious opal material originates in NSW, Queensl, S Aust (Ausl); Nev (USA); Mexico and Hun.

ZEOLITES

Zeolites are hydrated silicates of one or more alkali metals and aluminium. Analcite (p 118) may be a primary rock constituent, but the zeolites generally occur as fillings in basalt cavities and cracks in company with epidote and occasionally native metals or ores. They are trp or trl, with a vitreous or pearly LR, white STR, and low RIs; crystallise in various systems, but large well-formed xls are rare. More often than not the zs. take the form of massive botryoidal incrustations or radial ' puffs ' of thin needles. Natrolite and prehnite have been cut as gems; the remaining zs. are rather soft.

Apophyllite is a potassium-calcium silicate with fluorine, but no aluminium, colourless, white, reddish or yellowish white, and rose red; H $4\frac{1}{2}$–5; SG $2 \cdot 3$–$2 \cdot 4$; tetragonal system, tabular and pseudo-cubical habit, striated; also granular or foliaceous; exfoliates and fuses; dissolves in HCl. Main localities: Fife (Scot); Basin of Mines, NS (Can); Table Mt, Colo and Bergen Hill, NJ (USA); Ausl, Czsl, Ger, Iceland, Swd.

Chabazite is a calcium-sodium-aluminium compound, colourless, white, pink, yellowish to reddish brown; hexagonal system – rhombohedral or pseudo-cubical xls; also massive; H 4–5; SG $2 \cdot 1$–$2 \cdot 2$; decomposes in HCl with separation of shiny silica; often emits a blue glow after being heated on charcoal. Main localities: Skye, Renfrewshire (Scot); Giant's Causeway, Antrim (NI); Richmond, Vic (Ausl); Bay of Fundy, NS (Can); Conn, Mass, NJ, NY (USA); Aussig, Bohemia (Czsl); Haute Saône, Plombiers (Fra); Annarode (Ger); Greenland, Iceland, Poona (India) – occasionally in gneiss and schist.

In *harmotome* the alkalis are barium and potassium; H 4–$4\frac{1}{2}$; SG $2 \cdot 3$–$2 \cdot 5$; monoclinic, forms cruciform penetration twins, whence known as ' cross-stone '; sub-trp to trl; white, shades of grey, yellow and red; fuses with intumescence; is decomposed in HCl with gelatinisation. Occurrence: Strontian, Argyll (Scot); Rabbit Mt, Ont (Can); Bohemia (Czsl); Harz (Ger).

Laumonite or *hypostilbite*, is a calcium-sodium zeolite; trp or trl, cloudy when altered; white, red or yellow; LR pearly; STR colourless; monoclinic with prismatic habit, fibrous or columnar; H $3\frac{1}{2}$–4; SG $2 \cdot 25$–$2 \cdot 36$; readily fusible; gelatinises in HCl; also found in gneiss and schist. Occurrence: Dunbartonshire and Stirlingshire (Scot); NJ and Brewster, NY (USA); Brittany (Fra); Ger.

133

Natrolite is a sodium zeolite, white, yellowish or flesh pink; STR colourless or white; trp or trl; H 5–5½; SG 2·2–2·4; orthorhombic – simple prisms with pyramidal endings, also needles and ' puffs '; massive or fibrous; fuses in the light of a match; gelatinises in HCl; found in Glen Farg, Fife and other Scottish basalt localities; Antrim (NI); Gates Mt, NS (Can); Bergen Hill, NJ and New York Isl, NY (USA); Karroo (SA); Faroes, Iceland.

Phillipsite, bonite or *spangsite*, with calcium and potassium as the alkali, is trl with a vitreous LR; STR colourless; colourless, white, yellow, grey or reddish; H 4–4½; SG 2·2; monoclinic – prismatic xls, cruciform twins, also radial aggregates and ' puffs '; fusible; decomposes in HCl. Occurrence: Giant's Causeway, Antrim (NI); Vesuvius (Ita); Etna (Sicily); Ausr, Ger; also found in deep-sea deposits.

Prehnite is a hydrated calcium-aluminium silicate; H 6–6½; SG 2·8–3·0; orthorhombic – rare tabular xls; more often botryoidal, massive or in radial aggregates; trp to trl; green, yellowish green, yellow, colourless or white; fusible; decomposes in HCl; found in Dunbartonshire and Renfrewshire (Scot); Bergen Hill, NJ and Woodly, Conn (USA); Central Europe, Pyrenees, Africa.

Stilbite, with calcium and sodium, trp to trl, has a pearly LR; colourless, white, yellow, brown or red; STR colourless; monoclinic prisms, tabular xls or sheaves; H 3½–4; SG 2·1–2·2; fusible; decomposes in HCl. Main localities: Dunbartonshire and Stirlingshire (Scot); Giant's Causeway, Antrim (NI); Bergen Hill, NJ and Phillipstown, NY (USA); Transylvania (Rum); Alps, Faroes, Nor, Swd, India.

13

METAMORPHIC MINERALS

In theory a distinction is drawn between the metamorphism due to heat and that due to stress as each has different mineralogical consequences. Pure stress metamorphism, however, is comparatively rare, and where it does occur, eg along shear planes and faults in land movements, it is mainly destructive. In regional metamorphism, which affects large areas, both heat and pressure are involved, but pressure predominates. It will be recalled that contact metamorphism is due to the heat emanating from igneous intrusions and manifests itself within the metamorphic aureole around these. Both kinds of metamorphism may, but need not, produce the same minerals. Contact metamorphism is often accompanied by pneumatolysis and the formation of mineral lodes and thermal veins, but the corresponding minerals are considered in Chapter 14.

Metamorphic rocks commonly contain many of the minerals already described in other contexts, such as augite, beryl, felspathoids, hornblende, mica, sphene, spinel, tourmaline, zircon and quite a few others. Quartz, too, crystallises out in metamorphic rocks, and heat may cause fine crystals of amethyst and its other varieties to develop in sandstone or shale. The reader has to use his or her own judgement in the light of the information provided here, geological maps, and such further details as can be found in guidebooks, works on regional geology and mining reports.

In this chapter the minerals have been grouped under four headings: (1) regional metamorphic rocks, ie chiefly schists and gneisses; (2) garnets, which come mainly under (1) but form a distinct family of minerals; (3) metamorphic limestones, which may be the product of either regional or contact metamorphism; (4) contact metamorphic rocks (other than limestones). It will be understood that the listing of a mineral in any one of these divisions does not necessarily preclude its occurrence in other groups; it only means that it is, say, typically a limestone mineral and so will avoid siliceous rocks.

REGIONAL METAMORPHIC MINERALS

Regional metamorphism varies in intensity, and different minerals will appear in the rocks as it progresses. Thus chlorite and pyrite are the first to appear, then mica and garnet, followed by kyanite and staurolite, these in turn giving way to sillimanite, and finally cordierite, although garnet endures throughout the series right into gneiss, which is its end term. In any case it is the appearance of the more highly metamorphic minerals, and not the disappearance of the less metamorphic ones, that is significant.

Actinolite is a complicated compound, $Ca_2(FeMg)_3(Si_8O_{22})(OH)_2$, with a variable content of Fe and Mg, and so shading over into tremolite, qv and *nephrite* or ' Spanish jade ', a massive variety used as an ornamental stone. Act. is dark to pale green, white or pale grey, trp, trl or op; with vitreous LR and white STR; monoclinic, forms slender six-sided prisms; also columnar or fibrous (*amianthus* or actinolite asbestos); H 5–6; SG 2·9–3·2; fusible; insoluble in acids. It is of worldwide occurrence in metamorphic basic igneous rocks (actinolite schists), gneiss, impure limestone and dolomite, and even granite, eg in the Scottish Highlands, Alps and S W Africa; keeps company with talc, chlorite and serpentine.

Chlorites are a family of ferrous iron-magnesium aluminosilicates of variable composition, which may include ferric iron, chromium and manganese. They are scaly, monoclinic or pseudo-hexagonal, soft (H $1-2\frac{1}{2}$), green, blackish green to grey, with a silky, pearly or glassy LR and greenish-white STR; characteristic of low-grade metamorphism, in chlorite schists, phyllites and serpentinites; of widespread occurrence, eg in the Scottish Highlands, Pennsylvania (USA) and the Alps. *Prochlorite* is a member of this family, with Mg, Fe and Al as the main metals. It is leek green, very soft – H 1–2; monoclinic, but its small xls in the form of hexagonal plates are rare. *Clinochlore*, $Mg_5Al(OH)_8(AlSi_3O_{10})$, is darker, blackish green to blue–green, but fusible to a greyish–yellow bead, which prochl. is not. *Penninite* forms a yellow bead, is apple green to bluish green in colour, harder – H $2\frac{1}{2}$, mainly compact and resembles serpentine, with which it keeps company in olivine-rich metamorphic rocks; may also form pseudo-hexagonal monoclinic xls, often twinned. Chlorites are associated with pyrite, gold, sphene, diopside, augite and garnet.

Cordierite, dichroite or *iolite* is a double silicate of aluminium and magnesium, part of which is replaced by ferrous iron, with water of hydration; H $7-7\frac{1}{2}$; SG $2\cdot58-2\cdot70$; orthorhombic, forms thick short prisms with rounded edges; also massive, scaly or granular. It is trp or trl with a vitreous to dull LR, colourless STR, and a wide range of colourings: light blue, violet, smoky, greenish, yellowish or grey–blue, and strongly pleochroic (p 62). Good specimens are cut as gems (water sapphires). Cord. occurs in gneisses, norites, hornfels and some granites in Cornwall (Eng); Scottish Highlands; Donegal (Eire); N W Can; Conn and Mass (USA); Orijärvi (Fin); Bavaria (Ger); Tuscany (Ita); Kragerö (Nor); Cabo de Gata (Spn), Tunaberg (Swd); Ausl, Braz, Sri Lanka, Greenland, Hun, Jap, Madagascar, SA.

Epidote is a basic calcium-aluminium ferric-iron silicate; H 6–7; SG $3\cdot3-3\cdot5$; monoclinic – long lath-like xls with lengthwise striations, twins, radial aggregates – over 200 separate forms. The colour is very variable: pistachio green (*pistacite*), dark green, bluish green, blackish green, brown, yellowish brown and red (*withamite*); trl to op, seldom trp, strongly dichroic; STR grey; LR vitreous; melts to magnetic slag. Good specimens used as gemstones. Ep. is found in lime-rich metamorphic rocks, sometimes in granite pegmatites (eg in Jersey and Guernsey), with scapolite, garnet, hornblende and augite. Occurrence: Cornwall, Devon, Malverns (Eng); N Wal; Glen Coe (red) and other Highland sites (Scot); Antrim, Londonderry (NI); Arklow, Wicklow, Galway and Donegal (Eir); Lake Superior and Ariz (USA); Alps, Scandinavia, Urals etc.

Glaucophane is an amphibole (p 116); H 6–6½; SG 3·0–3·1; forms six-sided prisms of the monoclinic system; also fibrous, granular or massive; azure to lavender blue, bluish black or greyish; STR blue–grey; LR vitreous to pearly; fuses to glass. Gl. is found in mica-schist and gneiss in Anglesey (Wal); Calif (USA); Aosta (Ita); Croatia (Yug); Alps, N W Fra, Corsica, Grc, Jap.

Kyanite and *sillimanite* are of the same proportional composition, Al_2SiO_5, but different molecular structure. Ky. is transformed into sl. by increased metamorphic heat; both occur in schists and gneisses, sometimes together with staurolite and garnet. Kyanite or *disthene* (twostrength) has the peculiar property of being H 7 across the prism, but only 5 along it; SG 3·5–3·7. It belongs to the triclinic system and forms long prismatic xls with longitudinal striae, blades, rosettes or grains. The colour is typically sky blue, but may be white, red, green or yellow and tends to be patchy; dichroic; white STR; pearly LR; infusible; sometimes used as a gemstone. It is of widespread distribution in high-grade metamorphic rocks in the Scottish Highlands, USA, India etc.

Sillimanite is orthorhombic – usually acicular xls; also massive, nodular or foliaceous; H 6–7; SG 3·2. The colourings are faint greyish yellow, greyish green, brownish, or pale azure; trp or trl; LR vitreous; STR colourless; dichroic; sometimes cut as a gem; insoluble in acids. The distribution is similar to that of kyanite: Woster, Mass; Westchester Co, NY and Macon Co, NC (USA); Bohemia (Czsl); Saxony (Ger); Assam (India). *Lazulite* is an iron-magnesium phosphate of complicated composition; H 5–6; SG 3·0; monoclinic – xls rare, bipyramidal or tabular; mainly massive; LR vitreous; STR white; azure blue; trl at the edges; infusible, unaffected by acids. La. is found in veins, in quartzite, eg in Death Valley, Calif; Graves Mt, Ga and North Groton, NH (USA); Salzburg (Ausr); Vesuvius (Ita); Kola (USSR); Zermatt (Swz); Nor, Portugal, Bolivia and Greenland.

Pyrophyllite, $Al_2[(OH)_2Si_4O_{10}]$, is a soft mineral – H 1–2; SG 2·7–2·9; white, apple green, greyish green or brownish green, grey or yellow; LR pearly; STR white; forms radial, foliated or compact columnar aggregates, six-sided lamellae, or tabular orthorhombic xls; fuses with difficulty; is partly decomposed in H_2SO_4; occurs in crystalline schists, quartz veins and granites, nr Little Rock, Ark and in Mecklenburg Co, NC (USA); Ardennes (Belgium); Eifel (Ger); Urals (USSR); Spn and Swiss Alps.

Staurolite is an iron-aluminium silicate with some magnesium. of variable composition, reddish brown, yellowish brown or blackish brown, trl to op, seldom of gem quality; belongs to the orthorhombic system, forms long or short six-sided prisms, usually twinned crosswise (Fig 7, a and b, p 45); subvitreous LR; STR colourless or grey; H 7–7½; SG 3·7–3·8; infusible, insoluble in acids. It is found in mica-schists and gneisses with garnet and kyanite, in the Scottish Highlands; Donegal and Killiney nr Dublin (Eir); Litchfield, Conn; Dutchess Co, NY and Macon Co, NC (USA); Brittany (Fra); Alps and USSR.

Talc, soapstone or *steatite*, $Mg_3Si_4O_{10}(OH)_2$, is a hydrous magnesium silicate, monoclinic, but xls rare; usually granular, massive (soapstone) or scaly (talc); trp to op; pale green or greenish grey; LR pearly; STR colourless or white; soapy to the touch; marks 1 on Mohs' scale; SG $2 \cdot 7$–$2 \cdot 8$; hardly fusible; used as an ornamental stone. It is of widespread occurrence in low-grade metamorphic rocks, more particularly in the French Pyrenees and Italy, also USA and Manchuria.

Tremolite is a variation on the theme of actinolite (p 136); H $5\frac{1}{2}$–6; SG $2 \cdot 9$–$3 \cdot 1$; monoclinic, forms well-developed prisms or long blade-like and acicular xls; also massive or fibrous (Italian asbestos); trp or trl; colourless, white, grey or green, vitreous LR; white STR; may qualify as a gemstone; fusible. Occurrence: schists, metamorphosed basic and ultrabasic rocks, with talc, serpentine, nephrite; Scottish Highlands; Pontiac Co, Queb (Can); London Grove, NJ and St Lawrence Co, NY (USA); Gulsjö, Värmland (Swd); Tessin (Swz); Ger, Hun, S W Africa, USSR.

GARNETS

Garnets occur as accessory minerals in igneous rocks, but are typically metamorphic, found in mica-schists, gneisses, metamorphosed basic, limestone and dolomite rocks. The composition of the garnets is continuously variable, as in felspars or tourmalines. A garnet is a silicate of two or more metals in various proportions; eg almandine is an iron-aluminium garnet and the olive-green grossularite is a calcium-aluminium one. Traditionally the name ' garnet ' is associated with red or brown–red stones, but a garnet may be colourless or of any colour except blue.

All garnets belong to the cubic system and although they assume massive, compact or lamellar form, occur typically in twelve-sided beads, rarely cubes or more complicated solids of the cubic system, with a resinous, vitreous, occasionally dull LR, and usually white STR. They may be op, trl or trp, are single refracting with RIs between $1 \cdot 7$ and $1 \cdot 9$ in natural garnets, so that they have considerable fire. The synthetic strontium-aluminium garnet, marketed as *diamantite*, is colourless and rivals diamond in optical beauty but is unknown in natural state. The hardness varies from 6 to 8 so that any garnet could make a likely gem, but comparatively few specimens for minerals of such widespread occurrence attain this distinction. Some trp garnets – almandines – are so dark that they are usually cut as hollow cabochons (carbuncles) to admit as much light as possible.

The principal members of the garnet family are listed in Table 6. Since any intermediate composition may be possible no table can do full justice to reality.

Garnets are fusible: pyrope, which has a red streak, with difficulty; grossularite to a pale-green bead; andradite and almandine to a black magnetic globule. Pyrope gelatinises in acids.

Although *almandine* is, when trp, the *precious garnet*, it is one of the most common and of widespread occurrence in mica-schists and other metamorphic rocks of Scotland and Ireland, as well as Irish granites; also to be found in the Adirondacks, NY; Alas and Idaho (USA); Baffin Isl (Can); the Alps, Scandinavia, India, Madagascar etc. Most of the gem material hails from the Adirondacks, Alas, (USA); Ausl, Braz, Sri Lanka, India and Mexico.

Andradite may be found in Cornwall and Westmorland (Eng); Stanley Buttes, Ariz (USA); Pyrenees (Fra); Mt Somma (Ita); in igneous and metamorphic rocks of various types, with magnetite, epidote, nephelite and leucite.

Demantoid of gem quality comes mainly from Italy and the Urals.

Grossular, or *grossularite,* and *hessonite* are characteristic of contact metamorphic rocks, including marble, and are widely distributed, eg in Cornwall and Devon (Eng). Hessonite occurs in Aberdeenshire (Scot); and Wicklow (Eir); but most gem material originates in Sri Lanka and SA.

Melanite is an accessory mineral of leucite and nepheline syenites, where it keeps company with diopside, sphene and magnetite as well as, of course, leucite and nepheline.

141

Pyrope is the most popular garnet gemstone, and is often described as some kind of ' ruby ' – ' Elie ruby ' or 'Arizona ruby '. It is associated with ultrabasic rocks, and may be looked for at Elie Ness, Fife (Scot); Bohemia (Czsl); Saxony (Ger); and at Kimberley (SA). *Rhodolite* is found in NC (USA); Madagascar and Tanzania.

Spessartite may occasionally turn up in granite or rhyolite, but is typical of regional metamorphic rocks. It is known from several USA localities: Branchville, Conn; Salem, NC and Amelia Co, Va; Ausl, Braz and Sri Lanka.

Topazolite occurs in metamorphic granite on Mt Bischoff, Tasmania.

Uvarovite is usually described as ' emerald green ', but is more often of a bright vernal green, quite different from the emerald. It is found in chromium-rich rocks, on Fetlar and Unst, Shetlands (Scot); at Venasque, Pyrenees (Spn); and in the Urals (USSR).

The colourless *water garnet* has been recorded by Heddle in Banffshire (Scot), but this cannot be its only locality.

METAMORPHIC LIMESTONE MINERALS

Several of the minerals listed under the preceding headings are to be found in limestones and dolomites affected by regional or contact metamorphism, and some garnets may even be typical of such rocks. Their description is not repeated here, and the reader is referred to earlier pages. The usual caveats apply.

Apatite is a complex fluoro-chloro-hydro-phosphate of calcium in which fluorine and chlorine are largely interchangeable so that the composition ranges from pure fluor-apatite to pure chlor-apatite, and there are further varieties such as carbonate apatite and hydroxyl apatite. Apatite is Mohs' marker for H 5, but owing to this variable composition it may sink as low as H 4; SG, too, is variable between 3·17 and 3·23; and so is the colour. This may be absent, is typically green, but can be yellow, blue, pink, or mauve. The stone is trp to op, with a vitreous LR and white STR; birefringent. Although a little soft for such things as rings, it has often been cut and makes an attractive gem. Ap. may be massive, granular, radial or fibrous; but is typically crystalline, hexagonal, forming prisms, sometimes large, resembling those of quartz with which they are often found, many-faced beads, thick plates or bipyramids; fusible at the edges; soluble in HCl. Ap. is a primary accessory constituent of some acid and basic rocks and is of widespread occurrence in metamorphic rocks, especially limestones. Main localities are: Cornwall and Devon (Eng); Deeside and Ross-shire (Scot); Donegal and Killiney (Eire); Ont (Can); Calif, Me, Va and Pelham, Mass (USA); Spn, Bolivia and Mexico.

Axinite is another marginal gemstone, brittle but of adequate hardness – $6\frac{1}{2}$–7; SG 3·27; trp or trl, although not very colourful: clove brown, smoky grey, plum or greenish; LR vitreous; STR colourless. It may be massive or lamellar, but is usually found in deeply grooved triclinic xls, often thin and sharp edged, whence the name 'axe-inite'. Ax. is a complicated aluminium-calcium boro-silicate; readily fusible to a green bead; colours the flame pale green; found in Cornwall and Devon (Eng); Can; Calif at Coarse Gold, Pa at Bethlehem, Me at Phippsburg, Nev, NJ and NY at Cold Spring (USA); Harz and Saxony (Ger); Hun, Spn, Swz, Chile, Jap.

Braunite, $Mn_4 \ldots Mn_3 \ldots (O_8/SiO_4)$; H 6–$6\frac{1}{2}$; SG 4·7–4·9; massive, granular or tetragonal – small, usually octahedral xls; op, iron black to brownish black with a sub-metallic LR and black to brownish STR; found in metamorphic rocks, especially limestone and dolomite, but also as a primary mineral in porphyry veins in NSW (Ausl); Wellington (NZ); Harz (Ger); Elba and Piedmont (Ita); Upper Telemark (Nor); Gryhyttan, Jakobsberg, Långban and Örebo (Swd); India, SA.

Diopside, $CaMg(Si_2O_6)$, is a pyroxene gemstone; H 5–6; SG 3·20–3·38; monoclinic – prismatic xls with striated faces, often slender; also massive, granular or columnar; trp to trl, colourless, pale green, dark green to nearly black, grey or yellow; LR vitreous; STR white or grey; fuses on charcoal with difficulty to a magnetic globule. Dp. may occur in some granites, but is typical of crystalline schists and especially metamorphic limestones and dolomites; found in the Scottish Highlands; Que (Can); Calif and NY (USA); Piedmont (Ita); Baikal district and Urals (USSR); Alps, Finland, Nor, Rum, Swd, Braz and Sri Lanka.

Idocrase or *vesuvianite* is a very complicated basic calcium-aluminium silicate with magnesium and iron; potash and soda may likewise be present. It is a gemstone, trp or trl; brownish green, brown, red–brown or yellow; LR vitreous, fatty on broken surfaces; STR white; massive, granular or radiating, but usually crystalline – thick, sometimes long tetragonal prisms, rarely pyramids; H $6\frac{1}{2}$; SG $3 \cdot 3$–$3 \cdot 5$; fusible; partly decomposed in HCl. A green variety is called *californite* and a blue one *cyprine*. Id. keeps company with garnet, diopside, scapolite and wollastonite; found in Loch Tay limestones, (Scot); Donegal and Louth (Eir); Texada Isl, BC and Pontiac Co, Que (Can); Inyo Co, Cal; Phillipsburg, Me and Newton, NJ (USA); Eger (Czsl); Vesuvius (Ita); Urals (USSR); S Norway; S Ger.

Lapis lazuli, lazurite or *ultramarine*, $Na_{4-5}Al_3Si_7O_{12}S$; H 5–$5\frac{1}{2}$; SG $2 \cdot 3$–$2 \cdot 4$; is amorphous, rarely crystalline (cubic); azure to dark blue; LR vitreous; STR pale blue; often spangled with pyrite; readily fusible; discoloured by HCl with the evolution of H_2S (rotten-egg smell). It is a gemstone, found at the junction of limestone and granite, in Colo (USA); Alban Mts and Vesuvius (Ita); Ovalle (Chile); Baikal (USSR); Afghanistan, Iran.

Scapolite or *wernerite* is an isomorphous mixture of two minerals: marialite and meionite of complicated chemistry, the one with sodium, the other with calcium; H 5–6; SG $2 \cdot 54$–$2 \cdot 77$; seldom trp; white, colourless, pale yellow or pink, sometimes with a cat's-eye effect; LR pearly, resinous or vitreous; STR white; a minor gemstone; found in metamorphic limestones and amphibolites and as an alteration product of plagioclase in igneous rocks. Occurrence: Mass, NJ, Orange Co, NY and Chester Co, Pa (USA); Pyrenees, Scandinavia, Swz, Braz, Burma, Sri Lanka, Madagascar.

Scheelite, calcium tungstate, $CaWO_4$; H $4\frac{1}{2}$–5; SG $5 \cdot 9$–$6 \cdot 1$ (feels heavy in the hand); massive, reniform; but usually in tetragonal octahedral xls, pyramids, plates, twins; colourless, greenish white, yellowish; LR adamantine or resinous; STR colourless or white; occasionally cut as a gem; fluoresces lilac; crumbles and fuses in blowpipe; decomposes in HCl with a yellow residue. Sch. occurs in pegmatites and pneumatolytic veins, as well as in metamorphic limestones in Cornwall and Cumberland (Eng); Ariz, Calif, Nev (USA); Bohemia (Czsl); Saxony (Ger); Bolivia, Mexico.

Wollastonite, calcium silicate, $CaSiO_3$, monoclinic or triclinic – tabular xls, seldom good; massive, columnar, lamellar or radiating aggregates; H $4\frac{1}{2}$–5; SG $2 \cdot 8$–$2 \cdot 9$; trl, white or grey; LR pearly; STR white; fusible at the edges; decomposes in HCl with separation of silica. Occurrence: Mourne Mts (NI); Morin, Que (Can); Lewis Co, NY and Buck Co, Pa (USA); NSW (Ausl); Pargas (Fin); Swd and Mexico.

Zincite, the red oxide of zinc, ZnO, orange–red, blood red or hyacinth red; trl to trp; LR adamantine; STR reddish yellow; massive, granular, scaly or foliaceous; hexagonal – flat six-sided plates crowned with pyramids; H $4\frac{1}{2}$–5; SG $5 \cdot 4$–$5 \cdot 7$; infusible; soluble in HCl. The Smithsonian has some cut specimens from Franklin, NJ (USA); also found in Ita and Tasmania.

Zoisite is a variety of epidote (p 137f), $Ca_2Al_3[OH(SiO_4)_3]$, but unlike the latter it is orthorhombic – forms long striated prisms; also massive, columnar with longitudinal striations, or fibrous; colourless, greyish white, grey, green, yellowish brown or red; pleochroic, showing abnormal polarisation colours – usually inky blue; trp to trl; LR vitreous; STR colourless; H 6–$6\frac{1}{2}$; SG $3 \cdot 33$–$3 \cdot 38$; fuses to a trp bead. There is a rose pink variety called *thulite*, and a blue one from Tanzania, known as *tanzanite*. These are gemstones. Apart from limestones, zs. is found in 'greenstones' and amphibolites as well as copper lodes; eg in Glen Urquhart, Inverness-shire and Loch Garve area, Ross-shire (Scot); Tenn, Clay Co, NC and Chester Co, Pa (USA); Arendal (Nor); Alps etc.

CONTACT METAMORPHIC MINERALS

This section deals with contact metamorphic rocks other than limestones and dolomites, and so also with high-temperature forms of minerals.

Andalusite is a silicate of aluminium, Al_2SiO_5, and the high-temperature counterpart of kyanite (p 138), its high-pressure allomorph, while further application of heat to the latter turns it into sillimanite. However, and. is orthorhombic, forms simple thick prisms of square cross-section; a variety called *chiastolite* or *macle* is columnar and radial with cruciform markings in cross-section. And. with H $7-7\frac{1}{2}$; SG $3 \cdot 1-3 \cdot 3$; is whitish, rose red, flesh pink, reddish brown, pearl grey or violet; LR vitreous; STR white; usually op, but sometimes clear and cut as a gem. It occurs also as a granite accessory, found in Andalusia (Spn); but also in Cornwall, Devon and Cumberland (Eng); nr Ballachulish, Argyll (Scot); Leinster granite aureole (Eir); Calif and Nev (USA); Transvaal (SA); Urals (USSR); Braz, Alps.

Corundum is crystalline alumina, Al_2O_3; H 9; SG $3 \cdot 9-4 \cdot 1$; belongs to the hexagonal system – xls, steep pyramidal, barrel-shaped, spindle-shaped, sometimes tabular or rhombohedral; also massive or granular; trp, trl or op; LR adamantine to vitreous; STR white; colourless, blue, green, yellow, pink to deep red, violet, brown, grey or black. The coarse non-gem, grey, granular variety is *emery*. Red corundum, coloured by chromic oxide, is *ruby*; *sapphire* is blue, but all other gem corundums are described as sapphires, regardless of colour. Cor. is characteristic of rocks of low silica content, contact-metamorphic clayey and limey sediments, but may be found in some volcanics, peridotites and occasionally in veins of acid rocks as well as in detrital deposits. Coarse cor. is of widespread occurrence. Poor-quality sapphires are known from Cumberland (Eng); Arran, Ardnamurchan, Mull and Glen Clova (Scot); Crogan Kinshela Mts (Eir); rubies south of Dundonnell, N W Highlands (Scot). Gem material comes mainly from Queensl (Ausl); Mont and NC (USA); Burma, Sri Lanka, Kashmir and Thailand.

Graphite is pure carbon, C, and an allomorph of diamond, seldom crystalline – hexagonal, forming six-sided scales or laminae; usually massive, granular or earthy; black, brownish black, iron black or dark steel grey; op with a metallic or dull LR, and black shining STR (black lead); H 1–2; SG 2·1–2·3; feels fatty to the touch; infusible. Main localities: Cumberland (Eng); Sterling Hill and Ticonderoga, NY (USA); Buckingham, Que and Ont (Can); Ausr, Fin, Ger, Sri Lanka, Korea, Madagascar, Mexico, Siberia.

Hausmannite, the black manganese oxide, Mn_3O_4; H $5\frac{1}{2}$; SG 4·7–4·8; may be massive, granular or crystalline – tetragonal xls of pyramidal habit, often twinned and intergrown; iron black with a bluish tinge or brownish black; op to trl; LR submetallic; STR chestnut; infusible; soluble in HCl. It is found in association with magnetite, braunite, calcite and manganite. Occurrence: Whitehaven, Cumberland (Eng); Granan, Aberdeenshire (Scot); Obispo Co, Calif and Franklin, NJ (USA); Harz Mts (Ger); Pajsberg, Värmland (Swd).

Lievrite, *ilvaite* or *yenite*, is a basic calcium-iron silicate with a complex formula; H $5\frac{1}{2}$–6; SG 4·1; black, greyish or brownish black; op; LR sub-metallic; STR blackish; forms long orthorhombic prisms, lined lengthwise; also acicular, radiating aggregates, rarely granular; fusible; decomposed in HCl. Lv. keeps company with augite, sodalite, tin ores, zoisite and epidote; found nr Sommerville, Mass and in RI (USA); Saxony (Ger); Elba and Tuscany (Ita); Silesia (Pol); Grc and Greenland.

This account is not exhaustive.

14

METASOMATIC AND
HYDROTHERMAL VEIN MINERALS

INTRODUCTION

Most substances are more soluble in hot water than in cold, and as mineral-bearing waters find their way into the crevices and natural weaknesses of the rock they are cooled and begin to deposit their material. This process is accelerated by evaporation of the water on reaching the surface, and the result is that hollows and crevices in the rocks become lined with crystals, including valuable metal ores, and pleasing samples for the rockhound's collection. Such *hydrothermal* veins arise from waters released or invaded by the magmas in underground intrusions or those reaching the surface in volcanic activity.

The crevices into which water penetrates may already be veins of primary minerals with which the solutions react, depositing altered materials. Thus crocoisite is formed where solutions containing chromium compounds react with the lead ores frequently found in such veins. Where the rock itself is soluble, particularly in the case of limestones, the water will penetrate into the weaknesses and joints in the rock removing the original mineral and leaving the interstices filled with other materials. This *metasomatic* replacement of the calcite in limestones by magnesium salts occurs in the sea where coral reefs today are being converted into dolomite. It is thus not necessarily a hot-water process.

Hydrothermal (hot-water) and metasomatic (replacement) veins cannot be easily separated, and the same materials may occur in both. They shade naturally into volcanic deposits with minerals such as proustite (dealt with in Chapter 12) and include minerals found in salt beds, such as anhydrite, celestine and gypsum, and weathered iron and manganese ores, such as goethite, manganite and siderite, all of which are described in Chapter 15. Pyrargyrite, linnaeite and niccolite are also among the hydrothermal vein minerals, but because of their metallic appearance will be found in Chapter 9.

The following are dealt with here: barytes; zinc blende; fluorite; calcite, dolomite and magnesite; covelline; crocoisite; pitchblende; purpurite; rhodocrosite and rhodonite; strontianite and witherite; and wolfram.

SOME COMMON VEIN AND LIMESTONE MINERALS

Barytes, barite or *heavy spar* is barium sulphate, $BaSO_4$, usually found in tabular orthorhombic prisms, or comb-like (cockscomb) and coarse lamellar aggregates, also fibrous or massive; colourless, white or tinted red and yellow; LR vitreous; H $3-3\frac{1}{2}$; SG $4 \cdot 3-4 \cdot 6$. It is soluble in hot water, insoluble in cold; gives green flame of barium; found in veins with lead and zinc ores, or with fluorite. Occurrence: Dufton mines, Westmorland; Cumberland, Derbyshire, Shropshire (Eng); W Scotland; Grand Forks, BC (yellow xls) and Londonderry mines, NS (Can); St Lawrence Co, NY; Sterling and Hartsel (blue xls) and Gilman (yellow xls) in Colo, also Conn (USA); Ober-Ostern and Harz Mts (Ger); Bamle (Nor); Fra, and widespread elsewhere.

Blende, sphalerite or *black jack* is zinc sulphide, ZnS, usually containing some iron; forms tetrahedral xls, often distorted, frequently twinned; cubic system; also botryoidal aggregates and massive; yellow, red, brown or black; trl–op occasionally

149

trp; resinous or adamantine LR; STR brown or white; H $3\frac{1}{2}$–4; SG 3·9–4·2; dissolves in HCl giving H_2S (test for sulphides). Found replacing limestone as in the Mississippi valley (USA), usually in hydrothermal veins as at Broken Hill, NSW (Ausl); sometimes due to contact metamorphosis as in New Mexico (USA). Widespread, often with galena, in Cornwall, Derbyshire, Cumberland (Eng); Cardiganshire (Wal); Perthshire (Scot); Joplin Mo, Breckinridge, Col; Butte, Mon and Franklin, NJ (USA); Neudorf, Harz Mts (Ger); Alsace (Fra); Binnatal (Swz); Rio Tinto (Spn); Příbram (Czsl); Scandinavia, Jap, Korea.

Fluorite, fluor or *fluorspar*, calcium fluoride, CaF_2, is cubic, usually in cubes and octahedra, variously modified, sometimes twinned, also as granular aggregates; trp and colourless when pure, also white, black, brown and all rainbow colours; trp–trl with vitreous LR and white STR; rather soft – H 4; SG 3·0–3·3; fluorescent, sometimes showing a violet glow in addition to the normal colour. *Blue John* is a massive form mined in Derbyshire (Eng) for ornaments. Found in hydrothermal veins with galena, blende, quartz, barytes or tin ores, also in pegmatites: Weardale, Durham; Alston Moor and Cleator Moor, Cumberland; Devon and Cornwall (Eng); Thunder Bay area and Madoc area, Ont (Can); Westmoreland, NH; Clay Center, Ohio; Rossiclare, Ill and Ky (USA); Gersdorf (Ger); Scot, Eire, NI, Alps.

Calcite is the more stable allomorph of calcium carbonate, $CaCO_3$ (see aragonite p 126), with hexagonal xls in many different forms including *nail-head spar* prisms with flat end facets and *dog-tooth spar*: sharp pointed prisms. It is often twinned, also fibrous with silky LR (*satin spar*), massive, granular or earthy; colourless, white or tinted various shades; trp–op with vitreous LR; H 3; SG 2·7; high birefringence. Extremely widespread: as main constituent of limestone, chalk and marble, originally deposited in the sea; in druses, crevices and ore veins; as stalactites and stalagmites in caves; as *calcareous tufa* from volcanic waters; with barytes, gypsum and dolomite; with lead and zinc or tin ores; especially fine xls from Frizington and Egremont, Cumberland (Eng); Keeweenaw, Mich; NJ, Mass, Conn, in lead mines Okla, Kans and Mo, also Calif (USA); Helgustadir (Iceland); Mexico.

Dolomite is calcium and magnesium carbonate, $CaMg(CO_3)_2$, and is hexagonal, isomorphous with calcite and similar in appearance. Rhombohedral xls with faces slightly curved, twins like calcite, also massive and granular; usually trl; white or tinted yellow and brown with iron or pink with manganese; slightly harder than calcite – H $3\frac{1}{2}$–4 – with SG $2 \cdot 9$; widespread in magnesian limestones, eg in Dolomite Mts (Ita); xls are found in Cornwall, Cumberland and Isle of Man (Eng); Stony Point, NS; Niagara, Ont (Can), and the Great Lakes across to Ohio and NY in USA; also in the Mississippi valley, Colo and Calif (USA); Alsace and Savoy (Fra); Salzburg (Ausr); Piedmont and Tuscany (Ita); Binnatal (Swz); Minas Geraes (Braz); Colombia, Mexico, Algeria, Rum.

Magnesite is the magnesium carbonate $MgCO_3$ corresponding to calcite and dolomite with similar hexagonal, rhombohedral xls; also fibrous, massive and earthy; colourless, white, yellow or brownish; trp–op; H $3\frac{1}{2}$–$4\frac{1}{2}$; SG $3 \cdot 0$. It is found as the main constituent of sedimentary rocks from old salt beds at Bissell, Cal (USA); more often deposited by the action of hot solutions on limestone and dolomite, and in veins and fractures in serpentine formed by its weathering. It occurs on the Black River, Yukon and in Que (Can); Calif, Wash, Clark Co, Nev (USA); Tyrol (Ausr); Euboea (Grc); Urals (USSR); Manchuria, Czsl.

OTHER ASSOCIATED MINERALS

Covelline or *covellite*, cupric sulphide, CuS, forms thin hexagonal plates, but is usually found as incrustations; op, with submetallic to resinous LR; bluish black with black STR; H $1\frac{1}{2}$–2; SG $4 \cdot 6$; fuses easily in blowpipe flame. Covelline is found as secondary enrichment of copper deposits from solution in Alas, Colo, Mon, Utah, Wyo (USA); Kawau Isl (NZ); Baden, Hesse-Nassau, Saxony (Ger); Vesuvius (Ita); Salzburg (Ausr); Serbia (Yug); Chile, Argentina, Philippines.

Crocoisite or *crocoite*, chromate of lead, $PbCrO_4$, is vivid reddish orange and forms long monoclinic xls, often striated lengthwise, or plates, needles; also massive or in crusts; trl, with vitreous LR and orange–yellow STR; H $2\frac{1}{2}$–3; SG 5·9–6·1; rather rare, found at Dundas, Heazlewood and White River (Tasmania); Maricopa Co and Pinal Co, Ariz and Inyo Co and Riverside Co, Calif (USA); Umtali (Rhodesia); Rézbánya (Rum); Beresov district (USSR); Goyabeira, Minas Geraes (Braz); North Camarines province, Luzon (Philippines); Hun, Indonesia.

Pitchblende or *uraninite* is the primary ore of uranium with approximate formula UO_2. It is cubic with octahedral xls, or botryoidal, stalactitic, scaly or in amorphous gels; black, grey, brown or green, op; greasy LR; H $5\frac{1}{2}$ and very heavy – SG variable up to about 10; radioactive; soluble in HNO_3 and H_2SO_4. It is found in high-temperature veins, but also in granites. Widespread, including Can; Conn, S Dak, N Dak (USA); Saxony (Ger); Jachymov (Czsl); Katanga (Zaire); Swd, Nor, W Africa.

Purpurite is the mixed phosphate of iron and manganese, $(Fe,Mn)PO_4$, orthorhombic; prismatic xls or massive; purple with a purple STR and silky LR; H 4–$4\frac{1}{2}$; SG 3·3; occurs Wodgina, WA (Ausl); NC, Pala, Cal and Custer, N Dak (USA); Chanteloube (Fra).

Rhodocrosite or *diallogite*, $MnCO_3$, and *rhodonite*, $MnSiO_3$, are the carbonate and silicate of manganese, respectively. They are often found together in lead and zinc veins and in limestones. Both are pink or red, occasionally grey or brown, with vitreous LR, white STR and SG close to 3·6.

Rhodocrosite is hexagonal, rhombohedral, with bipyramidal crystals (see Fig 3e), but usually massive or as crusts, sometimes with a pink-and-white banded structure resembling agate, but much softer – H $3\frac{1}{2}$–$4\frac{1}{2}$; not fusible in blowpipe flame; dissolves in warm HCl. These facts and the hardness distinguish it from rhodonite. It is found at Okehampton and other places in Devon (Eng); Leadhills (Scot); Colo, Butte, Mon; Austin, Nev and Park City Utah (USA); Beierdorf and Freiberg, Saxony (Ger); Kapnik (Rum); Ljubija (Yug); Catamarca province (Argentina); Hun, Spn.

Rhodonite is triclinic with large tabular xls or massive; usually contains some iron and calcium. It is much harder than rcr. – H $5\frac{1}{2}$–$6\frac{1}{2}$, fusible, but only slightly affected by acids. Found with rcr. in Britain as above, and at Broken Hill, NSW (Ausl); also occurs in Dunedin area and Clutha River (NZ); Cummington, Mass (USA); Harz Mts (Ger); Pajsberg and Långban (Swd); Urals (USSR); Fra, Spn, Hun, Mexico, Braz.

Strontianite, strontium carbonate, $SrCO_3$, is orthorhombic and isomorphous with aragonite rather than calcite; prismatic, acicular, as radiating aggregates, fibrous or massive; trp–trl, colourless to grey or greenish; H $3\frac{1}{2}$–4 like arag. but heavier – SG $3\cdot6$–$3\cdot7$; gives a red strontium flame; found in ore veins or as nodules in limestone, with galena, barytes and celestine; Weardale, Durham (Eng); Strontian, Argyll (Scot); Cariboo district, BC (Can); Strontium Hills, Calif, Schoharie, NY and Mount Bonnell, Tex (USA); Freiberg, Saxony also Westphalia (Ger); Bixlegg, Tyrol (Ausr).

Witherite is barium carbonate, $BaCO_3$, with orthorhombic double pyramids, xls very frequently twinned, also fibrous or massive. It resembles str. with H $3\frac{1}{2}$ but is slightly heavier again – SG $4\cdot3$–$4\cdot4$ – and gives a barium green flame; often found with galena and barytes; Alston Moor, Cumberland; Northumberland and Durham (Eng); St Asaph (Wal); Thunder Bay, Ont (Can); Castle Dome, Yuma Co, Ariz and Platina, Shasta Co, Calif (USA); Ausr.

Wolfram or *wolframite* is a tungstate of iron and manganese, $(Fe,Mn)WO_4$, with the two metals in variable proportions. It is monoclinic, with prismatic or tabular xls, often striated; also bladed xls, massive or granular; black or dark brown; trl–op with sub-metallic LR and dark brown STR; H 5–5$\frac{1}{2}$; SG 7·1–7·9; decomposes in hot conc. HCl; occurs in high-temperature veins with tin ores in granite areas; St Austell, Cornwall and Caldbeck Fells, Cumberland (Eng); Queensl (Ausl); St Juan Co, Colo and Townesville, NC (USA); Zinnwald, Saxony (Ger); Llallagua (Bolivia); Spn, Czsl, Portugal, Braz, China, Korea, Malaysia; as placer deposits from gold-quartz veins in Lower Burma.

15

MARINE, LAKE AND SWAMP
DEPOSITS

EVAPORITES

This section deals with the soluble salts which are deposited
from the drying-up of inland seas and lakes. Among these
could be classed calcite and dolomite, which were, however,
described with the hydrothermal and metasomatic minerals in
the last chapter. Included here are celestine and gypsum,
which are found frequently in clay deposits of marine origin,
but often occur in hydrothermal veins as well, as does anhydrite.
Another evaporite is epsomite or epsom salts, which is a deposit
from springs and on the walls of caves, and is an alteration
product of the weathering of rocks as well as a constituent of
salt beds.

Sea water contains about 3·5 per cent of dissolved mineral
salts, and where salt-water areas are subject to evaporation in
hot and arid climates, these are progressively deposited, the
least soluble salts being precipitated first. This must have
occurred in the past when areas of the sea became wholly or
partly isolated, in many cases forming salt beds some thousands
of feet thick, which are mined today. In the vast beds at
Stassfurt, Germany, the salts are deposited in layers in the
following order: calcite and dolomite; gypsum and anhydrite;
and rock salt or common salt. Depending on the extent of
evaporation, these are followed by the so-called *bitterns*,

consisting of very soluble potassium and magnesium salts with a bitter taste: polyhalite; kieserite (a material similar to epsomite in composition); and carnallite.

The process of evaporation of inland seas can be witnessed today in the Caspian Sea in the USSR, the Dead Sea, and the salt lakes in Utah. Apart from Stassfurt, large salt beds are found in Cheshire (Eng); Ont (Can); Mich and NY (USA); Lorraine (Fra); Württemberg (Ger); Salzburg (Ausr); Wieliczka (Pol); USSR, India and China.

Salt deposits are light compared with other rocks, and have the interesting property that when compressed by overlying deposits, they flow, rising to the surface as salt domes and salt mountains. These frequently occur with deposits of oil, in the USA, Iran and other places.

The drying up of desert lakes may leave deposits of a different kind from the sea salts, obtained from the fierce weathering of rocks in the area. Typical of these compounds are the boron salts called borates. Of these borax and boracite are described here, the former being a desert material; the latter, found in the Stassfurt and other salt beds, may have been derived from it.

Celestine or *celestite*, $SrSO_4$, is the strontium equivalent of barytes (p 149), with which it is isomorphous. Some barium is often present; the orthorhombic xls are tabular or prismatic. Cel. also occurs as aggregates and fibrous or granular masses; colourless or white, often bluish, also red, green or brown. The blue colouring is often arranged as a series of growth zones, which distinguishes it from barytes, having a similar H – 3–$3\frac{1}{2}$ – but a slightly lower SG – $4 \cdot 0$. It gives a red strontium flame; occurs in clay, as at Yate, nr Bristol (Eng); also in salt beds, metasomatic in limestone and dolomite, in hydrothermal veins, and with volcanic sulphur deposits in Sicily. Widespread, including good xls at Syracuse and Rochester, NY; Clay Center and Portage, Ohio; Lampasas, Tex and Emery, Utah (USA); Muschelkalk and Gembock (Ger); Mexico and Morocco.

Anhydrite is the orthorhombic form of calcium sulphate, $CaSO_4$, with some water of crystallisation, one molecule to two of $CaSO_4$. It occurs as cube-like xls, also in fibrous, lamellar or granular form; trp–trl, colourless to white or bluish; H 3–4; much lighter than bar. and cel. – SG 2·9–3·0; found in salt beds, in rocks over salt domes, in gold-quartz and hydrothermal veins; La, Tex and Balmat, NY (USA); Bex-les-Bains (Swz); Chile, W Ausl.

Gypsum, $CaSO_4.2H_2O$, is the more common form of calcium sulphate, turning into anhydrite at 25 °C (77 °F). It is monoclinic, tabular, prismatic or acicular, often in ' swallow-tail ' twins, stellate groups, fibrous (*satin spar*) or massive (*alabaster*), the latter being used as an ornamental stone. It is colourless to white, grey, pink, or yellowish; soft – H $1\frac{1}{2}$–2; SG 2·3; pearly LR; slightly soluble in water; found in salt beds, clays and shales, dolomitised limestones and in ore veins: London and Oxford clays, satin spar at Matlock, Derbyshire, alabaster at Watchet, Somerset (Eng); Cavan and other places (Eir); Niagara Co, NY; Ellsworth, Ohio; Jet, Okla and Fremont River Canyon, Utah (USA); Cave of Swords (Mexico); Spn, Ita, Chile.

Rock salt or *halite* is common salt, NaCl; it belongs to the cubic system with cubes, often with hollowed faces, known as hopper xls; rarely octahedra; can be massive or granular; often contains some $CaSO_4$, $CaCl_2$ or $MgCl_2$; varies from colourless to white, yellow, red, blue or violet; vitreous LR; H 2–$2\frac{1}{2}$; SG 2·2; soluble in water, characteristic taste; usually in salt beds, sometimes as a sublimate from volcanoes.

Polyhalite is potassium, calcium and magnesium sulphate, $K_2Ca_2Mg(SO_4)_4.2H_2O$, forming elongated prisms in the triclinic system, but normally occurring in the salt beds as fibrous masses; colourless, white, grey, yellow, pink or red; vitreous to fatty LR; H 3–$3\frac{1}{2}$; SG 2·8; soluble in water, tending to decompose with the separation of gypsum.

Carnallite is potassium and magnesium chloride, $KMgCl_3$.

$6H_2O$; orthorhombic, forming hexagonally shaped pyramids, but usually in salt beds as granular masses; colourless to white, yellowish or reddish; vitreous LR, varying from shiny to dull; H 3; SG 1·6; deliquesces and is readily soluble in water, with a bitter taste.

Epsomite or *epsom salts* is magnesium sulphate, $MgSO_4.7H_2O$, occurring as small orthorhombic xls, fibrous aggregates and hair-like efflorescences; usually white; silky, vitreous or earthy LR; H 2–2½; SG 1·7; very soluble in water, with a bitter taste. Found in salt beds in the weathering zones of ores, as efflorescence in caves, or from springs as at Epsom, Surrey (Eng); from lakes in BC and Sask (Can); in Wash, Calif, Nev, N Mex, Utah, Wyo, Tenn, Ky, Ind (USA); Isère (Fra); Vesuvius (Ita); Saragossa (Spn); Bohemia (Czsl); Ger, Siberia, SA.

Boracite is a magnesium chloride and borate, with a complex formula; xls cubic, cubes and tetrahedra, but found in the salt beds in intergrown masses; trp–trl; colourless, white, grey, yellow, green or blue; LR vitreous; STR white; H 7, very much harder than any other of the salts; SG 2·9–3·0; soluble only in hot HCl, gives a green boron flame. Found in the salt beds at Stassfurt, etc; also Kalkberg, Hanover and Schildstein (Ger); Luneville, La Meurthe (Fra).

Borax, sodium borate, $Na_2B_4O_7.10H_2O$, forms large monoclinic xls with a tendency to dehydrate and crumble, also found massive and as efflorescent crusts; colourless, white or tinted yellow, green, blue or grey; vitreous LR; H 2–2½; SG 1·7; soluble in water, fuses readily to a glassy borax bead (p 70). Found in desert areas, Calif, Nev, N Mex (USA); Bolivia, Chile, Argentina, Iran, India, Tibet, USSR.

SEDIMENTS, IRON AND MANGANESE DEPOSITS

This section overlaps with the next chapter in that it includes minerals formed by the weathering of iron and manganese ores. These mostly occur in sediments deposited in the sea, in lakes and peat bogs. Among them siderite is also a hydrothermal vein mineral found in limestone and in tin veins; vivianite and goethite are likewise found in veins as secondary products from the weathering of pyrites. Among the manganese minerals, pyrolusite (which, being of metallic appearance, is dealt with in Chapter 9) and manganite occur in veins as well.

Despite these exceptions, it is generally true that products of weathering of iron and manganese minerals are eventually carried away in solution or suspension, and then often become deposited with organic materials in peat bogs and swamps. They are found associated with coal beds which have been formed from peat over periods of millions of years. There are good reasons to think that in some cases bacteria are responsible for the oxidation processes forming these sediments. The occurrence of iron phosphate as vivianite inside fossil bones in peat bogs shows the involvement of organic material, the phosphate radicals obviously being provided by the bones. The peculiar mineral struvite, also described here, is even more clearly a product of the decay of organic materials, as it contains ammonia as well as phosphorus.

In addition, glauconite is included; although it does not fit in particularly well with the other materials mentioned, it is a marine deposit known to be forming in the sea at the present time.

Siderite or *chalybite*, iron carbonate, $FeCO_3$, forms hexagonal xls of the rhombohedral type with typically slightly curved faces. Some manganese, magnesium and calcium is usually present; granular and globular masses common. Sid. is yellowish or brownish; trl–op; H $3\frac{1}{2}$–$4\frac{1}{2}$; SG 3·7–3·9; xls have vitreous to pearly LR; found replacing limestone, in veins with cryolite and tin ores, also in pegmatites; most commonly in clayey nodules as clay-ironstone associated with coal deposits, eg S Staffs, Northants (Eng); S Wal etc. Xls can be found in Cornwall (Eng); Gilman and Crystal Peak, Colo; Bisbee, Ariz, and Conn (USA); Morro Velho (Braz); Croatia (Yug); Spn, Ger and Greenland.

Limonite is a colloidal iron oxide, $2Fe_2O_3.3H_2O$ or FeOOH. nH_2O; amorphous; botryoidal, stalactitic, or as an earthy coating on iron ores or rocks; yellowish or brownish; op; silky LR, or dull and earthy; H 5–5½; SG 3·6–4·0 in the more compact forms. Widespread, including Cornwall (Eng); Conn, Mass, Pa, Mo, Tex (USA); Alsace-Lorraine (Fra); Bavaria, Harz Mts, Freiberg, Saxony (Ger); Rosenau (Czsl); Bilbao (Spn); Swd, Cuba.

Vivianite, phosphate of iron, $Fe_3(PO_4)_2.8H_2O$, forms long prismatic or bladed monoclinic xls, colourless, blue, greenish blue or purplish, with a pale blue STR; also reniform or globular aggregates; trp–trl with a pearly to vitreous LR, pleochroic; soft – H 1½–2½; SG 2·6–2·7; found in weathered pyrites veins or in clay deposits with organic material; St Agnes and Truro, Cornwall, also Devon (Eng); Shetlands and Isle of Man, in peat swamps; Wannon River Falls, Vic (Ausl); Leadville, Colo; Bingham, Utah; Yuba Co, Calif; Del and NJ (USA); Bavaria (Ger); Orodna, Transylvania (Rum); Crimea (USSR); Poopo and Llallagua (Bolivia).

Struvite, ammonium and magnesium phosphate, $NH_4MgPO_4.6H_2O$, forms orthorhombic crystals with sharp corners, sometimes intergrown; trl, yellow to pale brown; H 1½–2; SG 1·7; soluble in acids; found in peat bogs in Ausl, Ger, Guiana etc.

Psilomelane, a hydrated oxide of manganese with variable quantities of barium $(Ba,Mn)Mn_4O_8(OH)_2$, occurs as an amorphous colloidal precipitate; botryoidal, reniform, stalactitic; also powdery, known as *wad* or bog manganese; brown or black in colour and STR; op, with sub-metallic LR as if polished; H 5–6; SG 3·7–4·7; often with pyrolusite. Lead Geo, Orkney (Scot); Ark, Tucson, Ariz and Wythe Co, Va (USA); Schneeberg, Saxony (Ger); Minas Geraes (Braz); Transvaal (SA); India.

Manganite, MnOOH, is orthorhombic, with long prismatic xls, striated lengthwise, in bundles or radial aggregates; blackish to brownish; op–trl with red translucence; sub-metallic LR; H 4; SG 4·2–4·4; often in veins with pyrolusite; Cornwall and Cumberland (Eng); Hants and Picton Co, NS (Can); Negauriee, Mich and Woodstock, Va (USA); Harz Mts (Ger).

Goethite, FeOOH, is the equivalent iron compound, orthorhombic in thin plates or acicular, in radial aggregates, fibrous or massive; black, brown or yellow with yellowish STR; op, in small chips trl; adamantine LR, silky if fibrous; H 5–5½; SG 4·0–4·4; St Just and Lostwithiel, Cornwall (Eng); Lake Utah, in pegmatites Crystal Peak, Colo (USA); Saxony and Thuringia (Ger); Přibram (Czsl); Minas Geraes (Braz); Ausr, USSR, Chile.

Glauconite is a complex aluminosilicate of potassium, iron and magnesium, of monoclinic structure, but found in amorphous earthy masses consisting of rounded grains about 3mm in diameter, of various shades of green; op; dull LR; H 2; SG 2·2–2·4; occurs in the greensands, at Comely in Shropshire, Cheviot Hills, Kent and Sussex (Eng); NJ, Red Bird, Mo and French Creek, Pa (USA); Anvers and Havre (Belgium); Wal, SA, India, USSR.

16

PRODUCTS OF WEATHERING AND ALTERATION

LEAD AND ZINC ORES

The action of the air together with rain water and substances dissolved in it as it percolates into ore veins, is known as weathering and gives rise to secondary minerals. The primary sulphides and arsenic minerals are oxidised to sulphates and arsenates, and these are attacked by water containing dissolved carbon dioxide from the air to give carbonates and hydroxides, or basic salts which contain hydroxide and silicate, carbonate, chloride or other groups. Phosphates also appear among weathered minerals.

The primary lead and zinc ores are usually the sulphides, galena and blende, and these very frequently occur together. So, of course, do their products of alteration, which are described here. Mining areas, such as Cumberland and Derbyshire (Eng); Leadhills, Lanarkshire (Scot); Broken Hill, NSW (Ausl); Pa and the western states – Calif, Ariz, Nev, Col, N Mex (USA) are frequently mentioned as localities where they can be found.

Anglesite, sulphate of lead, or lead vitriol, $PbSO_4$, forms colourless, white or tinted xls in the orthorhombic system with cube-like shapes, and also granular and compact masses. It is trp–trl with a white STR and adamantine LR; H $2\frac{1}{2}$–3; SG 6·4; dissolves completely in KOH; formed from weathering of galena in the upper part of lead veins in Parys Mine, Anglesey (Wal); Cornwall, Cumberland and Derbyshire (Eng); Leadhills (Scot); Broken Hill, NSW (Ausl); New Caledonia, USA, Spn, USSR.

Cerussite, lead carbonate, $PbCO_3$, is orthorhombic and similar to ang. in appearance, but forms pyramidal xls, short or long prisms; also acicular, stellate, aggregated, massive or earthy: is slightly harder – H 3–$3\frac{1}{2}$ – with a similar SG – 6·5; dissolves completely in HNO_3, giving off carbon dioxide. It forms from the weathering of galena and anglesite in Cornwall, Derbyshire and Durham (Eng); Leadhills (Scot); Cardigan (Wal); Broken Hill, NSW (Ausl); Organ district N Mex, Tiger and Bisbee, Ariz and Colo (USA); Broken Hill (Zambia); Bohemia (Czsl); Tsumeb (S W Africa); Mindouli (Zaire); Transbaikalia (USSR); Sardinia (Ita), Ger, New Caledonia, Sardinia.

Pyromorphite, lead chloride and phosphate, $Pb_5Cl(PO_4)_3$, belongs to a family of minerals in which phosphate can be replaced by arsenate in *mimetite*, $Pb_5Cl(AsO_4)_3$, or vanadate in *vanadinite*, $Pb_5Cl(VO_4)_3$. These have the same chemical and crystal structure, ie they are isomorphous and often hard to tell apart without chemical tests. They are hexagonal, often in yellow or brownish prisms, usually trl, with resinous LR and white or yellowish STR and similar hardness and SG.

Pyromorphite is about the hardest of the three, H $3\frac{1}{2}$–4, with SG 6·5–7·1, and has the greatest variation in colour – from white and reddish to green and blue. It forms barrel-shaped prisms, reniform and globular masses, aggregates and crusts; in Cornwall, Derbyshire, at Roughton Gill near Caldbeck, Cumberland (Eng); Leadhills (Scot); Moyie, BC (Can); Broken Hill (Ausl); Chester Co, Pa; Coeur d'Alene district, Idaho and Cherokee Co, Ga (USA); Bad Ems and Moses (Ger); Huelgoat, Brittany (Fra); Přibram, Bohemia (Czsl) Durango (Mexico); Rhodesia.

Mimetite has hardness $3\frac{1}{2}$ and SG $7\cdot0-7\cdot3$ and is often pale in colour, white or pale yellow and of similar habit to pyr., found with it at Wheal Alfred, Cornwall and Dry Gill and Roughton Gill, Cumberland (Eng) and Leadhills (Scot). Other sites include 79 Mine, Ariz; Eureka, Nev and Phoenixville, Pa (USA); Bilbao Mine (Mexico); Badenweiler, Baden and Johanngeorgenstadt, Saxony (Ger).

Vanadinite is slightly softer, H 3, and often reddish in colour. It occurs in small prisms, pointed pyramids, often parallel aggregates; in Leadhills, also Wanlockhead, Dumfries (Scot); Alderley Edge, Cheshire (Eng); Pima Co and Globe district, Ariz; El Dorado Mine, Calif, Sierra Co and Black Canyon district, N Mex (USA); Tsumeb (S W Africa); Carinthia (Ausr); Berescovsk (USSR); Villa Ahamade (Mexico); Djebel Mahseur (Morocco); Spn. Comparatively rare.

Wulfenite, lead molybdate, $PbMoO_4$, resembles vanadinite in colour and physical properties, but is tetragonal with tabular, pyramidal, prismatic or massive habits. It is widespread in Ariz, N Mex, Nev and Pa at some of the places where pyromorphite minerals are found, also Utah (USA); Villa Ahamade (Mexico); Zinnwald, Saxony (Ger); Hun, Czsl, Yug, Alps and Zaire.

Greenockite, cadmium sulphide, CdS, occurs as a trl, yellow or orange crust on zinc blende, in which it was an impurity that has separated out by weathering. It sometimes forms small plates and hemimorphic xls in the hexagonal system; STR red or orange; H $3-3\frac{1}{2}$; SG $4\cdot9-5\cdot0$; at Wanlockhead, Dumfries and Bishopston, Renfrew (Scot); Pa, Topaz, Calif and Franklin, NJ (USA); Grc, Czsl, Bolivia etc.

Hemimorphite, a basic zinc silicate, $Zn_4(OH)_2Si_2O_7.H_2O$, forms orthorhombic xls with differently developed ends, and is thus the principal hemimorphic (literally ' half-shaped ') mineral (see Fig 4, f) with prismatic or tabular habit, frequently twinned, also fibrous, granular, massive and as crusts. It varies from trp to op; colourless to white, yellow, brown, green and even blue, with a vitreous LR and white STR; H $4\frac{1}{2}$–5; SG 3·3–3·5; Leadhills (Scot); Roughton Gill in Cumberland, Rutland mine nr Matlock, Derbyshire and Mendip Hills, Somerset (Eng); Sterling Hill, NJ; Elkhorn, Mon; Leadville, Colo and Wythe Co, Va (USA); Altenberg, Saxony (Ger); Iglesias (Ita); Moresnet (Belgium); Nerchinsk (Siberia); Durango (Mexico); Djebel Guergour (Algeria).

Smithsonite, zinc carbonate, $ZnCO_3$, resembles hemimorphite in its colourings and appearance, but is slightly harder – H 5–$5\frac{1}{2}$, and distinctly heavier – SG 4·0–4·5. It is, moreover, hexagonal with rhombohedral xls of high birefringence; more usually reniform, botryoidal, stalactitic or in granular crusts. It gives a carbonate reaction with acids. It often occurs as a replacement in limestone, and localities include the Mendip Hills in Somerset, Matlock, Derbyshire and Alston Moor, Cumberland (Eng); Leadhills (Scot); Broken Hill, NSW (Ausl); Yellville, Ark; Kelly, N Mex; Cerro Gordo district, Calif; Bamford, Pa and Mo (USA); Iglesias (Ita); Rhineland (Ger); Grc, Algeria, S W Africa, East Asia.

Hydrozincite, basic zinc carbonate, $2ZnCO_3.3Zn(OH)_2$, is monoclinic but microcrystalline, appearing as earthy or chalky crusts; op, white, pale yellow or other tints, with a dull, sometimes silky LR and gleaming STR; soft H 2–$2\frac{1}{2}$; SG 3·6–3·8. Found at Llandiloes, Montgom (Wal); N Kimberley, WA (Ausl); Cerro Gordo, Calif and Friedensville, Pa (USA); Silesia (Pol); Santander (Spn); Algeria, Ausr, Can.

Adamite, basic zinc arsenate, Zn_2AsO_4OH, is soft and relatively heavy, H $3\frac{1}{2}$; SG 4·3–4·5; forms small monoclinic xls, short or long prisms in aggregates in druses, normally trp with a vitreous LR, yellow or green, sometimes colourless, red or violet, usually with a yellow or green STR; fluoresces yellow–green; found often with limonite; Nev, Ariz, Utah (USA); Cap Garonne (Fra); Laurium (Grc); Durango (Mexico); Chile, Algeria, S W Africa.

COPPER AND OTHER ORE MINERALS

This section deals with the weathered copper minerals, except for turquoise which is under the next heading with the aluminium minerals. In addition, cobalt and nickel blooms, and autunite and torbernite, which are uranium minerals, are described here.

The weathering of copper ores from the primary sulphide and arsenide minerals, such as chalcopyrite, chalcocite, enargite and bornite, is similar to that of lead and zinc ores. These copper deposits are widespread together with lead and zinc in Pa and the western USA; with lead in Cornwall (Eng) and Tenn (USA); also Burra Burra, S Aust (Ausl); Chessy, nr Lyons (Fra); Katanga (Zaire); Chile.

Atacamite, basic copper chloride, $Cu_2Cl(OH)_3$, forms long spiky orthorhombic prisms; also fibrous, foliated or granular aggregates. It is trp–trl, green to greenish black, with adamantine or vitreous LR and apple-green STR; H 3–3$\frac{1}{2}$; SG 3·8; it is a product of weathering of copper ores, particularly in salty desert conditions, such as in the Atacama desert of S America. Specimens can be found at Botallack, Cornwall (Eng); Ravensthorpe, WA and Wallaroo and Burra Burra, S Aust (Ausl), also Cornwall and Moonta mines (Ausl); San Manuel, Ariz and Boleo and El Toro, Calif (USA); Vesuvius (Ita); Etna (Sicily); Chiquicamata (Chile).

Malachite is a basic copper carbonate, $Cu_2CO_3(OH)_2$, with a green colour, not as dark as atacamite, of similar appearance, forming thin needles which are, however, monoclinic, frequently in clusters. More commonly it is massive, with silky to dullish LR, or occurs as an earthy coating on other copper ores; H 3$\frac{1}{2}$–4; SG 3·9–4·0; of wide occurrence, at Redruth and nr Liskeard, Cornwall, at Alderley Edge, Cheshire and the Lake District (Eng); near Skull, Co Cork and at Tynagh, Galway (Eir); Burra Burra, S Aust (Ausl); Bisbee and Morenci, Ariz; Tintic, Utah; N Mex, Nev, Tenn, Pa (USA); Chessy (Fra); Harz Mts (Ger); Sverdlovsk and Nizhni Tagilsk (USSR); Tsumeb (S W Africa); Katanga (Zaire); Chile.

Azurite or *chessylite* is basic copper carbonate with a different formula, $Cu_3(CO_3)_2(OH)_2$, distinguishable from malachite by its azure-blue colour and pale-blue STR. Like mal. it is monoclinic; in long prisms, tabular plates, or massive and as crusts; at Broken Hill, NSW (Ausl); Chessy (Fra); Laurium (Grc); San Carlos (Mexico) and many of the localities mentioned for mal. Both are used as ornamental stones.

Chalcanthite, copper sulphate or blue vitriol, $CuSO_4.5H_2O$, is also blue with a pale-blue STR, forming triclinic prismatic xls, reniform, stalactitic or granular masses, and crusts. It is softer, H $2\frac{1}{2}$, and less dense, SG $2\cdot1-2\cdot3$, than azurite, and is water-soluble. On heating it loses water and shape, forming a bluish-white mass. From the weathering of sulphides in Cornwall (Eng); Wicklow (Eir); Ariz, Calif, Colo, Nev, Mon, Tenn, Pa, NC (USA); Rammelsberg, Harz Mts (Ger); Vesuvius (Ita); Rio Tinto (Spn); Bohemia (Czsl); Chiquicamata (Chile); Cyprus.

Chrysocolla, copper silicate, $CuSiO_3.2H_2O$, is amorphous, forming from colloidal gel in rounded masses; sometimes earthy; op to slightly trl at edges, vitreous LR, resembles enamel, but soft – H 2–4 – and lighter than other copper ores, SG $2\cdot0-2\cdot2$; colour blue, blue–green, sometimes green, with white to greenish STR; green hexagonal xls of similar composition and H 5 represent the rare mineral *dioptase*. Chrys. is found at the Lizard, Cornwall and in Cumberland (Eng); NS (Can); Adelaide, S Aust (Ausl); Calif, Ariz, Utah, Wis, Conn, Pa, NJ (USA); Schneeberg, Saxony and Kupferberg, Bavaria (Ger); Tyrol (Ausr); Etna (Sicily); Libethen (Hun); Nizhni Tagilsk (USSR); Katanga (Zaire); Rhodesia, Mexico, Chile.

Cuprite, Cu_2O, is the monovalent (cuprous) oxide of copper, forming trl, red to reddish-black cubic xls, with adamantine LR and reddish-brown STR; xls usually octahedral, also cubes and dodecahedra, and massive; H $3\frac{1}{2}$–4; SG $5\cdot8-6\cdot1$; somewhat similar to zincite (p 145); found at St Day, Cornwall (Eng); Bisbee Morenci and Globe, Ariz; Bingham, Utah and Santa

Rita, N Mex (USA); Lake Superior (USA and Can); Chessy (Fra); Burra Burra, S Aust; Broken Hill, NSW and Mt Isa, Queensl (Ausl); Westphalia (Ger); Linares (Spn); Timisoara (Rum); Perm district and Urals (USSR); Peru, Chile.

Cobalt bloom or *erythrite*, $Co_3(AsO_4)_2.8H_2O$, and *nickel bloom* or *annabergite*, $Ni_3(AsO_4)_2.8H_2O$, are arsenates formed by the weathering of smaltite, cobaltite and niccolite. They often occur together, and may partially replace each other; found as tiny monoclinic hairs or needles, more commonly earthy or massive, at Cobalt, Ont (Can); Humboldt Co, Nev (USA); Riesengebirge, Saxony (Ger); other localities mentioned below.

Cobalt bloom is trl, crimson-red, H $1\frac{1}{2}$–$2\frac{1}{2}$; SG $2 \cdot 95$, and occurs in Cornwall (Eng); Queensl (Ausl); Ariz, Calif, N Mex, Idaho (USA); Baden, Thuringia and Hesse-Nassau (Ger); Alsace and Isère (Fra); Salzburg (Ausr); Wallis (Swz); Tunaberg (Swd); Chile, Mexico, Morocco.

Nickel bloom is op, bright apple green with a green STR; H $2\frac{1}{2}$–3; SG $3 \cdot 0$–$3 \cdot 1$; might be confused with earthy forms of malachite. It is found in Bohemia (Czsl); Silesia (Pol); Laurium (Grc); Spn.

Autunite, $Ca(UO_2)_2(PO_4)_2.10$–$12H_2O$, and *torbernite*, $Cu(UO_2)_2(PO_4)_2.10H_2O$, are calcium and copper uranyl phosphates formed by the weathering of uranium ores, such as pitchblende. They are isomorphous, orthorhombic, usually found as square-looking plates in several places in Cornwall (Eng); at Mount Painter, S Aust (Ausl); in New England, at Mt Pine, NC and Maryville, Utah (USA); Schneeberg, Saxony (Ger) and as mentioned below.

Autunite is trl, yellow or yellow–green, with green STR, and pearly LR; H 2–$2\frac{1}{2}$; SG $3 \cdot 1$; intensely fluorescent; found at Katherine (Ausl); Colo and Spokane, Wash (USA); Margac and Autin in Saône et Loire (Fra).

Torbernite is trp–trl, green, with pale-green STR and adamantine to pearly LR; H also 2–$2\frac{1}{2}$; SG $3 \cdot 2$–$3 \cdot 5$; gives green or blue flame for copper; found at Callington, Cornwall (Eng); S Alligator Gorge, N Aust (Ausl); Lawrence Co in the Black Hills, SD and Grant Co, N Mex (USA); Jachymov (Czsl); Moctezuma (Mexico); Chinkolobwe (Zaire).

SERPENTINE AND ALUMINIUM MINERALS

The minerals described here are all associated with the weathering of silicates. Olivine, pyroxenes and amphiboles are all transformed by weathering into *serpentine*. As these form the main constituents of ultrabasic rocks, such rock is converted into *serpentinite*, consisting almost entirely of serpentine, together with smaller quantities of magnetite, and other minerals from the original rock. Serpentine is always massive, often showing the form of the crystals it has been derived from; ie it is pseudomorphous.

The further weathering of serpentine produces the nickel mineral *garnierite*, and *magnesite* (see p 151), which appears as whitish material filling cracks and veins in the serpentine.

The breakdown of the felspars characteristic of acid rocks and gneisses yields china clay or *kaolin*, and the final weathering product of aluminous rocks is aluminium oxide as *bauxite* or *gibbsite*, the former particularly requiring severe tropical weathering conditions to form.

Wavellite and *turquoise* are aluminium phosphates formed through the weathering of aluminosilicate rocks containing apatite.

Serpentine, basic magnesium silicate, $Mg_3Si_2O_5(OH)_4$, has the optical properties of the monoclinic system, but does not occur as xls, true serp. being compact and massive; *chrysotile*, the most common form of commercial asbestos, is a fibrous form. The gem variety *bowenite*, is trl, green and comparatively hard; found in NZ; Pa and RI (USA); Afghanistan and China. Common serp. is op, mostly green, also black, red, yellow and brown, frequently green streaked or spotted with red, making it an attractive ornamental stone; STR white; LR resinous to dull;

H $2\frac{1}{2}$–4; SG 2·5–2·6. Serpentinite occurs at the Lizard, Cornwall (Eng); Mona, Anglesey (Wal); Iona, Banffshire and Unst in the Shetlands (Scot); Connemara (Eire); Stillwater area (Can); NSW (Ausl) and other places; serp. is also found in smaller quantities in some schists and limestones.

Chrysotile is greenish white, green, yellow or brown, consisting of fine flexible fibres with a silky LR; found in seams traversing massive serp. in Lanark Co, Ont and Thetford area, Que (Can); Gila Co, Ariz; Montville, NJ and Lancaster Co, Pa (USA).

Garnierite or *noumeite*, $(Ni,Mg)_3Si_2O_5(OH)_4$, has some of the magnesium in serp. replaced by nickel; it is bright green to white, occasionally blue, always massive and amorphous, often earthy, a colloidal precipitate; op, with a dull LR and greenish-white STR; H 3–4; SG 2·2–2·8; occurs at Adelaide, S Aust (Ausl); in Noumea (New Caledonia); Riddle, Oreg and Webster, NC (USA); Vogtland (Ger); Malaga (Spn); Revda (USSR); Chile.

Kaolin, kaolinite or china clay is basic aluminium silicate, $Al_2Si_2O_5(OH)_4$, forming scales of hexagonal shape but triclinic structure, or clay-like masses; white, grey or yellow; op, with a dull LR; H 2–$2\frac{1}{2}$; SG 2·6; widespread, including Cornwall and Devon (Eng); Ark (USA); Limoges (Fra); Saxony (Ger); Silesia (Pol); Czsl, Ita, Jap.

Gibbsite is hydrated aluminium oxide, Al_2O_3, forming six-sided monoclinic scales or plates, nodular concretions and earthy coatings; xls are trl, other forms op; white, grey, greenish or reddish, with vitreous LR; H 3; SG 2·3–2·4; occurs with bauxite, in serpentine, talc-schists, and from the alteration of corundum in Ariz, Ark, Mass, Pa, NY (USA); Hesse (Ger); Vesuvius (Ita); Urals (USSR); Fra, Hun, N Swd, Nor, Turkey, India, Guyana, Tasmania.

Bauxite, of similar composition, is an amorphous colloidal deposit; earthy or nodular; white, grey, brown, green or yellow; op, with dull LR; H 1–3; SG 2·5; some in Ayrshire (Scot); Antrim (NI); also Wyo, Ark, Ala, Ga (USA); Arles

(Fra); Nassau (Ger); Ita, Yug, Hun, USSR, India, Africa, Braz, Jamaica, Guyana.

Wavellite, basic aluminium phosphate, $Al_6(PO_4)_4(OH)_6$. $9H_2O$, is orthorhombic, with acicular xls, usually found in distinctive globular aggregates; trp–trl, blue, green, white or colourless; vitreous LR and white STR; H $3\frac{1}{2}$–4; SG 2·3; dissolves easily in HCl; found at Barnstaple, Devon (Eng); Cork Co and Tipperary Co (Eire); Garland Co, Ark; Dunellen, Fla; Chester Co, Pa and Colo (USA); Saxony (Ger); Llallagua (Bolivia).

Turquoise is a hydrous copper aluminium phosphate, $CuAl_6(PO_4)_4(OH)_8.5H_2O$, of triclinic structure, but nearly always massive. It is an attractive gemstone; blue and bluish green to green in colour; trl–op with a waxy LR; H 5–6; SG 2·6–2·9; found in veins and seams, often with limonite and chalcedony in lavas; pale blue *rashleighite* occurs in the china clay in Cornwall (Eng); Turq. in Ariz, San Bernadino Co, Calif, Lake Co, Colo, Battle Mt, Nev and Campbell Co, Va (USA); Egypt, Iran, Chile.

17

ORGANIC MINERALS AND GEMS

ORGANIC MINERALS

The action of living things over long periods of time has given rise to vast sedimentary deposits, including the chalk beds, which consist mostly of calcite from the shells of tiny floating sea animals together with the larger shells of bottom dwellers, preserved as fossils. The remains of vegetable matter accumulating in forests and swamps turned into peat, as is still happening today, and eventually into coal, also forming extensive beds all over the world. We have seen (p 158ff) how the deposition of iron and manganese ores may be helped by bacteria in swamps and lakes, where fossil or more recent bones also provide a source of phosphate ions, giving rise to minerals.

There are several substances of organic origin which are valued as gem materials and are treated together here. They are: amber; jet; pearl; fossil ivory; and coral. Mention is also made of coprolites, which are not, however, gemstones. All of them have one thing in common: they were once part of the bodies of plants or animals and are non-crystalline solids.

VEGETABLE GEMSTONES

Amber is the fossil resin of conifers and similar trees, chiefly from the lower Tertiary times, found as rounded lumps in river deposits, and because of its lightness (SG appr 1·1) often washed up on sea beaches, as in East Anglia (Eng) and especially

172

on the Baltic coasts. The organic origin of amber is attested by the insects sometimes found entombed and preserved in it. They are fancifully known as ' dragons in amber '. Amber consists of carbon, hydrogen and oxygen in a variable ratio, approximating to the formula $C_{40}H_6O_4$, and a little sulphur, so that it is not a true chemical compound but a mixture. It contains volatile oils, resin acid and succinic acid, the latter of which is absent from copal, an otherwise comparable substance. Amber is trp–trl and resinous in LR, usually yellow, also whitish, reddish or brown with a white STR; H 2–2½; sometimes fluorescent; becomes negatively charged with electricity when rubbed. Other localities include mines in the north of England, Sicily, Poland, Rumania, Burma and Mexico. *Copal resin*, found in New Zealand, Zaire and Zanzibar, is a similar material, consisting of resin acids, resenes and essential oils, usually contemporary or recent fossil; it is more fusible than amber.

Jet is a form of *lignite*, which in turn is a form of coal. Over time the peaty remains of forests and marshes lose most of the hydrogen, oxygen and nitrogen they contain until they are reduced largely to carbon in an amorphous state. The highest form of coal is anthracite which is about 95 per cent carbon, and the lowest is lignite, containing about 72 per cent of carbon. Accordingly, lignite is quite moist and burns with a lot of smoke, while anthracite is nearly smokeless. *Lignite* is compact with a brilliant LR, and frequently shows traces of fossil leaves and other vegetable remains. *Jet* is simply lignite that is hard and compact enough to take a polish and not soil the hands. It is, of course, black, op, with a dull resinous LR and black STR; H 3–4 (coal is generally 2–2½); SG about 1·3. It burns with a bright smoky flame, and, like amber, becomes electrically charged when rubbed. It can be found near Whitby and Scarborough, Yorkshire (Eng); Sound of Bute (Scot); Spn and elsewhere. Jet was the favourite ornamental material in ancient Britain, and has been used for mourning jewellery in modern times; carved jet ornaments are still being made today, more particularly at Whitby.

Pearls are cysts forming inside the shells of molluscs, especially oysters and pearl-mussels, and consist mostly of calcium carbonate, $CaCO_3$, in the form of iridescent nacre (mother-of-pearl) deposited in concentric shells around a grain of sand or other body which is irritating the animal. The pearly LR and play of colour is due to reflection on thin layers of material in the pearl, as in opal (p 132). Natural pearls can be found in the sea, particularly in warmer climates, by divers rigorously trained in unaided diving, or perhaps with diving apparatus. But pearls can be farmed or 'cultured' by introducing suitable foreign bodies under the shells of the mussels.

Pearls, however, also form in fresh-water molluscs, and may be found in some unpolluted mountain streams and rivers in the British Isles and North America. Such mussels as *Anodonta cygnea* and *Unio margaritifera* produce river pearls. Searching for these requires a pair of good waders or wellingtons to keep out the cold and damp, a drum or bucket with a flat glass bottom, and a forked stick for poking about among the stones. Patience is also necessary, and June to August is the right season for the northern hemisphere.

Ivory comes from the tusks of elephants and walruses, and the ivory from the fossil mammoths of Siberia is of good commercial quality. Of course, it must be remembered that in this case even the bodies have often been remarkably, sometimes perfectly, preserved for thousands of years in the permafrost. Even so, as the most durable part of the skeleton, tusks of these animals have effectively resisted decay in many recent deposits – such as the clays of south-east England – together with other fossilised bones which may be loosely described as 'mineralogical ivory'.

The *coral* used in jewellery consists of the skeletons of certain coelenterates, known as polyps, which are found in warm seas, nowadays especially in Australasia and the Pacific and Indian Oceans, but also in the Mediterranean. The blood red to pink, sometimes white and yellow, branches of coral are used for beads and other ornaments and are chemically calcium carbonate, often altered to dolomite, and thus containing magnesium carbonate as well. The climates of the Earth have changed over geological time, and some shallow seas where corals used to grow have become dry land. Fossil remains of corals are not rare and may be found, for instance, in Devon (Eng) and Sutherland (Scot). Most of the colour is lost in fossilisation but the pattern survives and may look attractive in polished section, which is also true of many other fossils such as the silicified remains of sponges and bryozoa occasionally embodied in flints.

Also of organic origin are *coprolites*, or ' excrement stones ', made up of the fossilised droppings of fishes, reptiles and mammals, which have been transformed into calcium phosphate and carbonate. They have a corrugated or convoluted surface consisting of dispersed nodules, but sometimes form large masses of several tons.

Coprolite is grey, brown, sometimes black; H 2–4; SG 2·2– 2·5; occurs in the greensands of Kent and Sussex (Eng); N Wal; Ala, Fla, NC, SC (USA); Hudson Bay (Can); Belgium, France, USSR.

18

MINERALS IN COLLECTIONS AND JEWELLERY

COLLECTIONS

In museums minerals are commonly arranged according to chemical affinity and housed in shallow boxes with glass tops. The boxes may be raised at the back and slope forward for easier viewing. Alternatively, the exhibits, especially the large ones, are placed on glazed shelves or in glazed cabinets. A private collector may follow the same plan. But the usual difficulty is the shortage of space, which may mean that most of the finds will have to be kept in drawers or on bookshelves.

To make the best possible use of their varied shapes and to avoid confusion, it is recommended to arrange the specimens in shallow open trays, made of cardboard, metal, wood or plastic, which can be stacked on top of one another. If the specimens are arranged on a shelf, preferably supported on an outside frame with narrow ledges, any tray can be withdrawn without disturbing the others. It is also useful to secure the minerals in position to prevent them slipping about when the tray is moved and to label them, giving the name, place of origin and any other particulars that may be apposite. In the case of a cardboard tray, the minerals may be secured by making U-shaped incisions and bending back the cardboard tongues thus obtained so as to grip the specimen on the sides. This can also be done more elegantly by means of small blocks or angular pieces of wood, cardboard or plastic glued to the bottom of the tray.

All foreign matter such as lichen, mud, clay, ferruginous or calcareous coatings (see p 86) should be removed. This applies also to any excess of rock that is inessential or obstructs the view of the minerals we wish to display. Too much dressing and chiselling, however, tends to give the rock matrix an unnatural look, and should be avoided. Small loose crystals, waterworn pebbles, chips, or cut gems are best placed in open boxes (eg bottom halves of the plastic containers for typewriter ribbons) on cotton wool or lint. Water-soluble minerals, which absorb atmospheric moisture and run, or deliquesce, must be kept in hermetically sealed jars, or at least in sealed bags of transparent plastic.

As a rule the minerals are shown in their natural state, but in some cases, eg with agates, it is instructive to have a polished section which reveals the internal structure or some hidden beauties. Many mineral collections contain cut and polished stones, including species that are too soft for jewellery yet make very attractive gems.

Thus the dividing line between a collector and a *lapidary*, whose province it is to cut and polish gems, becomes somewhat blurred.

CUTTING AND POLISHING STONES WITHOUT MACHINERY

If a specimen has a reasonably even surface this can be smoothed down and polished with comparative ease. Minor roughnesses can be ground off or down with an ordinary steel file (H $6\frac{3}{4}$) on minerals up to about 5 on Mohs' scale; a diamond file (charged with diamond powder) would have to be used with harder stones. Minerals with distinct cleavage can be split along the cleavage planes with a hammer and chisel. But slicing hard minerals without a diamond saw (see p 188f) is a slow and laborious job.

Stones of up to H 5 can be primed with a file and cut with a metal saw. A more efficient way is to use a braided steel wire and a coarse silicon-carbide grit (grade 80–120). Quartz or, if available, garnet sand may be used instead with softer material not over H 6.

The specimen to be cut is firmly fixed to a flat stone slab or a wooden board with sealing or dopping wax (see p 190). The contiguous surfaces of the specimen and support must be cleaned with soap and water and methylated spirit or carbon tetrachloride to remove all traces of grease or fat and must be dry to enable the wax to grip. If possible, it is better to make a shallow groove in the stone along the line of the cut with a file first. The abrasive grit is then fed into the groove with a little oil, paraffin or water as coolant and lubricant, and the wire is drawn to and fro (reciprocated) over it. The cutting work is done by the grit, not by the wire, which acts simply as a carrier for it; and the cutting action is the same as in a mineralogical scratch (p 47), ie it relies on the grit being harder than the stone so that no great pressure is required. The groove can be made with wire and grit, without recourse to a file. Oil or paraffin should not be used with turquoise, opal and some other porous materials. The grinding slurry should be wiped or washed off from time to time. Malachite or serpentine can be cut quite easily in this way; with agate or quartz the progress is somewhat slow.

Once a good clean cut has been made, we have a reasonably even section to which it is not too difficult to give a high polish. This requires a piece of plate glass and an assortment of grits and powders of successively finer grade, indicated by an increasing number, which is that of the openings per square inch in the mesh used as a sieve in grading.

Silicon carbide of H $9\frac{1}{2}$–$9\frac{3}{4}$ will do for anything short of diamond; diamond grits are more effective for the very hard stones such as corundum and chrysoberyl – and, of course, necessary for diamond itself – but they are also much more expensive. The higher cost is somewhat offset by their greater efficiency – they also last longer. Silicon-carbide grits of grades 80, 120 and 400 or 120, 320 and 500 are successively used, and will give the treated face a dull sheen. The grits are mixed with water, paraffin or oil on the glass into a paste – not too thin and not too much of it – and the face to be polished is rubbed in the paste by a gentle figure-of-eight movement. Reversing the sense of rotation may help. The lubricant and abrasive may have to be added as the grinding proceeds.

The method consists in imparting to the surface progressively finer scratches until these become so fine as to be invisible without magnification. Strict *abrasive hygiene* must be observed, which means that not a single grain of a coarser abrasive should be allowed to infiltrate a finer grade. The abrasives of different grades must be kept separate in closed containers; the plate, the ' workpiece ' and the hands must be scrupulously cleaned before passing on to the next working stage. Abrasive grains can easily lodge under the fingernails, on cuffs and other clothing in the vicinity of the work and all these must be attended to. This is a general injunction and applies to all lapidary work.

For a good result it is advisable to spend some time at the last grinding stage before the final polishing, which is done with cerium oxide, tin oxide, levigated alumina or Linde-A (an American product) on a Perspex plate scored with a sharp knife or razor blade to hold the powder, a felt or leather pad lubricated with water. A well-polished face should be splendent (p 33) and show no scratches under a magnifying glass.

The necessary packaged abrasives and polishing powders of assorted grades can be purchased from lapidary outfitters.

Curved surfaces can be cut and polished in the same way by rocking the stone and/or using a Pyrex fruit bowl for support in the grinding and a curved piece of Perspex, eg from an old motor-cycle visor, for the polishing stage. Cabochons can be made fairly easily, but require mounting on a dopping stick (p 187). However, accurate faceting is difficult to obtain by hand, unless the stone be pre-cut on a machine, as every facet must be correctly angled and placed and the hand has a tendency to tilt the stone, which results in rounded edges.

TUMBLING

Tumbling is the lowest grade of lapidary work, but it does require simple power-driven machinery.

The method may be described as artificial erosion, and involves the same stages as have been described above. The erosion takes place in a watertight container, which holds the stones, water and abrasive, and is kept in gentle but constant motion, rotary or vibratory, by an electric motor through an appropriate gearing.

The object of the exercise is to produce pretty polished pebbles or *baroque* jewels of more or less irregular shape. These are mostly some kind of silica, but any massive or poorly crystallised material, including some rocks such as porphyries, rhyolites and obsidians, is suitable for tumbling provided that it is of substantially uniform hardness and lacks well-developed cleavage which may cause the stones to disintegrate in the process. The tumbling container, called *drum* or *barrel*, may be cylindrical or polygonal and be made of wood, plastic, rubber or rubber-lined metal. Such barrels are not expensive, and are best purchased ready-made. It is advisable to have a separate barrel for each of the four processing stages, and especially for the final polishing stage. Silicon-carbide grits are used almost exclusively for the grinding; levigated alumina, cerium oxide and tin oxide are used for polishing – the last-named being the most favoured.

As the barrel revolves or vibrates, the stones in the *charge* are rubbed against one another and the intervening abrasive, and so gradually become rounded, smoothed and polished. They should be of at least roughly the same hardness and toughness (for instance obsidian, which is splintery, should not be mixed with quartz balls) and approximately the same size, although it is good to add some small pea-sized stones, which act like ball-bearings and ensure more intimate contact between the main charge and the abrasive. Pebbles and hammer-broken material should not be mixed.

The action depends on gravity and so will not be effective unless there is enough weight. On the other hand, the stones must have room to move. A rotary drum should be between half and two-thirds full; in a vibratory drum the clearance is less important, but it, too, will become ineffective if jammed tight. If there are not enough stones the deficiency must be redressed with suitable ballast. Beach pebbles will do in most cases.

The abrasive makes about a tenth of the weight of the stones for H 7 and less for softer material. There should be enough water to cover up the charge. As the grinding proceeds water evaporates, and the rock flour removed from the stones forms a thick sludge. There is also an evolution of gases, which may cause wooden or metal drums to blow up like bottles with fermenting fruit juice, although commercial polythene and rubber-lined barrels are more or less immune to this danger. In any event a 6in drum should be inspected once every twenty-four hours or so; larger ones less frequently. The water and abrasive may need replenishing. If the sludge becomes too thick it may immobilise the charge. Should this threaten all the stones must be removed, washed and recharged with fresh abrasive and water. Incidentally, the tumbling sludge is like cement and sets to hard stone in an hour or so; it must on no account be poured down a sink.

The first stage is deemed complete when the stones have lost their blemishes and sharp corners, which will not happen simultaneously for the whole charge, so that some of the material may have to be taken out and replaced before the rest is ready.

A rotary drum is usually laid free between two shafts about

two-thirds of its diameter apart: one of these shafts is driven by a $\frac{1}{4}$hp or like motor through a V-belt and pulley transmission; the other is freely rotatable. For a round barrel 6in in diameter, 50rpm is usual; and 30rpm for an octagonal one of the same diameter. For larger and smaller drums the speeds are varied in inverse proportion to the square root of the diameter. A reduction of 25 per cent is recommended for polishing.

The processing time varies according to material, type of tumbler and barrel diameter. If we take chalcedonic silica and a round rotary 6in drum it takes five or six days for each of the first two grinding stages, and three days for the third stage. The polishing will again need five days or so, but the final rinse only six to eight hours. All times are less for larger and vibratory drums.

In passing from one stage to the next, abrasive hygiene must be scrupulously observed. Everything must be washed and rinsed and all traces of the coarser abrasive removed. It is advisable to wear rubber gloves.

Before the polishing operation all stones are carefully cleaned and examined for coarse scratches. If they have any, they are returned to the preceding stage. Those passed are placed in the polishing drum with the polishing agent, water and vermiculite to cushion the charge. If the water is hard a little detergent may be helpful. The proportion of polishing powder is about an ounce to a pound of stone. A further rinsing run in a thick mixture of water and detergent is recommended, but is not essential. As in the previous case the polished stones should be splendent and equally shiny, wet or dry. They are now ready for setting in jewellery.

TRADITIONAL TYPES OF CUT

A cut and polished stone is a gem (although strictly speaking this term applies to carved or engraved stones only) and may be either a rounded *cabochon* or faceted. Cabochons may be high or low and have various outlines: round, oval, square, polygonal, cruciform, which are available in the so-called *Bitner templates*. Since the stones so cut are usually opaque or translucent, the bottom of the ' beetle ' is usually left flat and unpolished. But in a *double cabochon* it has a polished surface of lower curvature; in a *hollow cabochon* the bottom part is polished and concave. This type of cut is used for very dark transparent stones, eg some garnets.

However, opaque stones, eg haematite, may have a faceted top part, or *crown* (p 101). The *rose* is a cut where only the crown is faceted; the *double rose* is like a faceted version of the double cabochon. The simple rose ends upwards in a six-sided pyramid, each triangular *star facet* of which adjoins the downward triangle of a *main facet* with the apex on the girdle. Between each pair of main facets there are two *cross* or *break facets* in the form of right-angled triangles standing on the girdle. These eighteen facets make up the *dentelle*.

The other faceted gems are developments of two standard types: the *brilliant* and the *step* or *trap cut*. Brilliants are used mainly for diamond and gemstones of high RI; steps for coloured stones of lower RI. But this is ultimately a matter of taste, and there are mixed cuts containing features from the rose, brilliant and/or step in various combinations.

A narrow *girdle* divides the crown from the pavilion of the *standard brilliant*. The girdle is itself faceted, but need not be polished, and is used for mounting the stone in a ring or other fitting. The crown is usually half as high as the pavilion, which may end up downwards in a *culet* point or *culet table*. The *crown table* is a horizontal octagonal facet, occupying about half of the gem's width, and has small *star facets* along its sides. Between these kite-shaped (deltoidal) *main facets* descend to the girdle, and between the main facets triangular *break facets*, exactly like those of the rose but twenty in number, stand upon the girdle. The pavilion has a similar set of *break facets* facing those of the crown across the girdle; and between the break facets the eight *main facets* of the pavilion lead to the culet,

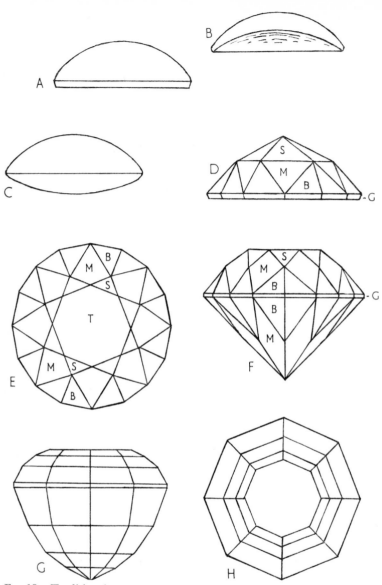

Fig 18   Traditional types of gem cut: A=cabochon with bevelled edge (to prevent chipping); B=hollow cabochon in section; C=double cabochon; D=rose cut from the side; E=standard round brilliant, crown from above; F=standard round brilliant from the side; G=example of step cut, side view; H=step cut, crown, from above (this is a 'round' variant, oblongs with unequal sides are more usual).   Facets: t=table; s=star; m=main; b=break.

where they may be cut off by a small octagonal table about an eighth of the gem in width.

This is the *round* standard brilliant of eightsome symmetry, to conform to the cubic system of diamond. But brilliants may be five-, six-, seven-, ten- or twelve-sided, oval, heart-shaped, pointed at one end (*pendeloque*) or at both ends (*marquise*); and various cuts, both simplified and ' complexified ' have been evolved from this pattern.

In the *step cut* we again have the crown and the pavilion, the former with a polygonal table; but there are no star facets and the facets along the sides of the table are steps of trapezium outline, progressively widening towards the girdle, usually in the ratio of 1:2:4. The pavilion is similarly stepped, the culet being a point, a ridge or a small table; in the former two cases all or the two end terminal facets respectively are triangular. The number of steps in the pavilion need not be the same as in the crown. Dark stones are cut shallow (low pavilion); pale ones are cut deep with more steps to the pavilion. There are variations on this theme; eg the *step rose*. A very simple variant of the step cut is the *table cut* in which the pavilion is a mirror image of the crown with only one or two steps between the table and the girdle. The steps may be replaced by star and break facets.

The *briolette* is a vertically elongated version of either the brilliant or the step cut, adapted for pendants.

The inclinations of the facets are adjusted to the critical angle in the way mentioned on p 57.

19
LAPIDARY WORK

BROAD OUTLINE

It will be appreciated that the compass of this book does not permit an exhaustive coverage of lapidary art and craft, and those interested must be referred to special works on this subject, such as V. A. Firsoff's *Working with Gemstones*, David & Charles (1974). The general principles, however, have already been broached in the preceding chapter and are easy enough to grasp.

The work of cutting and polishing a gem may be divided into several distinct stages: (1) the part to be cut is isolated as a blank; (2) the blank is trimmed; (3) it is roughly fashioned or *preformed* by grinding into shape; (4) smoothed by *sanding*; (5) polished. Each stage requires special tools and techniques, and a distinction must be drawn between cutting a cabochon and a faceted gem.

In some cases the cabochon is cut from a single crystal, chip or pebble. As a rule, however, the raw material takes the shape of a fairly large lump of stone which has to be *sliced* or *slabbed* with a *diamond saw*. The outline of the cabochons to be cut from the slab are then drawn upon it with an *aluminium pencil*, and a Bitner template (p 183) may be used for this purpose. Next the marked blanks are cut off with a *trimming saw*, which is somewhat smaller and thinner than the *slabbing saw* previously used although most amateurs rest content with a single general-purpose diamond saw. The isolated blank is trimmed to the marked outline, leaving an adequate margin, with the saw and/or file, and small salients may be pulled off with pliers.

At this stage, if not sooner, the stone becomes too difficult to hold in the hand and is mounted with *dopping wax, sealing wax* or other kind of cement upon a *dopstick, dopping stick* or *dop*, which is a piece of wooden dowelling or a metal rod, 4-6in long, of a diameter somewhat smaller than the shorter diameter of the finished cabochon. This done, the superfluous parts of the blank can be ground off on a *grinding wheel*. A grinding wheel is an artificial grindstone, 1-1½in thick and 4-8in in diameter, made with bonded silicon-carbide grit and driven in rotation by an electric motor. Flat surfaces can be preformed on the side of the wheel, but most of the grinding work is done by applying the stone gently to the perimeter against the sense of rotation. The wheel is lubricated with a trickle of water. As a rule, use is made of two wheels of grades 80, 100 or 120 and 220. This corresponds to the first two stages in tumbling. Alternatively this work can be done on horizontal revolving discs or *laps* charged with grits of the same grade.

Both cabochons and faceted gems are preformed on grinding wheels. Afterwards, however, the two part company for, whereas a cabochon can be given the correct shape on the wheels, the facets require great precision in the inclination and spacing round the gem. This necessitates a lapping machine with a *faceting head* which receives the dop in a *quill*, and whereby it can be given the right slope with a protractor and turned round through the correct angle, or *indexed*, for each new facet. Obviously every facet has to be taken through every cutting stage to the final polishing, and the pavilion and crown have to be worked separately, which involves reversing the stone upon the dop. This is a tricky operation as the two halves must be perfectly aligned, and is carried out by means of a *transfer jig*, a flat-topped dop being brought up against the table to

187

make sure that it lies true. Double and hollow cabochons likewise need reversing, the two halves being worked separately, but the alignment need not be so fine as in faceting. The concave part of a hollow cabochon is worked on a *button lap*.

To continue with our simple cabochon, the grinding is followed by the sanding in which use is made of silicon-carbide or diamond cloths, papers or plastic discs, exchangeably mounted on some kind of driven support. This support is traditionally a *sanding wheel* to which the exchangeable wet/dry paper or cloth disc is attached with non-hardenable adhesive. But there are also *drum* and *belt sanders*; and if we want to do it in style there are profiled hardwood cylinders charged with graded diamond abrasives, which do the work of grinders, sanders and polishers as well.

Sanding cloths or their equivalents of grades 220 and 320 or 400, 500 and 600 are successively used, and the 220 grade may be dispensed with if the stone has been done on a 220 grinder. The cloths are lubricated with water from a squeezy bottle or an automatic feed; but the diamond-charged wooden drums are run dry.

Abrasive hygiene must be strictly observed as usual.

Faceting involves the same processing stages on appropriately charged laps. The facets are not cut one after another, but alternately, beginning with the *mains*, and left somewhat undercut, ie not cut to their full depth, which allows for the material to be removed in subsequent working and the correction of minor faults. It is rather like salting food. Oversalted food and an overcut gem are hard to put right, and in the latter case the stone may have to be completely recut to a smaller size.

Polishing has some special features which are discussed at the end of this chapter.

DIAMOND SAWS

The operative part of a diamond saw is a rotary disc or *blade*, of mild steel or phosphor bronze, charged with diamond grit

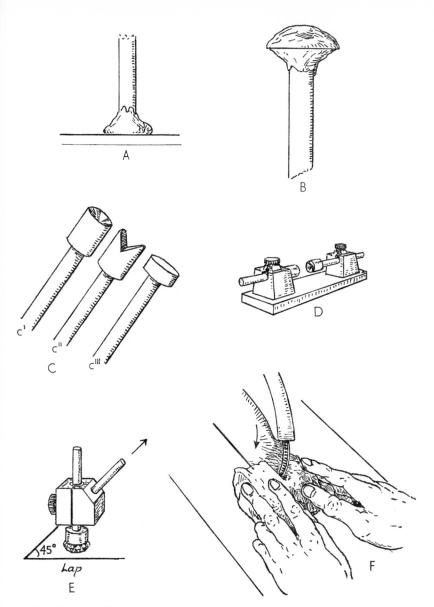

FIG 19   Lapidary tools: *A*=shaping a dopping button; *B*=cabochon rough dopped; *C*=faceting dopsticks: *c′* for round pavilion; *c″* for oblong pavilion; for checking the correct attitude of a table in the transfer jig, *c‴* is mounted on the one side and the stone is brought up against it; D=transfer jig; *E*=45° dop, used for cutting a table. The dop with the stone is inserted vertically downwards, and the permanent dop fits the faceting quill at 45°; the arrow points to the faceting head. *F*=feeding a stone by hand to a diamond saw. The arrow shows sense of rotation.

at the rim. The thickness varies from $\frac{1}{16}$ to $\frac{1}{8}$in with the diameter, which is anything between 4 and 36in, or their metric equivalents. Still smaller, very fine *slitting saws* are used in high-grade faceting work. The blade is thickest at the rim, to prevent its becoming jammed in the cut. There are two types of blade: in the one the abrasive is sintered into the rim all along it, in the other – in segments or notches. The sense of rotation of the first type is reversible; that of the second – fixed as specified by the makers.

The blade is usually mounted vertically in a suitable frame with a working table and driven by a $\frac{1}{8}$ to $\frac{1}{4}$hp electric motor at adjustable speed towards the operator, under a splash guard. Below the table the edge of the blade dips into a tank with coolant–lubricant, which is commonly a mixture of oil and paraffin, although Texaco 519 and Castrol 303 oils are preferable. Water is used for porous stones (p 178). After a time the lubricant becomes fouled with sawing waste and has to be replaced. The blade must not be allowed to overheat, and it is very important to present the workpiece at right angles to the blade and guide it accurately throughout the sawing. Towards the end, when only a thin bridge of stone remains, it is better to break this by hand. Correct guiding can be obtained by pushing the stone lightly on the two sides with the thumb and two fingers of both hands (Fig 19). Special feed clamps may be provided.

If the stone is too small to hold comfortably and/or too irregularly shaped, it may have to be mounted on wood or in a block made of vermiculite and white cement on which the cutting lines are marked. The mixture is placed in a paper-lined box and given four days to set.

After a time the blade grows dull, owing to the grit being driven into the metal. Reversible blades will benefit by remounting back to front, and any blade can be revived by sawing through a soft brick.

DOPPING

Sealing wax is quite adequate for dopping in most cases, especially if a scale of *shellac* is placed under the stone. Special *dopping wax* can be bought from lapidary outfitters or made according to the following recipe: sealing wax 4oz; shellac ½oz; plaster of Paris ¼oz; powdered resin ¼oz; heat and stir into a uniform mixture.

For use the wax is heated until plastic. But some stones, and opal in particular, are very sensitive to heat and easily crack under thermal stress. A mixture of cornflower and acetone adhesive may advantageously be used cold in this case and removed with acetone. The drawback of cold dopping is that the cement takes some time to set and has to be dissolved.

Otherwise there is no fundamental difference between the cold and hot dopping, except that the hot-dopping wax must be heated before application. This is best done on a hot plate, eg by placing the wax in a shallow tin on top of a U-shaped strip of sheet metal over a spirit lamp. The wax should flow easily, but must not boil, which makes it brittle. The dop is dipped into the molten wax and picks up a blob of it, which is flattened into a nailhead shape by pressing the dop lightly against a flat moist surface. Also, the stone must be heated slowly, say, in a dish with sand, to take the wax, which is moulded around its base into a bevel, leaving the working edge free (Fig 19, a and b.)

To remove the stone from the dop, it may be enough to give it a sharp knock, to put it into a refrigerator, or under a cold tap. If this does not work the wax will have to be reheated and the stone pulled off. Any wax left adhering to the stone can be washed off with methylated spirit or carbon tetrachloride. It is, however, very important to avoid sharp changes of temperature, which may cause the stone to crack; this applies equally to heating and cooling.

The dopsticks used in cabochon work may be of any thickness, but the metal faceting dops have to fit the quill in the head and are standardised, differing in thickness and shape at the receiving end. This may be shaped flat, as a hollow cone or a triangular trough, to accommodate the pavilions and crowns of faceted gems (Fig 19, c).

The *transfer jig* (Fig 19, d) consists of two clamping devices for the reception of the dop with the stone on the one side and of the transfer dop on the other. The former dop (not stone) is heated until the stone is sufficiently loose to accept the mouldable wax on the empty dop, which is then brought into contact with it to effect the transfer. A flat-headed dop is used to check up the alignment of the table.

MORE ABOUT LAPS AND WHEELS

As already mentioned, a *lap* is mounted horizontally and a *wheel* vertically, but the distinction is purely semantic as both may perform the same work. However, the essential difference is that vertical mounting necessitates ingrained abrasive, whereas loose abrasive will do for a horizontal lap. Thus if we want to economise and have one disc for different abrasives this must be a horizontal lap. On the other hand, omnibus combination machines, which do all the work from sawing to polishing with interchangeable discs, usually employ vertical mounting for reasons of structural convenience. They have to use ingrained abrasives accordingly. This reduces the risk of contamination with coarser particles, which can be troublesome in the case of an all-purpose lap. The offending grain may become embedded in it and be very difficult to weed out so that the lap may have to be resurfaced or even discarded altogether. The ordinary household dust contains grains of sand which make nasty scratches, so that when not in use laps should be protected against it, eg by polythene covers.

Not all laps are equally suitable for all jobs and materials, and a skilled faceter will have an assortment of them. Generally speaking, the harder the stone and the coarser the grade the tougher will be the corresponding lap.

Laps are made of cast iron, copper, tin, lead, type metal,

pewter, hardwood, such as teak and mahogany, plywood, plastic, leather, and for very soft materials even of beeswax with 10–15 per cent of carnauba wax, supported on muslin and set in wood. Bort or diamond powder is rolled into a copper lap with a copper roller. Usually, though, the abrasive is applied as and when necessary in the form of paste, mixed with oil or water, by means of a soft water-colour brush, working from the centre outwards. Special manufactured pastes and liquids are on the market, and diamond grits and powders are sold mixed with an *extender fluid* in disposable syringes, in different colours according to grade.

Since a lap revolves very fast, it has to be scored to hold the abrasive, unless this is rolled in. The scoring may be radial or concentric. Special scoring tools exist, but a one-inch-long segment of a hacksaw having twenty-four teeth to an inch will produce good concentric grooves if applied to a revolving lap. It is useful to have a broad, shallow, circular groove at the edge for working cabochons.

In time not just the abrasive but the disc or wheel itself is worn down. If the wear is uneven the surface becomes bumpy, inefficient and even dangerous. For this reason the stone should be moved about so as to cover as much of the lap's face or the grinding wheel's perimeter as possible. Even so, sooner or later, the lap or wheel will need resurfacing with a *trimming tool* or *scraper*. A razor-blade with a stiff backing inclined against the sense of rotation will serve for the softer laps. A *diamond wheel dresser* is used to revive an ailing grinder.

Another point to be borne in mind is that the surface speed of a disc increases in proportion to the distance from its centre, or hub, so that if a stone is kept in the same position it will be unevenly cut, to avoid which it should be rotated.

POLISHING

Polishing action differs somewhat from the grinding and cutting discussed so far in as much as it relies not so much on the wearing off and replacing of coarser scratches by finer ones as on the formation of a thin film of fused stone, known as the *Beilby layer*, due to frictional heat. This is how comparatively soft polishing agents, such as *putty powder*, can impart a high gloss to a hard stone; and also why coarse scratches are very difficult to remove by polishing alone, so that none should be allowed to survive the last sanding stage.

Most of the polishing is done on *buffing* laps or wheels (drums), made or covered with hard-packed felt or other fabric or leather, into which the polishing powder is rubbed with a little water. The powder, being very fine, forms an adhesive paste which does not need much water. In fact, it works best when nearly dry as otherwise it may not generate enough heat for a Beilby layer to arise. This is also why polishing requires high working speeds. But a Beilby layer is not an unqualified blessing, as it may recrystallise and produce a dull surface which has to be ground off. It is also dangerous to generate too much heat as this may cause the stone to crack. It should, therefore, be periodically inspected and the operation interrupted if necessary.

No Beilby layer is formed if fine diamond powders (size below 1 micron = 0·001mm), Linde-A (graded down to 0·3 microns) or Linde-B (down to 0·05 microns) are used for polishing. Tripoli, too, relies on plain abrasion. Such hard polishing agents operate at lower lap speeds, which largely eliminates the danger of overheating.

Not all materials respond equally well to the same method and polishing agent. Cerium oxide gives good results with chalcedony, but may not be equally effective on quartz, and so on. Most polishing powders are lubricated with water, but diamond powders are usually worked with paraffin (see also p 172). No water at all is used on wooden drums or laps charged with diamond. The stone, however, unless absorbent, may be periodically dipped in olive oil.

It is a mistake to charge a buff or lap with too much polishing powder; an old well-worked surface will have some powder, which has been ground down to smaller grain, embodied in it, and will yield a fine polish.

A well-polished gem should show no scratches under a linear magnification of 5–10.

TABLE 1 IGNEOUS ROCKS

Classification according to grain					Minerals	
Coarse	Medium	Fine	SG	SiO$_2$	Essential	Accessory
Acid High SiO$_2$ Low SG Pale colour Granite (orthoclase); adamellite (ortho = plag; hornblende); granodiorite (more plag than ortho)	Microgranite; quartz porphyry	Rhyolite; toscanite; dacite	2.5 2.7	66-80	Quartz orthoclase micas, maybe plagioclase, amphiboles, pyroxenes	apatite; zircon; magnetite; sphene; topaz; tourmaline; beryl
Intermediate Syenite (more ortho than plag); monzonite (ortho = plag); diorite (plag)	Microsyenite; porphyry; microdiorite; porphyrite	Trachyte; trachyandesite; andesite	2.6 2.8	55-66	Orthoclase and plagioclase hornblende, maybe micas, pyroxenes	quartz; apatite; zircon; sphene; iron ores
Basic Low SiO$_2$ High SG Dark colour Gabbro (olivine and augite); norite (olivine and hypersthene)	Dolerite	Basalt; tephrite (leucite, nepheline and analcite)	2.9 3.0	45-55	Plagioclase augite or diallage, maybe olivine, hornblende, nepheline, analcite	apatite; spinel; magnetite; ilmenite; biotite; hauyne; rutile; zeolites
Ultrabasic Peridotite (olivine) picrite (olivine, augite, some plag); perknite (pyroxenes)		Augitite (augite); limburgite (olivine and augite)	3.3	38-45	Olivine, magnetite, augite, hornblende or pyroxenes	

Ortho, orthoclase; plag, plagioclase

TABLE 2 METAMORPHIC ROCKS

Rocks	Colour	Texture	Parent rocks	Metamorphic process	Rock-forming minerals	Accessory minerals
Gneiss 1	as granites	coarse grained, banded	acid igneous or sedimentary	regional, high grade	quartz, felspar, mica, pyroxene; maybe andalusite, codierite, sillimanite	epidote, hornblende, garnet, apatite, rutile, zircon, iron ores
Granulite 2	as granites	granular	acid igneous or sedimentary	regional, high to medium grade	quartz, felspar, garnet, pyroxene; maybe biotite, kyanite	apatite, zircon, rutile, epidote, hercynite, iron spinel
Schist 3	pale, often greyish	foliated, crystalline	sedimentary	regional, medium grade	quartz, mica, paragonite; maybe garnet, staurolite	albite, epidote, rutile, graphite, calcite
Phyllite 4	dark grey, greenish	foliated, partly crystalline	sedimentary	regional, medium to low grade	sericite, chlorite, quartz	rutile, tourmaline, albite magnetite, ottrelite
Slate 5	greyish green, blue or purple	foliated, non-crystalline	shales	regional, low grade	none	no primary minerals
Amphibolite 'Greenstone' 6	dark green or green	foliated and fibrous, or massive	basic igneous and impure calcareous sediments	regional, high to medium grade	hornblende; maybe garnet, actinolite, tremolite, zoisite, glaucophane	albite, quartz, apatite, iron ores, sphene, rutile, epidote, chlorite
Serpentinite 7	green, streaked with red	massive	ultrabasic rocks	pneumatolytic	serpentine (alteration product of olivine)	garnet, bronzite, talc, tremolite
Quartzite 8	white, various other colours	massive	sandstone, gritstone	contact or regional	quartz	rarely
Marble 9	white, various other colours	massive or granular	limestone	contact or regional	calcite, dolomite	quartz, mica, talc, brucite, diopside, grossularite, idocrase
Hornfels 10	grey or brownish	massive	sedimentary, eg clay, shales etc	high grade, usually contact	quartz, felspar, mica	garnet, sphene, rutile, epidote, apatite, zircon, pyrites, corundum

TABLE 3 OPTICAL PROPERTIES OF MINERALS AND GEMSTONES

Mineral	RI	Dispersion	Refraction	Birefringence	Colour	Pleochroism
Amber	1.54	v low	single	nil	y, br	absent
Anatase	2.56-2.48	0.21-0.26	double	0.061	br, b	y-orange; pl b-dk b
Andalusite	1.64-1.63	0.013	double	0.010	y, br	strong rbr-g, yg
Apatite	1.64-1.63	0.013	double	0.003	various	y-gy; pl y-b
Axinite	1.69-1.68	0.015	double	0.010	br	strong b-br, yg
Azurite	1.84-1.73		double	0.110	azure b	b-dk b
Beryl:						
aquamarine	1.58-1.57	0.014	double	0.006	pl b	yg-b
emerald	1.59-1.56	0.014	double	0.006	g	yg-bg
morganite	1.60-1.58	0.014	double	0.009	pk, purple	pk-pl purple
Calcite	1.65-1.49	.008-.017	double	0.172	cls	absent
Cassiterite	2.09-1.99	0.071	double	0.096	br	distinct
Chalcedony	1.55-1.54			small	various	not seen
Chrysoberyl	1.76-1.75	0.015	double	0.009	y, g	weak g-y, r
Cordierite	1.55-1.54	0.014	double	0.008	b	strong ygy-dp b
Corundum:						
ruby					r	pl r-dp r
sapphires:	1.77-1.76	0.018	double	0.008	g	g-br
					b	bg-dp b
					v	pk-v
Datolite	1.67-1.62	0.016	double	0.044	cls, r, g	
Diamond	2.42	0.044	single	nil	various	absent
Diopside	1.70-1.67	0.016	double	.02-.03	g	very weak
Dioptase	1.70-1.64	.028-.036	double	0.053	g	dk g-pl g
Epidote	1.77-1.73	0.028	double	0.035	y, br, g	strong yg-dp br
Euclase	1.67-1.65	0.013	double	0.020	cls, g	weak cls, pl g-g
Fluorite	1.67-1.65	0.010	single	nil	various	absent
Garnets:						
almandine	1.82-1.78	0.024	single	nil	r, purple	absent
andradite	1.89-1.88	0.057	single	nil	brg, br	absent
demantoid	1.89-1.88	0.057	single	nil	g	absent
grossular	1.76-1.74	0.028	single	nil	pl olive g	absent
hessonite	1.76-1.74	0.028	single	nil	orange b	absent
pyrope	1.75-1.74	0.022	single	nil	dp r	absent
spessartite	1.81-1.80	0.027	single	nil	rbr, orange	absent
uvarovite	1.84-1.79		single	nil	emerald g	absent
Idocrase	1.72-1.71	0.019	double	0.004	g, br	weak g-y; br-r
Jadeite	1.67-1.65		double	0.013	g etc	weak
Kyanite	1.73-1.72	0.02	double	0.016	mainly b	pl b-dk b
Labradorite	1.57-1.56	0.012	double	0.008	gy	absent
Lazulite	1.64-1.60		double	0.036	b	strong cls-b
Natrolite	1.49-1.48		double	0.013	cls	absent
Oligoclase	1.55-1.54	0.012	double	0.007	cls, y	
Olivine						
(peridot)	1.69-1.65	0.020	double	0.038	olive g, br	weak g-yg, y
Opal	1.46-1.44		single	nil	various	absent
Orthoclase	1.53-1.52	0.012	double	0.010	various	absent
Phenakite	1.67-1.65	0.014	double	0.016	cls, y, bg	strong bg-rv
Prehnite	1.65-1.61		double	0.030	g, y, cls	
Quartz	1.55-1.54	0.013	double	0.009	various	very weak
Rutile	2.90-2.62	0.287	double	0.28	usu. dark	y, br-br, g, dk r
Scapolite	1.56-1.54	0.020	double	0.018	cls, y	
Sillimanite	1.65-1.63	0.015	double	0.020	cls	absent
Sinhalite	1.71-1.67	0.018	double	0.038	br	pl br-gbr-dk br
Smithsonite	1.85-1.62	0.14-0.31	double	0.230	b	
Sphene	2.06-1.91	0.051	double	0.1-0.15	br, y, g	yg-r; dp g-rbr
Spinel	1.72	0.020	single	nil	r, orange, b	absent
Spodumene	1.68-1.66	0.017	double	0.015	various	pk, cls-v; pl g-dk g
Staurolite	1.65-1.63	0.023	double	.011-.015	r, br	weak br-rbr
Topaz	1.63-1.62	0.014	double	0.008	various	distinct pl y-pl pk
Tourmalines:	1.65-1.62	0.017	double	0.035	various	strong pl-dk
	1.65-1.62	0.017	double	0.018	cls, br	
Zircons:						
high	1.99-1.92	0.038	double	0.07	b, various	pl b-pl y, cls
hyacinth	1.99-1.93	0.038	double	0.062	rbr	distinct r-y
low	1.78	0.038	double	low	various	unobservable
Zoisite	1.78-1.75		double	0.008	b, pk, etc	b-v-g (b stones)

b, blue; bg, blue green; br, brown; cls, colourless; dk, dark; dp, deep; gy, grey; pk, pink; pl, pale;
r, red; v, violet; w, white; y, yellow; yg, yellowish green.
Where two figures are given for dispersion, this shows the variation in different directions in highly birefringent stones.

TABLE 4 PHYSICAL PROPERTIES OF MINERALS

Mineral	Chemical formula	H	SG	Crystal system	Habit
Actinolite	$Ca_2(Fe,Mg)_5Si_8O_{22}(OH)_2$	5-6	2.9-3.2	mono	prismatic, radiating, fibrous
Adamite	$Zn_2(OH)AsO_4$	3½	4.3-4.5	ortho	small, many faceted prisms
Aegirine	$NaFeSi_2O_6$	6-6½	3.4-3.5	mono	striated prisms, fibrous
Agate, see chalcedony					
Albite (plagioclase)	$NaAlSi_3O_8$	6-6½	2.6	tric	tabular, often massive
Allanite (orthite) rare earth silicate		5½-6	3.5-4.2	mono	tabular, prismatic
Almandine (garnet), see also Table 6					
Alunite	$KAl_3(SO_4)_2(OH)_6$	3½-4	2.6-2.8	hex	rhombohedral, massive, earthy
Amalgam	Ag + Hg (variable)	3-3½	10-14	cubic	rhombododecahedral, massive
Amber	approx $C_{40}H_{64}O_4$ (variable)	2-2½	1.0-1.1	amor	amorphous nodules or plates
Analcite	$NaAlSi_2O_6.H_2O$	5-5½	2.2-2.3	cubic	xls, granular or massive
Anatase	TiO_2	5½-6	3.8-3.9	tetra	pyramids or tabular
Andalusite	Al_2SiO_5	7-7½	3.1-3.3	ortho	prismatic, granular or massive
Andesine (plagioclase 50-70% albite)		6	2.66	tric	commonly massive
Andradite (garnet), see also Table 6					
Anglesite	$PbSO_4$	2½-3	6.4	ortho	prismatic, tabular, massive
Anhydrite	$CaSO_4$	3-4	2.9-3.0	ortho	crystalline or massive
Anorthite (plagioclase)	$CaAl_2Si_2O_8$	6-6½	2.7	tric	prismatic or massive
Anorthoclase, similar to microcline					
Antimonite, see stibnite					
Antimony	Sb	3-3½	6.6-6.7	hex	pseudocubic, tabular, massive
Apatite	$Ca_5(PO_4)_3(F,Cl,OH)$	5	3.2	hex	crystalline or massive
Apophyllite	$KCa_4Si_8O_{22}(F,OH).8H_2O$	4½-5	2.3-2.5	tetra	prismatic, foliated, massive
Aragonite	$CaCO_3$	3½-4	2.9-3.0	ortho	prisms, fibrous or massive
Argentite	Ag_2S	2-2½	7.0-7.3	cubic	distorted xls, massive
Arsenic	As	3-4	5.6-5.9	hex	often granular or massive
Arsenopyrite	FeAsS	5½-6	5.9-6.2	ortho	prismatic or massive
Atacamite	$Cu_2Cl(OH)_3$	3-3½	3.8	ortho	prismatic, tabular, massive
Augite	$(Ca,Mg,Fe,Al)_2(Al,Si)_2O_6$	5-6	3.3-3.5	mono	usually prismatic
Autunite	$Ca(UO_2)_2(PO_4)_2.10-12HO$	2-2½	3.1	ortho	pseudo-tetragonal plates
Axinite	$Ca_2(Mn,Fe)Al_2BSi_4O_{15}.OH$	6½-7	3.3	tric	sharp blades, or massive
Azurite	$2CuCO_3.Cu(OH)_2$	3½-4	3.7-3.9	mono	prismatic, tabular, massive
Barytes	$BaSO_4$	3-3½	4.3-4.6	ortho	prismatic or massive
Bauxite	$Al_2O_3.2H_2O$	1-3	2.5	amor	earthy, oölitic
Beryl	$Al_2Be_3(Si_2O_6)_3$	7½-8	2.6-2.8	hex	6- or 12-sided prisms, massive
Biotite	$K(Mg,Fe)_3AlSi_3O_{10}(OH,F)_2$	2½-3	2.7-3.1	mono	tabular, foliated
Bismuth	Bi	2-2½	9.7-9.8	hex	pseudocubic, foliated, massive
Bismuthinite	Bi_2S_3	2	6.4-6.5	ortho	small needles, usually massive
Blende	ZnS	3½-4	3.9-4.2	cubic	tetrahedra common
Boracite	$5MgO.MgCl_2.7B_2O_3$	7	3.0	cubic	cubes, octahedra, or massive
Borax	$Na_2B_4O_7.10H_2O$	2-2½	1.7	mono	prismatic or massive
Bornite	Cu_5FeS_4	3	4.9-5.3	cubic	cube, octahedra, usually massive
Bournonite	$2PbS.Cu_2S.Sb_2S_3$	2½-3	5.5-5.9	ortho	often twin xls or massive
Braunite	Mn_2O_3 + some SiO_2	6-6½	4.7-4.9	tetra	octahedral, also massive
Bronzite	$(Mg,Fe)_2Si_2O_6$	5½	3.1-3.3	ortho	prismatic, usually massive
Brookite	TiO_2	5½-6	4.2-4.9	ortho	tabular xls
Brucite	$Mg(OH)_2$	2½	2.4	hex	xls, massive, fibrous
Bytownite (plagioclase 10-30% albite)		6-6½	2.7	tric	commonly massive
Calcite	$CaCO_3$	3	2.7	hex	rhombohedra, prisms, massive
Carnallite	$KCl.MgCl_2.6H_2O$	3	1.6	ortho	usually massive or granular
Cassiterite	SnO_2	6-7	6.8-7.1	tetra	xls, fibrous, massive
Celestine	$SrSO_4$	3-3½	4.0	ortho	tabular, fibrous, granular
Celsian	$BaAl_2Si_2O_8$	6-6½	3.4	mono	prismatic, acicular, massive
Cerussite	$PbCO_3$	3-3½	6.5	ortho	prismatic, granular, massive
Chabazite	$(Ca,Na)Al_2Si_4O_{12}.6H_2O$	4-5	2.1-2.2	hex	rhombohedral or massive
Chalcanthite	$CuSO_4.5H_2O$	2½	2.1-2.3	tric	flat xls, also massive
Chalcedony	SiO_2	6½-7	2.6	hex	cryptocrystalline quartz
Chalcocite	Cu_2S	2½-3	5.7-5.8	ortho	prismatic, tabular, massive
Chalcopyrite	$CuFeS_2$	3½-4	4.1-4.3	tetra	bisphenoidal, massive
Chlorite, see prochlorite clinochlore, penninite					
Chromite	$FeCr_2O_4$	5½	4.5-4.8	cubic	octahedral, usually massive
Chrysoberyl	$BeAl_2O_4$	8½	3.7	ortho	prismatic, tabular, stellate
Chrysocolla	$CuSiO_3.2H_2O$	2-4	2.0-2.2	amor	botryoidal or earthy
Chrysotile, fibrous form of serpentine					
Cinnabar	HgS	2-2½	8.0-8.2	hex	rhombohedra, tabular, massive
Clinochlore	$(Fe,Mg,Al)_6(Al,Si)_4O_{10}(OH)_8$	2	2.5-2.8	mono	tabular, massive, scaly
Cobalt Bloom	$Co_3As_2O_8.8H_2O$	1½-2½	2.95	mono	prismatic, usually massive or earthy
Cobaltite	CoAsS	5½	6.0-6.3	cubic	cube, pyritohedron, usually massive

adam, adamantine; met, metallic; op, opaque; prly, pearly; res, resinous; trl, translucent; trp, transparent; vit, vitreous; xls, crystals; b, blue; bk, black; br, brown; cls, colourless; dk, dark; dp, deep; g, green; gy, grey; pk, pink; pl, pale; r, red; s, silver; sbk, colour of iron or steel; sgy, colour of tin; tint, tinted; v, violet; w, white; xls, crystals; y, yellow; yg, yellowish-green

Cleavage	Fracture	Trans-parency	Colour	Lustre	Streak	Page ref
prismatic, good	uneven	op	g, w, gy	vitreous	w	136
perfect	uneven	trp	cls, w, y, g	vitreous		165
prismatic, distinct	uneven	op	br, bk, g	vit-res	y, g	115f
perfect basal	uneven	op-trp	w. tint	vit-pearly	cls, w	119f
poor	uneven	op	bk, br	vitreous	gy, g, br	109
basal, good	conch	op	w, gy, r	vitreous	w	128
absent	conch	op	s	metallic	s	93
absent	conch	trp-trl	y, br	resinous	w	172f
cubic, poor	uneven	trp-trl	cls, w, tint	vitreous	w	118
perfect basal	uneven	trp-op	br, bk, b, r	adam	cls, w, y	123
poor	uneven	op-trl	w, pk, br, gy	vitreous	w	146
perfect basal	uneven	op	w, tint	vit-pearly	w	120
rectangular, good	conch	trp-trl	cls, w	adam	cls	162f
rectangular, perfect	uneven	trp	cls, w, b, gy	vitreous	w, yg	157
perfect basal	uneven	op-trp	cls, w, gy, g	vitreous	w	119f
perfect	uneven	op	sgy	metallic	gy	91f
poor	conch	trp-op	g, bg, y, b, pk	vitreous	w	142f
perfect basal	uneven	trp-trl	w, tint	vit-pearly	cls	133
poor	conch	trp-op	cls, w, y	vitreous	cls, w, y	126f
poor	uneven	op	dk gy, bk	metallic	shiny gy	100
perfect	uneven	op	sgy	metallic	sgy	92
prismatic, distinct	uneven	op	s, gy	metallic	gy-bk	94
perfect	conch	trp-trl	g, g-bk	adam-vit	g	166
good, prismatic	uneven	op	bk, g-bk	vitreous	w, gy	118
2 perfect, direct	uneven	trl	y, yg	pearly	y	168
distinct to 1 face	conch	trp-trl	br, gy, b, g	vitreous	cls	143
perfect	conch	trl-op	dp b	vitreous	pl b	167
rectangular	uneven	trp-trl	cls, w, tint	vitreous	w	149
none	earthy	op	w, gy, br, y	dull	w	170f
indistinct, basal	conch	trp	various	vitreous	w	109f
laminated	uneven	trp-op	br,bk,g	pearly	w	107f
perfect basal	granular	op	s,reddish	metallic	s	92
perfect	conch	op	gy	metallic	dk gy	99f
perfect polyhedral	conch	trp-op	bk,br,y,w	res-adam	br,w	149f
poor tetrahedral	conch	trl	cls,w,y,g	vitreous	w	158
two distinct	conch	trp	w or tint	vitreous	w	158
indistinct	conch	op	r,br	metallic	gy-bk	98
one distinct	conch	op	gy-bk	metallic	gy-bk	101
poor	uneven	op	br-bk	metallic	br-bk	143
rectangular	uneven	trl-op	w,gy,g,br-y	vit-prly	w,br	120f
poor	uneven	trp-trl	y-br,br,bk	adam-met	cls,y,br	123f
perfect basal	uneven	trl	w,b,g,gy	vit-prly	w	
perfect basal	uneven	op-trp	gy,b	vit-prly	w	120
rhombohedral	conch	trp-op	cls,w,tint	vitreous	w	150f
none	conch	trp-trl	w,pk	vitreous	w	157f
incomplete	conch	op-trp	br,br-bk	adam	w,y	110
prismatic	conch	trp-trl	w	vit-prly	w	156
perfect basal	conch	trp	cls,w,r,gy	prly,vit	w	106f
good,variable	conch	trp-trl	w,gy	adam-vit	cls	163
rhombohedral	uneven	trp-trl	cls,w,pk,y,br	vitreous	w	133
imperfect	conch	trl	b	vitreous	pl b	167
none	hackly	trl-op	various	waxy	w	129ff
poor prismatic	conch	op	dk sgy	metallic	dk sgy	100
indistinct	conch	op	brassy	metallic	g-bk	96f
none	uneven	op	bk,br	metallic	br	121
weak prismatic	conch	trp	g,yg,br	vitreous	cls	110
none	conch	trl-op	bg,b,g	vit,earthy	w,g-w	167
perfect prismatic	uneven	trl-op	r,gy,br	adam-met	r	127f
laminated	splintery	trl	g-bk,bg	vit-prly	g-w	137
laminated		trl	r,gy,g	adam-vit	r,gy,g	168
perfect	conch	trl	s,reddish	metallic	gy	94

continued overleaf

Mineral	Chemical formula	H	SG	Crystal system	Habit
Copper	Cu	2½-3	8.5-9.0	cubic	octahedra, massive, arborescent
Copperas (melanterite)	$FeSO_4.7H_2O$	2	1.9	mono	prismatic, usually massive powdery
Cordierite	$(Mg,Fe)_2 Al_3 AlSi_5)O_{18}$	7-7½	2.6-2.7	ortho	pseudohexagonal, massive, granular
Corundum	Al_2O_3	9	3.9-4.1	hex	rhombohedral, also massive
Covelline	CuS	1½-2	4.6	hex	hex plates, usually massive
Cristobalite	SiO_2	6-7	2.3	cubic	octahedral
Crocoisite (crocoite)	$PbCrO_4$	2½-3	5.9-6.1	mono	prismatic, granular
Cryolite	$Na_3 AlF_6$	2½-3	2.95	mono	cuboidal xls, usually massive
Cuprite	Cu_2O	3½-4	5.8-6.1	cubic	octahedral, massive, or earthy
Datolite	$CaBSiO_4 (OH)$	5-5½	2.9-3.2	mono	prismatic, massive, granular
Demantoid (garnet, see also Table 6)					
Diallage	$Ca(Mg,Fe,Al)Si_2 O_6$	5-6	3.3-3.4	mono	foliated augite/diopside
Diamond	C	10	3.5	cubic	cubes, octahedra, pebbles
Diopside	$CaMgSi_2O_6$	5-6	3.2-3.4	mono	prismatic, massive, granular
Dioptase	$CuSiO_3.H_2O$	5	3.2-3.3	hex	rhombohedral, also massive
Dolomite	$CaCO_3.MgCO_3$	3½-4	2.8-2.9	hex	rhombohedral, massive, granular
Dyscrasite	Ag_3Sb	3½-4	9.4-10.0	ortho	pyramids, massive, granular
Enargite	Cu_3AsS_4	3-3½	4.4	ortho	usually massive or granular
Enstatite	$MgSiO_3$	5½-6	3.2-3.9	ortho	prismatic, also massive
Epidote	$Ca_2 (Al,Fe)_3 (SiO_4)_3 (OH)$	6-7	3.3-3.5	mono	elongated xls, granular
Epsomite	$MgSO_4.7H_2O$	2-2½	1.7	ortho	prismatic, usually massive, fibrous
Erubescite, see bornite					
Euclase	$BeAlSiO_4 (OH)$	7½-8	3.1	mono	prismatic xls
Euxenite (compound of rare metals)		5½-6½	4.7-5.0	ortho	prismatic, also massive
Fluorite	CaF_2	4	3.0-3.3	cubic	cubes etc, also granular
Franklinite	$(Fe,Zn,Mn)(Mn,Fe)_2 O_4$	6-6½	5.0-5.2	cubic	octahedral, granular, massive
Galena	PbS, some AgS etc	2½	7.2-7.6	cubic	cubes, octahedra, massive
Garnets (see also Table 6)	$M_3^{II}M_2^{III} (SiO_4)_3$	6-8	3.4-4.2	cubic	cubes, various beads, massive
Garnierite	$(Ni,Mg)_6 (OH)_8 Si_4 O_{10}$	3-4	2.2-2.8	amor	massive or earthy
Gibbsite	$Al_2 O_3 3H_2 O$	3	2.3-2.4	mono	tabular, usually concretionary
Glauconite	$K(Fe,Al)_2 (Si,Al)_4 O_{10} (OH)_2$	2	2.2-2.4	mono	amorphous, granular or earthy
Glaucophane	$Na_2 (Mg,Fe)_3 (Al,Fe)_2 Si_8 O_{22} (OH)_2$	6-6½	3.0-3.1	mono	prisms, fibrous, granular, massive
Goethite	$FeO(OH)$	5-5½	4.0-4.4	ortho	prisms, tabular, massive, fibrous
Gold	Au	2½-3	15.5-19	cubic	cubes, usually massive, arborescent
Graphite	C	1-2	2.1-2.3	hex	usually scaly, massive, granular, earthy
Greenockite	CdS	3-3½	4.9-5.0	hex	hemimorphic xls, crusts
Grossularite (garnet, see also Table 6)					
Gypsum	$CaSO_4.2H_2O$	1½-2	2.3	mono	prisms, stellate, granular, fibrous
Haematite	Fe_2O_3	5½-6½	5.2-5.3	hex	rhombohedral, usually scaly or fibrous masses
Harmotome	$(K,Ba)Al_2 Si_5 O_{14}.5H_2O$	4-4½	2.3-2.5	mono	always cruciform twins
Hausmannite	Mn_3O_4	5½	4.7-4.8	tetra	pyramidal, massive, granular
Haüyne	$(Na_2, Ca)_4 (AlSiO_4)_6 (SO_4)_2$	5½-6	2.2-2.4	cubic	crystal beads, granular
Hemimorphite	$Zn_4 Si_2 O_7 (OH)_2.H_2O$	4½-5	3.3-3.5	ortho	hemimorphic, massive, granular crusts
Heulandite	$(Na_2, Ca)_4 Al_6 (Al, Si)_4 Si_{26}O_{72}.24H_2O$	3½-4	2.2	mono	tabular, globular masses
Hornblende	(silicate with Al,Mg,Fe,Ca,Na)	5-6	2.9-3.4	mono	prismatic, bladed, fibrous, massive, granular
Hornstone, see chalcedony					
Hydrozincite	$2ZnCO_3.3Zn(OH)_2$	2-2½	3.6-3.8	mono	usually massive, fibrous, crusts
Idocrase	$Ca_{10}Al_4 (Mg, Fe)_2 (Si_2O_7)_2 (SiO_4)_5 (OH)$	6½	3.3-3.5	tetra	prismatic, massive, granular
Ilmenite	$FeTiO_3$	5-6	4.5-5.0	hex	rhombohedral, plates, scales
Iridium	Ir	6-7	22.7	cubic	usually granular
Iron	Fe	4-5	7.3-7.9	cubic	usually scales, plates, grains
Jadeite	$NaAlSi_2O_6$	6½-7	3.2-3.5	mono	usually massive (=jade)
Jasper (form of chalcedony SiO_2)		7	2.5-2.6	hex	cryptocrystalline silica
Jet	over 70% C	3-4	1.3	amor	compact form of lignite (coal)
Kaolin	$Al_4 Si_4 O_{10} (OH)_8$	2-2½	2.6	tric	pseudohexagonal plates, earthy
Kupfernickel, see niccolite					
Kyanite	$Al_2 SiO_5$	5-7	3.5-3.7	tric	prismatic, bladed
Labradorite (plagioclase 30-50% albite)		6	2.67	tric	tabular, usually massive
Lapis lazuli	$3NaAlSiO_4.Na_2 S$	5-5½	2.3-2.4	cubic	usually amorphous
Laumonite	$(Ca, Na_2)(AlSi_2O_6)_2.H_2O$	3½-4	2.2-2.4	mono	prismatic, fibrous, columnar
Lazulite	$(Mg, Fe) Al_2 (PO_4)_2 (OH)_2$	5-6	3.0-3.1	mono	pyramidal, massive, granular
Lead	Pb	1½	11.4	cubic	cubes, capillary, wiry
Lepidolite	$K(Li, Al)_3 (Si, Al)_4 O_{10}(OH, F)_2$	2½-4	2.8-2.9	mono	usually scaly or granular masses
Leucite	$KAlSi_2O_6$	5½-6	2.4-2.6	cubic	cubic form, tetra properties
Lievrite	$CaFe_2 (FeOH)(SiO_4)_2$	5½-6	3.8-4.1	ortho	prisms, acicular, radiating
Limonite	$2Fe_2O_3.3H_2O$	5-5½	3.6-4.0	amor	colloidal masses or earthy
Linnaeite	Co_3S_4	5½	4.8-5.0	cubic	octahedral, massive, granular
Magnesite	$MgCO_3$	3½-4½	3.0	hex	usually massive or fibrous

adam, adamantine; met, metallic; op, opaque; prly, pearly; res, resinous; trl, translucent; trp, transparent; vit, vitreous; b, blue; bg, blue-green; bk, black; br, brown; cls, colourless; dk, dark; dp, deep; g, green; gy, grey; pk, pink; pl, pale; r, red; s, silver; sbk, colour of iron or steel; sgy, colour of tin; tint, tinted; v, violet; w, white; xls, crystals; y, yellow; yg, yellowish-green

Cleavage	Fracture	Trans-parency	Colour	Lustre	Streak	Page Ref
none	hackly	op	r	metallic	r	95
one perfect	conch	trl	w,g	vitreous	cls	--
poor pinacoidal	uneven	trp-trl	b,g,v,y	vit-dull	cls	137
none, basal partings	conch	trp-op	various	adam-vit	w	146f
perfect basal	even	op	b-bk	resinous	bk	151f
none			w, tint	dull		129
prismatic	conch	trl	r,orange	vitreous	orange	152
prismatic	uneven	trl	r,br,cls,w,bk	vit-prly	w	110f
poor octahedral	conch	trl-op	r	adam	r-br, shiny	167f
none	conch	trp-trl	cls,w,tint	vitreous	w	121
none	uneven	op-trl	g,bk,br	pearly	gy-w	118f
perfect octahedral	conch	trp-trl	various	adam	gy	122
good prismatic	uneven	trp-trl	cls,g,bk,gy,y	vitreous	w,gy	143f
good rhombohedral	conch	trp-trl	emerald g	vitreous	g	167
perfect rhombohedral	conch	trp-trl	w,tint	vit-prly	w,gy	151
two distinct	uneven	op	s,y	metallic	s	93
good prismatic	uneven	op	gy-bk,sbk	metallic	bk	
good prismatic	uneven	trl-op	gy,g,y,br,bk	vit-prly	gy,cls	120f
perfect basal	uneven	trl-op	g,b,bk,br,r	vitreous	gy	137f
one good	conch	trp-trl	cls,w	vitreous	w	158
one perfect		trp-trl	cls,g,b,y,w	vitreous	cls	
	conch	trl-op	bk,br,g-bk	adam-vit	br,y,g	
perfect octahedral	conch	trp-trl	various	vitreous	w	150
poor octahedral	uneven	op	sbk	metallic	bk,br	102
perfect cubic	even	op	gy	metallic	gy	100
poor	uneven	op-trp	v,r,y,g,bk	res-vit	w	140ff
none	earthy	op	w,g,b	dull	g-w	170
one perfect	uneven	trl	w,gy,g,r	vit-prly	w	170
none	earthy	op	g,y,gy,bk-g	dull	g	161
perfect prismatic	uneven	trl	b,bk,g	vit-prly	b-gy	138
one good	uneven	op-trl	br-bk,y,r	adam	br,y	161
none	hackly	op	y	metallic	y	96
perfect laminar	uneven	op	b, br-bk, sbk	met-dull	bk, shiny	147
one distinct	conch	trl	y, y-orange	adam-res	r, orange	164
perfect laminar	conch	trp-trl	cls, w, gy, y	pearly	w	157
poor	uneven	op	sgy, sbk, r	metallic	r,r-br	101f
indistinct	uneven	trl	w, gy, y, r	vitreous	w	133
good basal	uneven	op-trl	sbk, b, br-bk	met-vit	br	147
rhombododecahedral	conch	trp-trl	b, gy, g, r, y	vit-res	cls, w, pl b	128
perfect prismatic	uneven	trp-op	w,y-br,g	vitreous	w	164f
one perfect	uneven	trp-trl	w, r, br	vit-prly	w	
two perfect at 120°	uneven	op	gy, g, br-bk	vitreous	gy, g, br-bk	116
one perfect	uneven	op	w, pl y	dull-silky	gleaming	165
indistinct	uneven	trp-trl	g-br, r-br, y	vitreous	w	144
none	conch	op-trl	sbk, br-bk	met-dull	bk	122
poor	hackly	op	s	metallic	s	95
perfect cubic	hackly	op	sbk, bk	metallic	sbk	99
prismatic	splintery	op-trl	g, w, pl v	vit-prly	cls	122f
none	conch	op	r,br,y,g,v,b,bk	dull	w	130
none	conch	op	bk	dull	bk	173f
perfect basal	conch	op	w, gy, y	dull	w	170
pinacoidal	fibrous	trp-op	b, w, r, g, y	pearly	w	138
perfect basal	conch	trl-op	gy-br	vitreous	cls	120
imperfect	uneven	op	b	vitreous	pl b	144
perfect	uneven	trp-trl	w,r,y,b	vit-prly	cls	133
indistinct	uneven	op-trl	b	vitreous	w	139
none	v. soft	op	gy, bk	metallic	sgy	99
perfect laminar	uneven	trl	r, v, w	pearly	w	108
imperfect	conch	op-trp	w, gy, cls	vit-res	w	128f
two good	uneven	op	bk, gy, br-bk	met-vit	bk	147
none	conch	op	br, y	silky	y-br	160
imperfect	uneven	op	s, gy	metallic	gy-bk	94
rhombohedral perfect	conch	trp-op	w, gy-w, y, br	vitreous	w	151

continued overleaf

Mineral	Chemical formula	H	SG	Crystal system	Habit
Magnetite	Fe_3O_4	5½-6½	5.0-5.2	cubic	octahedra, massive, granular
Malachite	$CuCO_3.Cu(OH)_2$	3½-4	3.9-4.0	mono	usually fibrous masses, granular, earthy
Manganite	$MnO(OH)$	4	4.2-4.4	ortho	prismatic, aggregates, columnar
Marcasite	FeS_2	6-6½	4.8-4.9	ortho	tabular, aggregates, nodules
Melanite (garnet, see also Table 6)					
Mercury	Hg		13.6		liquid globules
Microcline	$KAlSi_3O_8$	6-6½	2.56	tric	prismatic, tabular, granular
Millerite	NiS	3-3½	5.3-5.6	hex	needles, fibrous, massive
Mimetite	$(PbCl)Pb_4(AsO_4)_3$	3½	7.0-7.3	hex	trigonal, botryoidal, crusts
Mispickel, see arsenopyrite					
Molybdenite	MoS_2	1-1½	4.7-4.8	hex	usually foliated, massive
Monazite	$(Ce,La,Yt)PO_4$	5-5½	4.8-5.3	mono	tabular, twins, massive, sandy
Muscovite	$KAl_3Si_3O_{10}(OH)_2$	2-2½	2.8-3.0	mono	pseudohexagonal plates, massive
Natrolite	$Na_2Al_2Si_3O_{10}.2H_2O$	5-5½	2.2-2.4	ortho	prismatic, acicular, radial aggregates, massive
Nepheline	$Na_3K(AlSiO_4)_4$	5½-6	2.6	hex	prismatic, aggregates, massive
Nephrite (massive actinolite-tremolite)		5-6½	2.9-3.1	mono	fibrous masses similar to jade
Niccolite	$NiAs$	5-5½	7.3-7.8	hex	usually irregular masses, botryoidal
Nickel bloom	$Ni_3(AsO_4)_2.8H_2O$	2½-3	3.0-3.1	mono	capillary xls, earthy coatings
Nosean	$3NaAlSiO_4.Na_2SO_4$	5½	2.2-2.4	cubic	dodecahedral, granular
Oligoclase (plagioclase 10-30% albite)		6-6½	2.64	tric	usually cryptocrystalline masses
Olivine	$(Mg,Fe)_2SiO_4$	6½-7	3.3	ortho	prismatic, tabular, granular
Opal	$SiO_2.nH_2O$	5½	1.8-2.2	amor	reniform, stalactitic, etc
Orpiment	As_2S_3	1½-2	3.4-3.5	mono	prismatic, usually massive, crusts
Orthoclase	$KAlSi_3O_8$	6	2.5-2.6	mono	prismatic, tabular, granular masses
Osmiridium	$Os + Ir$	6-7	19-21	hex	rhombohedral xls, grains
Palladium	Pd	4½-5	11.3-12	cubic	usually small grains
Paragonite	$NaAl_3Si_3O_{10}(OH,F)_2$	2½-3	2.85	mono	usually laminated masses
Penninite	$(Mg,Fe,Al)_6(Si,Al)_4O_{10}(OH)_8$	2½	2.6-2.8	mono	pseudohexagonal, massive
Pentlandite	$(Fe,Ni)S$	3-3½	4.6-5.0	cubic	usually granular or massive
Phenakite	Be_2SiO_4	7½-8	3.0	ortho	pseudohexagonal xls
Phillipsite	$(Ca,K_2)_2(AlSi_2O_6)_4.9H_2O$	4-4½	2.2	mono	prismatic cruciform twins, radial aggregates
Phlogopite	$KMg_3AlSi_3O_{10}(OH,F)_2$	2½-3	2.8	mono	tabular, laminar, scales
Pitchblende (uraninite)	UO_2	5½	6.4-10	cubic	octahedra, usually massive, granular
Platinum	Pt	4-4½	21.5	cubic	usually granular
Polyhalite	$K_2MgCa_2(SO_4)_4.2H_2O$	3-3½	2.8	tric	prismatic, usually platy or fibrous
Prehnite	$Ca_2Al_2Si_3O_{10}(OH)_2.nH_2O$	6-6½	2.8-3.0	ortho	hemimorphic tabular, radial aggregates
Prochlorite	$(Mg,Fe,Al)_6(OH)_8(Al,Si)_4O_{10}$	1-2	2.8-2.9	mono	plates, irregular scaly aggregates
Proustite	Ag_3AsS_3	2-2½	5.6	hex	hemimorphic, granular, usually massive
Psilomelane	$(Ba,Mn)Mn_4O_8(OH)_2$	5-6	3.7-4.7	amor	massive, botryoidal, stalactitic
Purpurite	$(Mn,Fe)PO_4$	4-4½	3.3	ortho	prismatic or massive
Pyrargyrite	Ag_3SbS_3	2½-3	5.9	hex	hemimorphic prisms, massive
Pyrite	FeS_2	6-6½	5.0-5.2	cubic	striated cubes etc, massive, nodular
Pyrolusite	MnO_2	2-2½	4.8	ortho	usually fibrous, massive, pseudomorphous
Pyromorphite	$3Pb_3(PO_4)_2.PbCl_2$	3½-4	6.5-7.1	hex	trigonal prisms, aggregates, crusts
Pyrope (garnet, see also Table 6)					
Pyrophyllite	$Al_2(OH)_2Si_4O_{10}$	1-2	2.7-2.9	ortho	tabular, foliated, radial aggregates
Pyrrhotite	FeS (up to 5% NiS)	3½-4½	4.6	hex	tabular, foliated, massive, granular
Quartz	SiO_2	7	2.6-2.7	hex	prismatic, twins, aggregates
Realgar	As_4S_4	1½-2	3.5-3.6	mono	prisms, needles, massive, granular
Rhodocrosite	$MnCO_3$	3½-4½	3.5-3.6	hex	usually massive, globular, crusts
Rhodolite (garnet, see also Table 6)					
Rhodonite	$MnSiO_3$	5½-6½	3.4-3.6	tric	large tabular xls, massive
Rock salt	$NaCl$	2-2½	2.2	cubic	cubes, octahedra, massive, granular
Rutile	TiO_2	6-6½	4.2-4.3	tetra	prisms, twins, massive, granular
Scapolite (wernerite)	$(NaCl,CaCO_3).3(Na,CaAl)AlSi_3O_8$	5-6	2.5-2.8	tetra	prismatic, massive, granular
Scheelite	$CaWO_4$	4½-5	5.9-6.1	tetra	pyramidal, granular, massive
Scolecite	$CaAlSi_2O_{10}.3H_2O$	5-5½	2.2-2.4	mono	prismatic, radiating, fibrous
Serpentine	$Mg_6Si_4O_{10}(OH)_8$	3-4	2.5-2.6	mono	massive, granular, foliated, fibrous
Siderite	$FeCO_3$	3½-4½	3.7-3.9	hex	rhombohedral, massive, granular
Sillimanite	Al_2SiO_5	6-7	3.2	ortho	acicular, massive, foliated, nodular
Silver	Ag	2½-3	9.6-12	cubic	cube etc, usually massive arborescent
Sinhalite	$MgAlBO_4$	6½	3.5-3.6	ortho	prismatic xls, pebbles
Smaltite	$CoAs_2$	5½	6.4-6.6	cubic	cube, octahedra, massive, granular
Smithsonite	$ZnCO_3$	5-5½	4.0-4.5	hex	usually massive, granular, crusts, earthy
Sodalite	$3NaAlSiO_4.NaCl$	5-6	2.2-2.4	cubic	dodecahedral, massive
Sperrylite	$PtAs_2$	6-7	10.6	cubic	cubes, cube and octahedron
Spessatite (garnet, see also Table 6)					
Sphalerite, see blende					

adam, adamantine; met, metallic; op, opaque; prly, pearly; res, resinous; trl, translucent; trp, transparent; vit, vitreous; b, blue; bg, blue-green;
bk, black; br, brown; cls, colourless; dk, dark; dp, deep; g, green; gy, grey; pk, pink; pl, pale; r, red; s, silver; sbk, colour of iron or steel; sgy,
colour of tin; tint, tinted; v, violet; w, white; xls, crystals; y, yellow; yg, yellowish-green

Cleavage	Fracture	Transparency	Colour	Lustre	Streak	Page ref
poor octahedral	uneven	op	sbk,br-bk	met-dull	bk	102
basal	conch	trp-op	g	silky-vit	pl g	166
good	uneven	op-trl	sbk,br	met-vit	dk,r-br	160f
very poor	uneven	op	pl bronze	metallic	gy	98
		op	s	metallic		93
perfect basal	uneven	op-trl	w,tint,g	vitreous	w	106f
perfect rhombohedral	uneven	op	bronze	metallic	g-bk	97
indistinct	uneven	trl	pl y,br,w	resinous	w	163f
perfect laminar	soft	op	gy-v	metallic	dk gy	99
imperfect basal	conch	op	pl y,dk r-br	resinous	w	111
perfect laminar	uneven	trp-trl	w,bk,br,y,g	pearly	cls	107f
perfect prismatic	conch	trp-trl	w,y,pk	vit-prly	cls,w	134
distinct prismatic	conch	trp-trl	w,cls,pl gy	res-vit	w	116
fibrous	uneven	op-trl	pl g, w	vit-dull	w	136
rarely seen	conch	op	copper r	metallic	br-bk	96
rarely seen	earthy	op	apple g	silky-vit	g	168
poor	uneven	op-trl	gy,b,br,w	vit-res	various	129
perfect basal	conch	op-trl	w,g,r,gy,y	vit-prly	w	120
poor	conch	trp-trl	g,yg,br,r	vitreous	w	119
none	conch	trl-op	various	res-prly	w	131f
perfect laminar	uneven	trl	y	res-prly	y	127
perfect basal	conch	op-trp	w,gy,tint	vit-prly	w	106f
poor	hackly	op	sgy,sbk	metallic	gy	95
none	hackly	op	sgy,s	metallic	sgy,s	93f
perfect laminar	uneven	trp-trl	y,g	pearly		108
one perfect	uneven	trp-trl	g,bg	pearly	pl g	137
granular	conch	op	bronze y	metallic	bk	98
indistinct	conch	trp	cls,pl y,pk	vitreous	w	111
	uneven	trl	w,y,gy,r	vitreous	cls	134
perfect laminar	uneven	trp-trl	cls,br,r,w	pearly	cls	108
	conch	op	bk,gy,br,g	met-res	bk,dk g	152
none	hackly	op	sgy,s	metallic	sgy,s	98f
one good	conch	trl	pk,r,w,y,g	vit-res	cls,pk	157
one distinct	uneven	trp-trl	g,yg,y,cls,w	vit-prly	cls	134
scaly	uneven	trl	g	vit-prly	pl g	137
one good	conch	trl	r	adam	r	127f
none	uneven	op	bk,br	met-dull	br-bk shiny	160
one good	uneven	op	purple	silky	purple	152
rhombohedral	conch	op-trl	dk r,b-gy,bk	met-adam	r	95f
indistinct cubic	conch	op	brassy	metallic	g-bk	97
one good	uneven	op	sbk,dk gy	metallic	b-bk	100
indistinct prismatic	uneven	trl	g,y,br,b,r	resinous	w,y	163f
perfect basal	uneven	trl	w,g,gy,br,y	pearly	w	139
distinct basal	uneven	op	bronze,br	metallic	dk gy	97
none	conch	trp-op	various	vit-res	w	104ff
one good	conch	trl	r,orange	res-adam	orange	127
perfect rhombohedral	uneven	trl	r,y,br,gy	vit-prly	w,pk	152f
perfect prismatic	uneven	trp-op	r,br,g,y,bk	vitreous	w	152f
perfect cubic	conch	trp-trl	cls,w,tint	vitreous	cls,w	157
poor prismatic	uneven	trl-op	br,bk,r	met-adam	pl y,g	123
distinct prismatic	conch	trl-op	w,y,pk	vit-prly	w	144f
one good	uneven	trp-trl	pl g,y	adam-res	cls,w	145
good prismatic		trp-trl	w	vit-silky	w	
one distinct	conch	trl-op	g,bk,r,y,br	res-dull	w	169f
perfect rhombohedral	uneven	op-trl	y,br,br-bk	prly-vit	w	159
one perfect	uneven	trp-trl	gy-g,gy-y,br,pl b	vitreous	cls	138f
none	hackly	op	s	metallic	brilliant	93
none		trp	pl y,dp br	vit-adam	w	119
various, poor	uneven	op	sgy,pl gy	metallic	dk gy	94
perfect rhombohedral	uneven	trl-op	w,gy,g,br	vit-prly	w	165
distinct	conch	trp-trl	b,cls,gy,y,g,r	vit-res	cls	116
poor	conch	op	sgy	metallic	bk	95

continued overleaf

Mineral	Chemical formula	H	SG	Crystal system	Habit
Sphene (titanite)	$CaTiSiO_5$	5-5½	3.5	mono	wedge shapes, twins, massive
Spinel	$MgAl_2O_4$	7½-8	3.5-4.1	cubic	octahedra, twins, granular
Spodumene	$LiAlSi_2O_6$	6½-7	3.1-3.2	mono	8-sided prisms, massive
Stannine (stannite)	Cu_2FeSnS_4	4	4.3-4.5	tetra	tetrahedra, twins, usually massive, granular
Staurolite	$FeAl_4(SiO_5)_2(OH)_2$	7-7½	3.7-3.8	ortho	6-sided prisms, often twins
Stibnite	Sb_2S_3	2	4.6-4.7	ortho	needles, radial aggregates, fibrous, massive
Stilbite	$(Na_2,Ca)Al_2Si_6O_{10}.6H_2O$	3½-4	2.1-2.2	mono	tabular, twins, aggregates
Strontianite	$SrCO_3$	3½-4	3.6-3.7	ortho	prismatic, needles, fibrous, granular
Struvite	$NH_4MgPO_4.6H_2O$	1½-2	1.7	ortho	sharp xls, intergrowths
Sulphur	S	2	1.9-2.1	ortho	bipyramids, granular, fibrous, nodular
Talc	$Mg_3Si_4O_{10}(OH)_2$	1	2.7-2.8	mono	usually granular, massive or scaly
Tellurium	Te	2-2½	6.1-6.3	hex	prismatic, needles, usually massive
Tenorite	CuO	3-4	6.25	mono	usually scaly, massive, powdery
Tetrahedrite	$(Cu,Fe)_{12}Sb_4S_{13}$	3-4½	4.4-5.4	cubic	tetrahedral, massive, granular
Topaz	$Al_2SiO_4(OH,F)_2$	8	3.4-3.6	ortho	striated prisms or massive
Topazolite (garnet, *see also* Table 6)					
Torbernite	$Cu(UO_2)_2(PO_4)_2.12H_2O$	2-2½	3.2-3.5	ortho	pseudotetragonal plates, foliated
Tourmaline	$Na(Mg,Fe)_3Al_6(OH)_4(BO_3)_3(SiO_3)_6$	7-7½	3.0-3.2	hex	trigonal prisms, massive
Tremolite	$Ca_2Mg_5Si_8O_{22}(OH)_2$	5½-6	2.9-3.1	mono	prisms, bladed, fibrous, massive
Trydimite	SiO_2	6½-7	2.3	hex-ortho	plates, often twins
Turquoise	$CuAl_6(PO_4)_4(OH)_8.5H_2O$	5-6	2.6-2.9	tric	usually massive, stalactitic, crusts
Uvarovite (garnet, *see also* Table 6)					
Vanadinite	$Pb_5(VO_4)_3Cl$	3	6.7-7.1	hex	trigonal pyramids, aggregates, crusts
Vivianite	$Fe_3(PO_4)_2.8H_2O$	1½-2½	2.6-2.7	mono	small prisms, aggregates, crusts
Wavellite	$Al_6(PO_4)_4(OH)_6.9H_2O$	3½-4	2.3	ortho	usually globular aggregates, crusts
Witherite	$BaCO_3$	3½	4.3-4.4	ortho	prismatic twins, massive, granular
Wolfram	$(Fe,Mn)WO_4$	5-5½	7.1-7.9	mono	prismatic, tabular, bladed, massive
Woolastonite	$CaSiO_3$	4½-5	2.8-2.9	mo-tri	tabular, massive, lamellar
Wulfenite	$PbMoO_4$	3	6.3-7.0	tetra	various xls, massive, granular
Wurtzite	ZnS	3½-4	4.0	hex	prisms, pyramids, usually massive, fibrous
Zincite	ZnO	4½-5	5.4-5.7	hex	massive, granular or foliated
Zinnwaldite	$K(Li,Fe,Al)_3(Si,Al)_4O_{10}(OH,F)_2$	2-3	2.6-3.2	mono	tabular, 6-sided plates
Zircon	$ZrSiO_4$	7-7½	3.9-4.8	tetra	prisms and pyramid, small grains
Zoisite	$Ca_2Al_3(SiO_4)_3OH$	6-6½	3.3-3.4	ortho	long prisms, massive, fibrous

adam, adamantine; met, metallic; op, opaque; prly, pearly; res, resinous; trl, translucent; trp, transparent; vit, vitreous; b, blue; bg, blue-green; bk, black; br, brown; cls, colourless; dk, dark; dp, deep; g, green; gy, grey; pk, pink; pl. pale; r, red; s, silver; sbk, colour of iron or steel; sgy, colour of tin; tint, tinted; v, violet; w, white; xls, crystals; y, yellow; yg, yellowish-green

TABLE 5   SYMBOLS OF ELEMENTS AND SALT RADICALS

Elements				Salts	
Ag,	silver	Mg,	magnesium	Fluorides,	F group
Al,	aluminium	Mn,	manganese	Chlorides,	Cl
As,	arsenic	Mo,	molybdenum	Bromides,	Br
Au,	gold	N,	nitrogen	Iodides,	I
B,	boron	Na,	sodium	Hydroxides,	OH
Ba,	barium	Ni,	nickel	Oxides,	O
Be,	beryllium	O,	oxygen	Sulphides,	S
Bi,	bismuth	Os,	osmium	Sulphates,	SO_4
Br,	bromine	P,	phosphorous	Borates,	BO_3
C,	carbon	Pb,	lead	Carbonates,	CO_3
Ca,	calcium	Pt,	platinum	Nitrates,	NO_3
Cl,	chlorine	S,	sulphur	Phosphates,	PO_4
Co,	cobalt	Sb,	antimony	Silicates,	SiO_4
Cr,	chromium	Si,	silicon		Si_2O_7
Cu,	copper	Sn,	tin		etc
F,	fluorine	Sr,	strontium		
Fe,	iron	Te,	tellurium		
H,	hydrogen	Ti,	titanium		
Hg,	mercury	Tl,	thallium		
I,	iodine	U,	uranium		
Ir,	iridium	W,	tungsten		
K,	potassium	Zn,	zinc		
Li,	lithium	Zr,	zirconium		

Cleavage	Fracture	Transparency	Colour	Lustre	Streak	Page ref
good prismatic	conch	trp-op	y,g,br,bk	adam-res	w	111
very poor	conch	trp-op	various	vitreous	w	124
one good prismatic	conch	trp-trl	v,pk,y,g	vit-prly	w	112
indistinct	uneven	op	sbk,sgy	metallic	bk	101
interrupted	conch	trl-op	br,bk	vit-res	cls,gy	139
one perfect	conch	op	sgy	metallic	gy	99-100
one perfect	uneven	trp-trl	cls,w,y,br,r	vit-prly	cls	134
distinct prismatic	uneven	trp-trl	pl g,y,gy,w	vit-res	w	153
good		trl	y,pl br	vitreous		160
imperfect	conch trp-	trp-trl	y,br	resinous	pl y	128
perfect laminar	uneven	trp-op	g,gy,w	pearly	cls,w	139f
good		op	sgy	metallic	w	92
poor	conch	op	sbk,gy	metallic		--
none	uneven	op-trl	sbk	metallic	bk,br,r	101
perfect	uneven	trp-op	cls,tint	vitreous	cls	112
perfect laminar		trp-trl	g	adam-prly	pl g	168f
poor rhombohedral	uneven	trp-op	various	vitreous	cls	112-3
one perfect	splintery	trp-trl	cls,w,gy,g	vitreous	w	140
scaly		trp-trl	cls,w	vitreous	w	129
perfect basal	conch	trl-op	b,bg,g,gy-g	waxy	w,pl g	171
poor prismatic	uneven	trp-trl	r,br,y	resinous	w,y	163f
perfect laminar	fibrous	trp-trl	b,g,w,cls	prly-vit	pl b	160
one perfect	uneven	trl	w,g,br,y	vit-prly	w	171
one good	uneven	trl	w,y,gy	vit-res	w	153
one perfect	uneven	trl-op	rbr,bk	met-dull	dk br	153f
one perfect	uneven	trl	w,gy,y,br	prly-vit	w	145
pyramidal good	uneven	trp-trl	y,gy,br,r	res-adam	w,pl y	164
one good	fibrous	op	br	vitreous	pl br	--
perfect basal	conch	trl-trp	r	adam	orange	145
perfect laminar	uneven	trl-op	v,y,br	pearly	w	108
indistinct	conch	op-trp	various	adam	cls	113-4
one perfect	uneven	trp-trl	cls,gy,g,br,r	vitreous	cls	145f

TABLE 6   THE GARNET FAMILY

Name	Chemistry	Colour	H	SG	RI
Almandine	$Fe_3 Al_2 (SiO_4)_3$	deep red	$7\frac{1}{2}$-8	3.83-4.20	1.78-1.82
Andradite	$Ca_3 Fe_2 (SiO_4)_3$	brown to brownish green	$6\frac{1}{2}$-7	3.80-3.90	1.88-1.89
Demantoid	variety of above	green	$6\frac{1}{2}$-7	3.80-3.90	1.88-1.89
Grossularite	$Ca_3 Al_2 (SiO_4)_3$	pale olive green	7-$7\frac{1}{2}$	3.60-3.70	1.74-1.76
Hessonite or cinammon stone	variety of above	honey to orange red	6	3.50-3.70	1.74-1.76
Melanite	variety of andradite	black	$6\frac{1}{2}$-7	3.80-3.90	opaque
Pyrope	$Mg_3 Al_2 (SiO_4)_3$	red to purple	7-$7\frac{1}{2}$	3.65-3.80	1.74-1.75
Rhodolite	variety of above	soft rosy purple	7-$7\frac{1}{2}$	3.65-3.80	1.74-1.75
Spessatite or spessartine	$Mn_2 Al_2 (SiO_4)_3$	brownish red to orange	6	3.98-4.25	1.80-1.81
Topazolite	variety of andradite	yellow or greenish	$6\frac{1}{2}$-7	3.80-3.90	1.88-1.89
Uvarovite	$Ca_3 Cr_2 (SiO_4)_3$	green	$7\frac{1}{2}$	3.42-3.55	1.84

SUGGESTIONS FOR FURTHER READING

Anderson, B. W. *Gem Testing*, Temple Press, London (1958)

Blakemore, K. and Andrews, G. *Collecting Gems and Ornamental Stones*, Foyle, London (1967)

Börner, R. *Minerals, Rocks and Gemstones*, Oliver & Boyd, Edinburgh and London (1967)

Cooper, Lyn and Ray. *New Zealand Gemstones*, A. H. & A. W. Reed, Wellington, Auckland and Sydney (1969)

Correns, C. W. *Introduction to Mineralogy*, Allen & Unwin, London (1969)

Deeson, A. F. L. (ed). *The Collector's Encyclopedia of Rocks and Minerals*, David & Charles, Newton Abbot (1973)

Delair, J. B. *Collecting Rocks and Fossils*, Batsford, London (1966)

Desautels, P. E. *The Mineral Kingdom*, Hamlyn, London (1969)

Ellis, Clarence. *The Pebbles on the Beach*, Faber & Faber, London (1957)

Evans, I. O. *Rocks, Minerals and Gemstones*, Hamlyn, London (1972)

Firsoff, V. A. *Gemstones of the British Isles*, Oliver & Boyd, Edinburgh and London (1971)

———. *Working with Gemstones*, David & Charles, Newton Abbot (1974)

Frondel, C. *The (Dana's) System of Mineralogy*, Wiley, New York (1962)

Heddle, F. M. *The Mineralogy of Scotland,* David Douglas, Edinburgh (1901)

Kirkcaldy, J. F. *Minerals and Rocks,* Blandford Press, London (1963)

Kraus, E. M. and Slawson, C. B. *Gems and Gem Materials,* McGraw-Hill, New York and London (1947)

Pearl, R. M. *Introduction to the Mineral Kingdom,* Blandford Press, London (1966)

Perry, Ron and Nance. *Australian Gemstones,* A. H. & A. W. Reed, Wellington, Auckland and Sydney (1970)

Read, H. H. (ed). *Rutley's Elements of Mineralogy,* Murby, London (1970)

Rogers, Cedric. *A Collector's Guide to Minerals, Rocks and Gemstones in Cornwall and Devon,* Bradford Barton, Truro (1968)

Shepherd, Walter. *Rocks, Minerals and Fossils* (Young Scientist Series), Weidenfeld & Nicolson, London (1962)

——. *Flint,* Faber & Faber, London (1972)

Sinkansas, John. *Standard Catalogue of Gems,* Van Nostrand, New York (1968)

——. *Gemstones of North America,* Van Nostrand, New York (1972)

Smith, H. G. F. *Gemstones,* Methuen, London (1952); rev ed Chapman & Hall, London (1973)

Tennissen, A. C. *Colourful Mineral Identifier,* Sterling Publishing Co, New York (1969)

Webster, Robert. *Gemmologist's Compendium,* N. A. G. Press, London (1964)

——. *Practical Gemmology,* N. A. G. Press, London (1966)

——. *Gems,* Butterworth, London (1970)

Weinstein, M. *Precious and Semi-precious Stones,* Pitman, London (1946)

Zim, H. S. and Shaffer, P. R. *Rocks and Minerals,* Hamlyn, London (1965)

INDEX

(For reference to minerals see Table 4)

208